About the Author

Ali Millar was born in Edinburgh and raised in the Scottish Borders. Her writing has appeared in the *Guardian, Stylist, The London Magazine, The Quietus* and other publications. Her debut novel, *Ava Anna Ada,* is forthcoming in 2024 from White Rabbit Books. She lives in London.

Praise for *The Last Days*

'Courageous stuff . . . intense, compelling, raw' *The Times*

'Poetically unpeels the layers of fear and shame built into the psyche of children who are raised as Witnesses' *Telegraph*

'A coming-of-age story like no other, *The Last Days* is about finding voice through desire, authentic connection and creative expression. It sings with the strength and bravery it takes to step away from what has defined you, particularly when those you love follow a different truth. A searingly honest memoir' Lily Dunn, author of *Sins of My Father*

'I loved this book. It's a thing of beauty. Ali Millar pulls you heart first through an extraordinary life, somehow making sense of an experience that should make no sense at all. A sublime talent' David Whitehouse

'This is a dam-burst of a book ... so gracious and deft, so carefully weighted, so tender yet flinty, so cinematic and earthed' Darran Anderson, *Caught by the River*

'A great prison break, except the walls she has to tunnel through have been there since birth' Lias Saoudi, author of *Ten Thousand Apologies, The Fat White Family and The Miracle of Failure*

'Elegiac and propulsive' Stuart Kelly, *The Scotsman*

'A memoir that touches peoples' hearts and souls; utterly moving' Estelle Paranque, author of *Blood, Fire and Gold*

'Extraordinary, I can't think what it took to begin to write' Helen Mort, author of *A Line Above the Sky*

'Relentless' Rachel Cooke, *Observer*

'A visceral cult classic' Dan Richards, author of *Outpost*

'A real-life *The Handmaid's Tale*' Phillip Adams, ABC National Radio

The
Last Days

An extraordinary story of
one woman's fight for freedom

ALI MILLAR

1

Ebury Press, an imprint of Ebury Publishing,
20 Vauxhall Bridge Road,
London SW1V 2SA

Ebury Press is part of the Penguin Random House group of companies
whose addresses can be found at global.penguinrandomhouse.com

Penguin
Random House
UK

Copyright © Ali Millar, 2022

Ali Millar has asserted her right to be identified as the author of this
Work in accordance with the Copyright, Designs and Patents Act 1988

First published by Ebury Press in 2022
This edition published by Ebury Press in 2023

www.penguin.co.uk

A CIP catalogue record for this book is available from the British Library

ISBN 9781529109535

Printed and bound in Great Britain by Clays Ltd, Elcograf S.p.A.

The authorised representative in the EEA is Penguin Random House
Ireland, Morrison Chambers, 32 Nassau Street, Dublin D02 YH68

Penguin Random House is committed to a sustainable future
for our business, our readers and our planet. This book is made
from Forest Stewardship Council® certified paper.

MIX
Paper | Supporting
responsible forestry
FSC® C018179

This book is for Elizabeth: impossibly, always.
In memory of Chris.

'In the morning it was morning and I was still alive.'

Charles Bukowski

CONTENTS

CONTENTS

THE WORLD WITHIN THE WORD

IT IS 1982 AND IN the Kingdom Hall we are Jehovah's Witnesses.

Outside the Kingdom Hall is the world. We know the whole world is lying in the power of the wicked one, whose sole mission is to lead us away from Jehovah and his life-giving ways. The state of the world, where men have become lovers of pleasure rather than of God, shows us the end is close and Satan is like a roaring lion, seeking to devour us. Our five meetings a week keep us safe, as does studying our Bible-based literature.

Inside the Kingdom Hall we are all brothers and sisters who speak the pure language. We are one happy family, part of the worldwide association of Christian brothers. We are here to receive Jehovah's instructions.

We have a few simple beliefs, and these are not burdensome.

We believe the Bible is the infallible word of God. We believe every word of it to be true.

We do not believe in a heavenly hope. Instead we believe Jehovah God has anointed 144,000 humans to serve at His side for eternity. Everyone who survives His coming judgment will live forever on earth.

We do not believe in hellfire. Jehovah is a God of love.

We do not believe in the Trinity, because it is an impossibility.

We believe Jesus is God's Son and was sent to the earth to deliver us from sin.

We believe Eve's sin brought pain, suffering and death into the world.

We believe the earth was created in six days, although we do not know exactly how long a Biblical day is.

We know birthdays, Christmas and Easter are all of pagan origin. We shun false worship and do not celebrate any worldly holidays. Instead, we annually observe the death of Christ. This is a time to reflect on the value of the ransom sacrifice and what it means for us as Jehovah's people.

We believe blood is sacred, and under no circumstances would we accept a blood transfusion. If we should die because of this we know we have made Jehovah's heart glad, and he will reward us with everlasting life.

We believe our bodies are holy. We do not pollute them with drugs, tobacco or excessive alcohol. We do not engage in pre-marital sex.

We believe homosexuality is a sin from which we flee. We believe we must live according to the gender assigned to us at birth.

Husbands are the head of the family; wives and children must be submissive.

We believe worldly education is of little value, and avoid further education. We know the love of money is a trap and take care not to be ambitious. Brothers often work for themselves, sisters raise the family.

To keep the congregation clean, we disfellowship unrepentant wrongdoers, taking care not to associate with them afterwards. This is an act of love.

We know Jehovah is our best friend. This heavenly friendship is more important than all earthly ones. Jehovah has chosen to save us personally from the darkness of the world. We draw close to Jehovah by praying to him three times a day.

We believe the dead will be resurrected. This gives us much hope and comfort. We see death as a temporary state, akin to sleeping.

We have a direction and purpose that worldly people lack. Our purpose is to warn others the end is coming. The battle of Armageddon will bring the end, and only baptised members of Jehovah's earthly organisation will survive. After this we will live forever in paradise.

These are the beliefs that unite us in worship; these are the beliefs we teach others in our Christian ministry; these are the beliefs you listened to and laughed at to begin with, until you needed to believe them, until they were the comfort and salve they were intended to be; these are the beliefs that sound both facile and monstrous now from a distance; these are the beliefs that were mine too, so short a time ago; these are the beliefs you fed to me; these are the beliefs you said would save my life and neither of us knew, not then, what they would do to us.

BOOK ONE: GENESIS

1. CRITICAL TIMES

'But know this, that in the last days critical times hard to deal with will be here. For men will be lovers of themselves, lovers of money, boastful, haughty, blasphemers, disobedient to parents, unthankful, disloyal, having no natural affection, not open to any agreement, slanderers, without self-control, fierce, without love of goodness, betrayers, headstrong, puffed up with pride, lovers of pleasures rather than lovers of God.'

2 Tim. 3:1–4 NWT

'This good news of the kingdom will be preached in all the inhabited earth for a witness to all the nations; and then the end will come.'

Matt. 24:14 NWT

REMEMBER THE DAY YOU SAT *me on your knee and slipped the wide, worn silver band from your middle finger? You ran your fingers around the edge of it, bending your head over mine. See, you said, it has no end and no beginning: look.*

I looked.

I saw you caress the indentations on the metal with your long, slender fingers, your hazel eyes gazing down at it. I took it from you and felt its cold weight beneath my own fingers.

This is how you explained God to me.

When I asked who had made the ring you did not answer.

Then you said, It's like you and me. We will be together, always, like it says in the Bible.

I didn't tell you that you'd shortened the verse. You should have said we would be together always, even until the end of the world. But you'd told me the world wouldn't end, that it would go on forever.

All I can think of now is you and the ring. I want to know where your desire for God came from. How do you remember the memories of someone else, Agnès Varda wondered, and so do I. I want to feast on yours. I want to eat them up. I want to consume you in the hope I can make sense of you. I want to remember my conception and how it led to everything after. I want to be there in the beginning, before the earth took form and void, before the light and long before the darkness, before your Christ was impaled and risen. I will cannibalise you to take us both back there, to where this began with you and him, so long ago.

IN THE BEGINNING

1979

The sun put itself to bed hours ago and now
the village street is full of fog and winter dark. The
woman sits in the pub, twisting her hands together on
her knee. She tells herself he's coming, he will come.

This isn't something she's done before. She's never
left her five-year-old with a babysitter to meet someone she's only spoken to once on the phone; this isn't
what she does, this isn't who she is.

And yet, she liked the way he spoke, the long, slow
unspooling of his voice, an intimate whisper, snaking
into her ear. She taps her fingers on the table in front
of her, then stops: the barmaid is watching. She needs
to look confident, as if she knows he'll come.

The door swings open, and he stands in it for just
a second too long, the mist balling itself up onto his

wool coat. He peels it from his long body as he walks across the room towards her. The barmaid tucks a loose strand of hair behind her ear.

He smiles at the woman, stretches out his hand to take hers as he leans across the table towards her.

You must be, he says.

Yes, she giggles, yes. It's me.

He stares at her. Notices her high cheekbones and the hollows beneath them, her long nose, her delicate fingers, her deep brown eyes. He sees her chestnut-dark hair and the way it shines as the light catches it, hears the breeding in her low voice; a perfect specimen, he thinks. He smiles at her and the edges of his light blue eyes crinkle. This is the moment she knows they are soulmates.

He puts his coat over the back of the chair. Would you like a drink, he asks and, deep in the points of her stilettoes, she curls her toes. Please, she says. A Cinzano would be perfect.

She thinks she catches the faint peaty smell of whisky on his breath. Surely he's not been drinking already? But she tells herself not to be so suspicious as she sees his taut body cross the room. She hears the high-pitched laugh of the barmaid as he rests his elbows on the polished surface of the bar.

She leans back against the fake-leather banquette, hoping she's not sweating too much, and tugs slightly at the hem of her skirt. The barmaid pours the drinks then pulls a packet of Big D peanuts from the chest of the cardboard woman hanging behind the bar. He points to it, and she hears more laughter, but can't make out the exact shape of the words.

He comes back and puts their drinks down; she picks hers up immediately, trying to resist wiping the white bloom off the table. She worried beforehand about silence, but she shouldn't have. He talks for both of them. He's practised this often enough to know what he's doing now. He tells her about his ex-wife in South Africa, and how sad he is to not see his two sons, but some things can't be helped, and at least his work is fascinating. And she is wide-eyed, falling, hook, line, sinker, for all of it.

She nods a lot, giggles a lot. When she tells him about her daughter, she expects him to leave. But he only smiles and asks more questions.

She excuses herself to go to the bathroom, where she sits in the cubicle with the whole history of the village engraved on the wall, all the fights and fucks, the hastily scrawled phone numbers to call for good times, the break-ups, the make-ups. She tries to avoid the lurid details as she thinks maybe this is it, maybe this is how she escapes the weight of this place. Newcomer, they still call her, but soon she won't be anymore, she'll be packing up and leaving now she's found him.

Or he's found her. Hard to tell which way round fate works.

He's half slumped on the bar when she comes back; the barmaid is flushed and laughing as she pulls out another packet of peanuts and he laughs. Risky, he says.

The third drink turns him maudlin; he says he's lonely, he says he wants to settle down. He neglects to mention he's already fairly settled and on to his second wife, who is pregnant with his fourth child.

In the months to come, he fills her head full of dreams the way she's always wanted someone to. He doesn't call them dreams, he calls them plans. When she begins to feel sick and dizzy he tells her she's all he's ever wanted as she twists her new diamond ring on her finger and pats her growing, stretching, itching stomach, where inside I tumble and stretch and she feeds her blood to me, and, symbiotic already, I eat her up.

She gives up her job and knows everything will be fixed now he's here. That's what men do for her, they fix things.

He manages to stay nine months before the fruit is too tempting elsewhere. Her brother discovers the other wife and the *other* other woman; his holy trinity, each of them pregnant or lactating.

He leaves me mewing in her arms and she sits, shaking, with an empty bank account.

The wolves come knocking then. What she still needs is a man, a real man, someone to wrap her up and keep her warm; someone to tell her what to do and what to think and what to believe, and men come in many guises. It isn't long before He comes, before He is there, omnipresent and eternal, giving her the comfort she's been waiting for, and when I am two and too young to remember life outside in the garden, she weds herself to Him in the swimming pool, held under by four strong arms, and she rises, washed clean, spotless and unblemished in the blood of the Lamb. From that day on, He holds her in His teeth.

*

Is this how you remember the memories of someone else? I don't know. What I do know is that I dreamt last night that I could remember all your memories. It was one of the worst dreams I've ever had. It was a warning, I know, to leave your memories alone, and stick to mine only. What follows is what I remember happening.

Maggie Nelson wrote, 'I want you to know, if you ever read this, there was a time when I would rather have had you by my side than any one of these words; I would rather have had you by my side than all the blue in the world.'

I want you to remember that, Mum: all the blue, always.

WASHED CLEAN IN
THE BLOOD OF THE LAMB

1982

THERE IS A PHOTOGRAPH, OR there was a photo-graph, and in it is the little girl I don't want to remember being.

In the photograph I'm standing under a tree, wearing stiff brown shoes, and I'm scowling into the camera lens. I like to make this face a lot because I think I have a pretty frown. My sister tells me I will have a face full of lines when I'm old. I know she is stupid because I'm not going to get old. Mummy has told me Jehovah's new system will be here before I start school. I will be young and pretty and perfect for forever and ever. Safe in this knowledge, I scowl.

I'm under the tree because five minutes earlier I

made a huge fuss. Huge fusses are things I am good at making. Huge fusses are things I am not to make today, not on Mummy's special day.

Her special day is happening in the box near the tree. They say it is a swimming pool, but it looks like a big box to me. I don't like swimming pools. They don't make sense like the sea does. Swimming pools have rules and the sea does not. The aunty Mummy left me with says she's being baptised in the pool inside the box. I am not sure exactly what this means, and I don't want to find out.

Mummy knows I do not go in boxes. She should have known I wouldn't go in this box. I am not a parcel, I say when I see a lift; I will not go in it. And then I try to make my feet stick to the ground so she can't pick me up and put me in. Sometimes Mummy says I am opinionated and her breath comes out her mouth like a hiss; that's how I know opinionated is a bad thing to be.

Aunty Hazel says, You are missing your mummy being dunked under the water. You are missing your mummy start her new life. I know she is playing a game and the game is to make me feel bad. I will not feel bad about not going in the box. She says, It is a happy day and you have made a huge fuss. Your poor mummy.

People always say Mummy is a poor mummy. I know we're poor, but don't know why people tell me about it all the time. They tell me to look after my mummy and they tell me to be big and brave for her. This feels sort of upside down.

I will not let Aunty Hazel's game work, so I stand scowling in my stiff brown shoes for the invisible photographer.

I am always already too obstinate, too hard of heart.

This is how it is I miss my mother's rebirth; how I miss her marrying herself to her new God; how I miss the ending wrapped up as a beginning.

NOT FORSAKING
THE GATHERING OF
OURSELVES TOGETHER

1986

E VERY WEEK HAS THE SAME routine. This keeps us strong in the faith. This is an important thing to be, because otherwise we are easy prey for Satan who is like a roaring lion seeking to devour someone. I have to be careful that that someone is not me. Mummy has made sure I know this.

The week's routine looks like this: Sundays are for the two-hour meeting, with ministry afterwards; Monday is studying at home with Mummy and my sister Zoe; Tuesday is the book study I am trying hard not to hate (but not trying hard enough); Wednesday is studying the *Watchtower* for Sunday and practising the answers we will give; Thursday is the two-hour meeting, the one I am tired after; Friday is preparing for Tuesday and Thursday *and* practising what to say on the ministry; Saturday morning is ministry and then cake at someone's house afterwards, and Saturday night is for an interchange of encouragement, but sometimes for Granny and Grampa's house, which is good because we don't have to say prayers out loud there. We still have to say them in our heads, but we are not to talk about Jehovah and His life-giving ways at Granny's house because Granny and Grampa do not love Jehovah and will die at Armageddon. I like it there. I get to watch *Bergerac*. Granny says John Nettles has such lovely eyes.

I am always tired from all of this. Sometimes I think bad thoughts. Sometimes I think how I would like to wake up on a Saturday morning and watch TV like the other kids at school do. We don't have a television though. Mummy says they bring demons in.

There are no birthdays or Christmases to mark time. I know when things happen because I know the years of famines or earthquakes or new wars. These are things worldly people call bad news, but we know are good news. These are things that mean we must be thankful and happy, because the end is very close.

Mummy always tells me how lucky I am to be one of Jehovah's people. I am going to live forever. I am lucky because I don't have to decide what to do for a job or to go to university like worldly people. The end will be here soon. The end is when Jehovah will kill all the bad people and let all his faithful servants live forever on paradise earth. Imagine, Mummy says, how exciting it'll be to live forever. We will be able to pat lions and all the bad people will be gone for good.

NOT CELEBRATING
PAGAN HOLIDAYS

1986

IT IS THURSDAY NIGHT IN the Kingdom Hall and I am swinging my legs back and forward. Mummy reaches across and puts her hand on my knee. Her hand means I'm to stop. Jehovah does not like little girls who fidget. I am trying to be a little girl Jehovah likes because I don't want to die when the end comes. But I'm not very good at pleasing Jehovah. I don't close the doors on my cupboards properly or fold my clothes the right way or manage to keep my eyes shut during the whole prayer. Mummy says these are things good girls do. I need to work harder.

I stop kicking.

I'm supposed to be listening to the speaker who is telling us life-giving things, but I am like a sleeping dog with one ear open and one ear switched off. My ear that is off is busy thinking other things. I'm thinking about the Kingdom Hall ceiling with long bumpy lines on it. I think they look like Hebrew. I know what Hebrew looks like because I've seen pictures of it in *My Book of Bible Stories*. I think after the meeting I will tell the other children it's Hebrew, and they'll give me an impressed look. I think this is naughty because it will be a lie, since I don't exactly know what the lines really are. Lies are from the devil.

The speaker's voice sounds far away. He's talking about things I don't understand. My eyes are heavy. The air is too warm.

I say sorry to Jehovah in my head for this lie I've almost told and still might. I say I'll not eat my pudding if Mummy doesn't find out what I have been thinking.

I wriggle my bottom on the hard seat. I want to sit on Mummy's knee and go to sleep, but I am too old for that now. I try to lick my lips, but my mouth is dry. I can still taste the taste from earlier: at school I did one of the worst things I have ever done. I betrayed Jehovah, and this, maybe, is why I'm not able to sit still. I've done bad things before. Once, I dropped a rattle on my baby cousin's head and it made her cry. That was a bad thing. I washed the tail of my cat with laundry powder and it changed colour. That was a bad thing. But none of these things are as bad as betraying Jehovah's trust. Mummy said that once trust is broken it doesn't fix properly.

The taste sits there in my mouth. If I can still taste it then maybe someone will be able to smell it. Big people know the smells of most things. I especially do not want Zoe to know about what I did. If she knows she'll tell Mummy, the way she always tells her everything. Zoe is six years older than me and can tell all the bad things I think and say and do just by looking at me.

At school they said it would be nice to make Christmas cards with Santa on. I love Christmas. I love Granny's sitting room with all the pretty cards hung in long rows, I love the tree with its white lights and glass balls. I love *The Snowman* on the television, and Christmas cake with its white icing that cracks as Granny tries to cut it with the special silver knife. A long time ago, until I was four, we were allowed to do Christmas on a different day at Granny's house, but Mummy stopped that.

True Christians do not celebrate Christmas. For us, Christmas is a normal day. Mummy says it is a chance to show Jehovah our loyalty. We show our loyalty by not making cards at school or singing carols or going to church services. We sit loyally in the sitting room on Christmas Day not thinking about the things that are happening in other houses.

I thought it would not be such a bad thing to make a card. I drew two boots on the black gummed paper. With sharp scissors I cut the boots out. I licked them and stuck them onto white card that looked like new snow. This is the taste that is making my mouth dry.

I pulled apart two balls of cotton wool to make his beard. I can still feel the dry pull of them between my fingers. Some glue is stuck to my skin. When I pull at it, it feels like it'll rip my skin off. That would serve me right.

I wonder where the teacher put the card. Did she put it on the drying rack? Did she put it in my tray? Did she put it in my school bag? How long until Mummy finds out the terrible thing I've done? I think of the sack I cut out, all fat with presents for other children, and how I wrote in the card: 'Dear Santa, I would like a new doll and pram for Christmas, even though Mummy says Santa is a lie made up by the devil.' I asked for things I don't need, this means I am greedy, and greed is a sin. It is a sin to want things you can't have, Mummy once said. It is better to not want too much from life, she said in a quieter voice.

I think I could say a silent prayer of repentance to Jehovah. But I know I can't ask for my sins to remain undiscovered, so I don't pray. I just sit there and think of all the things that mean I'm a bad little girl and not a good one. Actions speak louder than words, Mummy says. Mine are screaming at me.

Doing this bad thing means I'll die when the end comes. This means birds will peck my eyes out. This is what the Bible says will happen to all the people who die at Armageddon. On the platform the elders say bodies will line the streets after the great tribulation. In the magazines there are brightly coloured pictures of wars and famines and diseases and earthquakes.

Mummy says we need to be joyful because our deliverance from this sinful world is close at hand. I'm not good at being joyful because I know these things mean I am about to die too. When I die, Mummy will discover what a naughty little girl I really am.

Jehovah only kills naughty little girls.

I will make her sad.

I bite my lips. The speaker says we are to sing song number 15 and I jump up and sing it loudly because it's my favourite. It's about the new system, lions lying down with lambs. When the song finishes, I bow my head to pray and I say, AMEN, loudly at the end, even though I know Jehovah will not listen to me because I'm too bad.

After the meeting finishes, I go up to the magazine counter with Mummy to help her collect the literature. We take the jam jar that holds the money for them with us and count out the change to pay the elder behind the counter. Even if there's no money for sweeties, or chicken, or real butter, even if Mummy is crying on the phone to Granny about having to stretch the budget again, there's always money for the magazines. When we distribute the magazines, we have to ask the householder for money, and then we put the money in the jam jar to buy more, but we also have to add our own money and then put it all in the box at the back of the Kingdom Hall every week to support the worldwide preaching work.

Mummy takes a big pile of magazines and gives some to me to hold. Why don't you sit and read one of them while you wait to go home, she says. I sit down and look at the cover with a big picture of what looks like a giant dusty mushroom on the front. I know it's an atomic bomb because I know the nuclear war is about to come. Below the cloud it says in big writing: WORLD ON THE BRINK.

That night, when I go to bed, I dream the dream I am always dreaming, the one I am most afraid of. I am not afraid of spiders or bugs but I am scared of the dark, of war, of the Great Tribulation, of clearing the dead from the streets or being one of the dead cleared from the street. I should not be scared of any of these things, but I am scared of them because I don't have enough faith. The thing I am the most scared of is the dream I am always dreaming, because it is right there happening in my head and I can't stop it. It's a dream of things that look like clouds. That is all it is. There are only clouds and clouds and clouds.

In the dream I'm in the clouds and I need to get somewhere. My legs will not move. I try to make them, but they don't work. The clouds get closer and thicker, and as they do, they change colour. They go from being white to grey to clouds all black and thick all around me. I am in the middle of them as they eat me up.

I scream.

I scream so loudly I wake up. I'm sitting up in bed screaming when I hear Mummy's door creak open.

I feel the sticky feeling of pee as it dries on my leg.

Mummy comes into my room and pulls the covers

back sharply, telling me to stand up. She strips the sheet from my bed and says, I'll need to take you back to the doctor again, the pills aren't working anymore.

I sit in the not-cold-but-not-hot bath with the night outside the window. It wants in. I shut my eyes to keep it out but when I do my dream is there, clouds and clouds and clouds all eating me up.

THIS GOOD NEWS OF THE
KINGDOM WILL BE PREACHED

1985

I AM FIVE YEARS OLD AND already an expert on doorbells.

I know there are big fat round ones that are black with white buttons in the middle. I know there are some that play tunes. I know others need to be pressed hard and fully and that there's a trick to these ones, where it's possible to make it look like they've been pressed when they haven't been and the householder will never come. I should feel bad about this. But I don't, because when we leave we write down the addresses of the people who aren't at home and then we keep going back and back and back until we get them. Mummy says Jehovah will make sure everyone with the right heart attitude is saved before the end comes.

My favourite of all the doorbells is one I have only seen on a single house. It has a big winding mechanism, like on the bottom of my jewellery box, that needs to be turned round and round until it's wound so tightly it can't help but spin in the opposite direction. Then from deep inside the house, I hear the bell ring, before hurried footsteps bring tiny Mrs Honeywell to the door. She has a dovecote in her garden that she sometimes lets us look at after I've done my presentation. I like her, she always gives me 40 pence for the magazines. As she gives me the money she smiles and says, Don't spend it all at once, as if she thinks I get to keep it all and not give it to Mummy to put in the jar for more magazines.

Mr Snowball doesn't have a doorbell; instead he has a big brass fox's head that I like to lift and drop and listen to as it echoes in the bones of his big house. He shuffles along his red floor tiles, his feet making a swishing sound. When he answers the door his big toe in his thick grey socks is poking through the fur-lined leather of his slippers. I love his name and I love his overgrown, tangled garden smelling of lavender and rosemary, which I try to rub against so the scent of them sticks to my hands and I can sniff them later.

Once, after it has rained the rain makes itself into thick drops that brush their way onto my duffel coat. We've been in Mr Snowball's garden for long enough for my hands to turn red and puffy and my nose to get drippy. I'm away somewhere else in my head when suddenly I see a giant turtle. It's huge, like something from the Galapagos Islands. It ambles along, lifting each thick leg deliberately, placing its feet down on the crunchy path. Its shell is so thick and pointy it looks like it would survive the nuclear holocaust. Look, Mummy, I shout, before I remember to be quiet. A turtle. Mummy and Mr Snowball laugh. A tortoise you mean, Mummy says. It'll probably outlive me, Mr Snowball says, like a stupid person who doesn't understand that all the people who love Jehovah will live forever, maybe even people who only take the magazines.

You can see it next time, he says, but the next time the tortoise is hibernating. When he stops taking the magazines, we stop visiting him.

Mr Snowball is not a study, he is only a return visit. Studies are people who Mummy is trying to help become baptised Witnesses of Jehovah. She visits them and together they read the literature from the society, and the studies answer questions. I like studies best, because I get to see inside their houses. It's like looking at a tiny piece of their lives. Theirs are lives I'd never get to see otherwise. Behind every doorbell is a life as different as the bell is.

Mummy has lots of studies. She has Mrs Lyon, who has a fancy doorbell and a big white house full of antiques. I love antiques the best. Her coal fire spits and splutters all day, throwing tiny black pieces out onto the carpet and making a funny smell. Because of the fire, her house is always too hot and, because it is always too hot, I want to sleep when we visit. My head starts to nod and drop to my jumper as Mummy tells her about Babylon the Great and false religion and how the end will come just as it did in Noah's day. I'm supposed to read a scripture but sometimes Mummy needs to remind me because I'm too busy looking at the pictures lining her walls as a way to stay awake. My favourite painting is also the most sinful. It's a lady with no top on. Instead of a top she has long hair covering both of her breasts. Her hair is thick and golden and stretches all the way down to her belly button. She stares out of the painting at me as if she doesn't care that I'm looking at her. One day, Mrs Lyon's son, David, comes in and tells me that my hair will be like that soon. I have very long and thick blonde hair but have never thought of it in the way David describes. I feel strange, like I want to shiver. David is a character, Mummy says. She says this around Christmastime when he gives me a glass of watered-down sherry and Mummy a glass of whisky, and we both have thick slices of fruitcake because it would be rude not to, and Mummy's nose is pink when we walk home in the dark with the streetlamps making golden haloes in the snow where my boots sink, the frost sticking to my tights.

Mrs Cow is another study. She has a simple, white doorbell stuck to the side of her door. Next to it is a giant number 3, all thick and curly, like it's made from toothpaste squeezed from the tube. Mrs Cow has been a study for a long time. She should be progressing to baptism. Some people progress more slowly than others, Mummy says. I think Mrs Cow progresses slowly because she is very bad at reading. She studies from a simplified brochure with huge writing and pictures. When Mummy asks her a question, she reads the answer and smiles when Mummy says, Well done. Mummy says, The beautiful thing about the truth is anyone can learn it.

Mummy likes teaching people the truth. In fact, she used to be a teacher.

Mummy says Mrs Cow lives in a bungalow, but I'm not sure she's right, because her house isn't like the bungalows at the end of the village that are long and fancy with big gardens wrapping around them. Mrs Cow lives in two rooms and has a concrete path going up to the front of her house. Her door creaks as she opens it, and I try not to giggle, remembering I am not allowed to suggest that she oils it because that would be rude. Mrs Cow lives in her two rooms all on her own and is so lonely, I think, that she sometimes forgets to open her curtains. I make a plan to make her less lonely. My plan is that I will give her my second favourite doll to keep her company for a week. When I take her my doll, with a tiny blue suitcase packed with changes of clothes, she says, You are a very kind girl. I don't tell her it is only my second favourite. At the end of the week my doll is wearing different clothes and smells a bit funny too. Mummy and the aunties laugh about it afterwards when they have tea and biscuits. I'm not sure what's funny.

Because Mummy has so many studies she doesn't have a job. Mummy is doing Jehovah's work, which is far more important than working for worldly people and money. We get our money from the post office every Thursday when her special book is stamped and a whole lot of crisp notes with the special money smell are handed over. Mummy says this is playing the system and is something Jesus would be proud of.

Soon, I will have to start school and won't get to go with Mummy anymore on the weekday ministry. It is important, she says, that I make the most of it before it's only Saturdays and Sundays I'll be left with. To make the most of my time we visit Vivien who has just come out of the mental hospital after having her baby. Vivien cries about not being able to give him breastmilk or disposable nappies. We visit the family who don't have a doorbell, just a long letter box the same as us. There the children sit on the floor and play with empty tape boxes. Before we go in, Mummy says that even if I am desperate to go to the toilet, I must not go, the same as she says when we visit Mrs Trotter. Mrs Trotter asks who we are every time we visit but still asks us in. She wears giant nappies and hangs them on the fireguard to dry them out so the whole of her tiny sitting room smells of pee. Mummy tells me to sit on the side of the sofa when we are there. I try not to notice that the carpet makes a sucking and squelching sound as we walk over it. Mrs Trotter likes to give us cups of tea and before we leave Mummy takes them to the kitchen and pours them down the sink.

The life-giving work we are doing is essential, Mummy says, and so do the elders to make it doubly

true. We wouldn't let people die in a burning building; they say this is why we can't let people die in
Satan's burning world.

Seeing all these pieces of other people's lives is a bit
like watching television without the screen. Sometimes it feels too close. I worry about what my life
will look like when I'm older. Mummy tells me what
life was like for her when she was little, and I know
from the faraway sound of her voice that it is different
to her life now. I can't decide if she thinks this is a bad
thing or a good thing. I tell her when I'm big I will
live in Germany and have a fitted kitchen, but she
says, It's not always possible to get what you want
from life.

I think of all the people we visit in their houses
and wonder what it was they wanted and still want. I
worry I'll get stuck like them here behind the hills
and the trees that suck people in where the rest of the
world feels very far away, all the time.

RESIST THE DEVIL

1986

A T THE ASSEMBLY ALL THE congregations meet together so we can learn lots of exciting new things, and also because Jesus used to do it with the Israelites. Because we follow Jesus, we try to do the same things he did.

On the platform an elder gives a talk to warn us about things that could contain demons. He tells us about a sister who bought a china cat from a charity shop; once she got the cat home, strange things began to happen. One night as she was sleeping, she felt something lying on her, but when she woke there was nothing there. She sat up but could still feel something touching her. That was when she realised there was a demon right there in her bedroom. She got the china cat and was careful to take it outside before she smashed it. If she'd broken it inside, well, the trouble that could have caused, all the demons caught in the cat would have escaped into her house and who knows the chaos they'd bring with them. What faith she had, the elder says, and everyone claps very loudly to show how much they agree.

This is why we need to avoid charity shops from now on. This is not handy. Mummy needs to go to the charity shop, because they are cheaper than the normal shops.

When the elder continues to explain that demons might send messages in records, I write that down in my new notebook. He says, They hide messages that people can only hear if they play them backwards. It's helpful of him to explain this because I am finding it all a little bit confusing.

It also sounds like an exciting thing, but I don't write that down. I say to my thought, Go away. I write down: 'Demons are very good at pretending to be other people, just look at Satan the devil, the father of the lie, who transformed himself into the snake who misled Eve.'

This time after the assembly finishes we don't stop at the chip shop on the way home like we do sometimes as an extra-special treat. Mummy says, We need to get home as quickly as we can. At home she takes all the records out of the white spinning bookcase that is also a drinks cabinet. It isn't like Granny's drinks cabinet. Hers has all sorts of pretty bottles with all different coloured liquid in, and but Mummy's only has one bottle in it that she never takes out apart from when she makes the special ice cream I'm not allowed to eat for visitors. She takes out Fleetwood Mac last and puts it on the floor.

I know we aren't allowed to listen to that one because it has my daddy's name, which is also my real name, on it. I'm not allowed to talk about him because we don't know if anything he told Mummy was true, and he broke her heart, and it wasn't that long ago. Mummy says, You only think it is a long time ago because you have nothing to compare time to.

Soon there is a huge stack of records on the floor, all slipping off each other. Let's take them outside, Mummy says. I don't know what we are going to do but I help to pick them up. Zoe has a great pile of them in her arms even though she said, Do I have to? and Mummy said, Yes, it's really important we follow directions.

I follow Mummy to the park behind the house. It's hard to scramble up the grass banking without free hands to grab onto it. I am out of puff by the time I get to the top. The sky is beginning to think about getting dark and is all different blues and reds and oranges that make my tummy feel sore. There are children playing at the park. Bad boys are on the swings and some of them are walking up the slide, taking the mud on their shoes up it with them. The bad boys shout names over to us, they shout, Hovis Witness, and rude words. Mummy says, It's OK, think of Elijah and how the bears attacked the bad children. I think of bears coming out from the line of trees at the back of the park and baring their teeth and ripping the boys into tiny pieces until I'm not so sure that I want to think about Elijah anymore. I wonder how it must feel to be one of the boys; I think climbing the slide and jumping off swings looks like good fun.

Mummy takes a record out of its sleeve and tries to bend it. This is surprising because she always tells me to be extra careful with records. It doesn't want to bend. Zoe says, Here, give it to me, and holds her hands out. I'm not sure what they're doing. She takes it from Mummy, puts it on the ground and then stamps hard on it. Nothing much happens; it bends a little bit and mud flies up onto Zoe's pink tights.

When Mummy jumps on it, a piece breaks off and lies in the grass. Mummy and Zoe laugh. It breaks into smaller and smaller pieces and then Zoe gets the hang of it too, and together they jump on the records, making them smaller and smaller and less and less useful.

I try. I am too little to make them break. Come on, Thunder Thighs, jump, Zoe shouts. I try, the records still don't break. They just bend more on the damp grass, and my feet get wet. I want to go back inside. Pick up the pieces then, Zoe says, do something useful. I begin to collect the bits and worry that maybe I'm collecting all the demons back together so they can be trapped inside a bin and then what will happen to them after that? I'm scared that the demons are now roaming around in the park just outside the back door of our house. Surely they will find their way back in or maybe even hang around in the garden outside the guinea pigs' hutch, just waiting for me to come out with vegetable scraps to throw into the run. I will try not to think of them like this, not when I am feeding the animals in the dark.

There are too many pieces to hold all at once. Mummy says, I'll go and get a binbag, you collect all the bits. After she leaves, the boys come across from the swings with some bigger boys. They smile at Zoe as they walk in a circle around us.

They all laugh. Fucking weirdos, they say. But they run away when Mummy comes back. They aren't as brave as they want us to think they are.

It begins to get dark, a deep blue dark like the ink I spilt on the new sofa. We go home with white air coming out of our mouths. I pretend it's smoke. After dinner when Mummy gives me carrot tops and cabbage leaves to take out to the piggies, I run down the path, afraid of the dark. There are hundreds of tiny snowflake shapes on the paving stones as the frost forms. To try to stop the afraid feeling growing in my tummy and moving up to my throat, I look up at the stars and remember the promise God made to Abraham and how Jehovah delivered him, like one day he will deliver us.

SINS OF THE FLESH

1986

DINNERS AT GRANNY'S HOUSE ARE the best. Because Granny is rich she always has lots of food in the kitchen. She has beef and butter, brown bread and biscuits, seedless grapes and dates, it is a house full of food. Mummy says it wasn't always like this. She says, We were poor growing up just like we are now. Granny tells me about the sailing boat she had when she was little and shows me the pearl necklace the villagers gave to her granny when she was 21 because they loved how well she looked after them from her big house. This makes my head hurt and time make no sense. All this poorness, this richness, it feels like a changeable thing, a thing to move between, even though Mummy cries a lot about money and not having a job, and when she cries to Granny about it Granny says she should go back to teaching, and when she cries to the elders they say she should trust in Jehovah. I guess Mummy is a very trusting person.

Sometimes I like to just stand in Granny's larder and look at all the food stretching up high on the shelves above my head. She even has a SodaStream machine, which is a sort of magic thing that makes water fizzy and then you can pour juice into it to flavour it however you want. When I'm there with my cousins, which isn't very often because they are worldly and Mummy is still sad about her big brother finding out my dad had another wife, we make all sorts of flavoured drinks. I like my cousins. Mummy says they are high spirited, and I think she might be right, although she says it like it's a bad thing but I think it's a good thing because they are fun. They teach me to make tropical juice with the SodaStream and tell me that Grampa doesn't realise pick-and-mix is sold by weight so when he buys it just fills the whole bag up. They are always running around and being loud and so when I'm with them I do the same thing and it feels like being at home with people the same as me, which is a strange and bad thing to think about people who are worldly, especially when the brothers and sisters in the Kingdom Hall say they are family now. They say to Mummy, It doesn't matter what you've given up, we are your spiritual family. I am not too sure.

Granny even has ice pops in her freezer. She has a big freezer in the outhouse that she fills with dead lambs and pigs and cows and ice pops at the top. These big long poles of frozen juice are like miracles when we've been running round the garden or hitting croquet balls as hard as we can. We don't even need to ask if we can have one, we can just take them and tear the plastic off the top with our teeth. The ice squeaks as we crunch it. The juice melts at the bottom and we tip the plastic up to get the last bits of the melted ice out and the syrup escapes our mouth and onto our chins and sometimes onto our tops, where it leaves round stains even the hot wash can't take out. The best thing is we can do this over and over. As many times as we like. The ice pops are like manna from heaven. They never run out. I like the cola ones the best, followed by the orange. We all do. We learn not to fight about this. Although sometimes we pull each other's hair, nip each other's skin. Tiny things for no one to see.

Granny's table is like Christmas all the time. I still remember when we used to have our different-day Christmas at Granny and Grampa's. Granny would make a Christmas dinner, which was like no other meal we had for the rest of the year. There would be fish knives and butter knives and a starter and a fish course and turkey and cranberry jelly she'd made herself, all winking and pink in a crystal bowl in the middle of the table. There would be red and green candles and the smell of so much food in the air would make my tummy happier than anything I could ever describe. One time, Mummy reached across the candles and the mohair her jumper was made from caught itself into a tiny fire and the room smelt like burnt cat and everyone laughed with flushed cheeks and Grampa filled up their glasses with the German wine from a blue bottle. After lunch Granny and Grampa would give us a big present. It felt how I think Christmas must feel. We don't do it anymore. Now we sit in our house and pretend nothing is happening on that day. The thing about pretending a thing isn't happening is it becomes the only thing it's possible to think about.

It's not too bad. Granny makes a fuss of us. I don't think this is to make us feel special. She makes a fuss of everyone. Granny loves people like no one else I know. Apart from me. Mummy says Granny can't love me because I look like my dad. Because I look like him, I remind her of him. This is my fault for still being here. The good thing is I still get to eat her food. I'm sitting at the table thinking of ice pops and how nice it would be if it was still summer but the leaves have fallen from the trees. We went on a walk earlier and trampled through them and now I am hungry and on my plate there is new meat I haven't eaten before. It is sort of like a cross between chicken and lamb, which is a bit weird, but I like it. It is a heavy sort of a meat. Mummy eats some. Then she frowns. Then she pushes it with her fork to pick it up and looks under the meat where pink juices are running from it. She swallows. Grampa takes something out his mouth from where he's sitting on his special big chair at the top of the table. Louise, he says to Granny, holding up a round thing, you nearly took my teeth out! Granny laughs at him, and tells us to be careful, we need to watch for shot.

I don't know what shot is. I hate food with things in. That's why I am suspicious of the sausages Mummy gives me with hard white lumps in them. That's why I don't trust fish with bones just waiting to choke me.

Shot! Mummy shouts, then she looks at Granny a bit like she would like to shoot her. You said, Mummy says, this was bled, and now you're saying it's shot.

Granny doesn't say anything back quickly, which is not how Granny usually works. Well dear, she says after a while, I'm sure it's been bled, it was just shot before it was. Mummy pushes her chair back and stands up. Her cheeks are red and her eyes are the cold eyes you don't want to look at you. No, Mum, she says, you tried to trick me. You knew these pheasants were shot and hadn't been bled before you fed them to us. Girls, Mummy shouts as she turns to us, stop eating!

Then Mummy runs out the room shouting something about needing to phone the elders immediately, and Zoe runs after her, and then Granny runs out too and me and Grampa are left sitting there. Grampa looks at me, and then he picks up the piece of shot on his plate and holds it up to me. It's a tiny little round ball. Who would have thought, he says to me in his warm voice, that something so little could cause so much fuss? Then he starts to carry on carving the meat up, pushing it with his knife onto his fork. Go on, he says, eat it if you want to. I look at the meat and then I think of Jehovah telling us that all meat needs to be bled, as it was when our people were in the wilderness. I said to Mummy once that I wasn't sure it was our people who'd been given the Ten Commandments but rather the Israelites, but she said they prefigured the Witnesses, and it was Jehovah who'd given them the commandments, and those commandments they were given so long ago were ours too, so we were in many ways also the same people. This confused me. Especially since Mummy says the Jews are the worst for killing Jesus. I think the reason she's always saying things about Jews is because my dad is one. Sometimes I wonder if that makes me one too, but that's another thought I make go away until it gets bigger and bigger. Thoughts are a pest like that. I look at Grampa and see how much he's enjoying this sinful flesh and I remember what it tasted like and know I won't be allowed to eat it ever again and so I put it on my fork and eat it. It doesn't taste so good anymore.

I hear Mummy on the phone through the dining-room hatch, she is saying, Thank you, thank you, thank you, to the elder she's talking to. She is saying, I didn't mean to eat it, I was tricked into it. When she comes back into the room her cheeks are all puffy and her eyes are all red. I put my fork down. She says, We're going home now. Granny says, But it's strawberry bavarois for pudding. This is my favourite. Granny serves it with langues de chat, which is French for cats' tongues, which I think is an excellent name for sponge biscuits lumpy with sugar. I use them to scoop the soft pudding up and don't use a spoon and Mummy can't tell me to stop or say it's rude because it's Granny's house and Granny doesn't care about that. So long as I use the right fork for the right course, by the time it gets to pudding, I can do what I like.

But today there will be no pudding. No end of dinner, when Granny says we are not to fold our napkins but instead leave them at the side of our plates to show we've finished our dinner, because whoever doesn't wash their napkins after every meal. Mummy, I said once, and Mummy was not happy, just like Mummy is not happy now about the pheasant and the blood and the trick and Jehovah and it is dark in the car when we drive home. It is a long time after that until I see Granny or Grampa again. It's OK, Mummy says when I ask about them, Aunty Ingrid and Uncle Liam are like your granny and grampa now.

AND DEATH WILL BE NO MORE

1987

I'M SEVEN WHEN MUMMY'S SISTER, Aunty Liz, who is not a Witness, teaches me the trick of leaving myself.

The fields are golden and the farmers, knowing it won't be long before the first frost, have sent their combines out to gather the last of the harvest. The fields look like the syrup we put on our pancakes as a treat. I watch them on my way home through the window of the big bus. The long rectangular windows along the top are open to let the air in. It rushes in too loud and too cold, but it brings with it the sound of the combines moving up and down and down and up. I like the rhythm of them, their slow hum. The other children are in harvest assembly, but because it is a pagan celebration, I'm allowed to go home early. I'm excited to be going home because Zoe will not be there. I like the times without her the best.

Mummy isn't at the bus stop when the bus gets in. I stand under the big clock with the racing car on it and watch it tick and tick. I worry she isn't coming. Then I see her running up the hill. Her eyes are puffy, as though she has hay fever.

We walk down the steep hill holding hands. I swing Mummy's arm back and forth and make my ponytail swish. I pretend I am a real horse. I don't tell Mummy how that morning other children brought in vegetables and tins and big cakes for the harvest festival. I want to ask her if I didn't take anything for the altar because Jehovah doesn't like celebrating things or if it was because we are poor. But I don't.

At home, I sit on the front step and play with Zoe's baby rabbit. Her fur is so thick my hand sinks into it when I pat her, and deep inside it I can feel her tiny body. I have to hold her very firmly close to me otherwise she might hop out of my arms, which means that I'm never comfortable when I hold her and am always a little bit worried she'll jump out and hop away down the street. We don't have a front gate to stop her. Usually, I'm not allowed to hold Wispa because she's Zoe's rabbit but today Mummy said I could, and I don't want to remind her of the things I shouldn't be doing.

I tickle Wispa's ears and she sits there gently, with the sun warming both of us, and even the hard stone step feels warm under my bottom. In that moment the whole world is warm and at peace even though I know the Bible says the opposite.

Mummy comes and stands in the doorway.

Her face looks strange, almost as if she's suddenly very old. She says, There's something I need to tell you, you better come inside.

The world is too loud. The birds shout and tractors roar. I think of all the things I do that I shouldn't, and know that's why Mummy's telling me to go in. I worry that somehow she knows I want to be a make-up designer when I grow up and not a missionary preaching to all the poor godless Africans.

The doorstep feels cold now. I stand up. I squeeze Wispa too tightly as I put her in her cage and follow Mummy inside.

In the sitting room she sits down and pats her knee. This means I am to sit on it. I'm too big now to fit myself easily onto her knee. I try to. I put my head on her jumper. It scratches my face.

She says, Aunty Liz is dead.

The room spins and goes black. When I am back in it, it has become a strange room I haven't seen before; all the pictures on the walls seem new, the plants new, the sewing machine new, even Mummy looks like someone else.

I don't know why she thinks it's funny to lie to me.

She picks me up and puts me on the floor, as if I'm holding her too tightly, as if I'm something she needs to remove. The room still feels black. I don't like it. She pulls her lips tight in the new way she's discovered

50

overnight, and tells me I need to put my shoes on as she walks out the room.

I sit there puzzled about why she's lied to me. It is a very strange thing to make up, even though Aunty Liz is in hospital because she's sad and sad people die. I know when Mummy comes back into the room she'll say, Tricked you, only joking.

She'll say sorry for getting it wrong. She'll kiss the top of my head.

When she comes into the room I wait for those things to happen. They don't. She says, Hurry up, put your shoes on.

I put my top teeth hard against my bottom ones to stop myself crying.

My shoes are made from stiff brown leather. I polish them every Saturday night so they are shiny for Jehovah on Sundays. Jehovah is a holy God; He likes clean shoes and clothes and bodies and faces and houses and gardens and organised insides of drawers and cupboards. But I am dirty on the outside of me and messy on the inside of me, Jehovah must find it hard to like me.

I wish my feet would hurry up and grow so I can get new shoes. I've tried to make them look old, but Mummy just makes me polish over the scuffs. When I tell her they aren't comfy she says, They're perfectly fine. Mummy isn't good at getting tricked, at least not by me. I would like slip-on shoes like the worldly girls at school wear.

I put my shoes on and my feet feel like they are being swallowed.

Halfway to Granny's house, just past the paper mill that makes everything stink of eggs, Mummy stops the car. Come on, she says, climb over into the front seat. I need to tell you something else. I sit next to her feeling like I'm grown up, even though my knee is sore because I just bumped it on the gear stick as I climbed over.

I make lots of noises as I clamber over, to exaggerate how difficult it is. The kind of noises that would usually make her smile but her face is wet behind her glasses. I sit down and stare out the front windscreen. I begin to worry that what she said might be true. I begin to wonder how it would feel if Aunty Liz was really, actually, stone dead.

Aunty Liz didn't just die, she says. She killed herself.

I think about this. Mummy can't be lying because Satan is the father of the lie and she hates Satan. I should've thought of that earlier. So, Aunty Liz is dead. This is a difficult thing to imagine. Aunty Liz has really shiny eyes and moves fast and laughs lots and gets into all sorts of tricky situations and goes away into the hospital for a while. But she always comes out of it, and when she does she's slowed down, and I like her best this way because she looks more like a grown-up then and less like a child. It is a bit scary when she's like a child. Like something is a bit wrong with her.

My forehead begins to hurt. I want the pain to go away.

I will not cry.

It makes sense now. Sad people die, I've watched enough Disney films to know that.

We sit there in the silence. I don't try to fill it up with words the way I usually do. I just sit, thinking about Aunty Liz. People either make me feel comfortable or uncomfortable, and I don't know if everyone else feels the same because I know it would be rude to ask people a question like that. I know asking too many questions is rude because it's something I used to do, before I was old enough to realise quite how rude I was. Grampa makes me feel good and comfortable. He feels like summer and running in the garden with my shoes off. He always smiles when he sees me even if he has been crying and his eyes crinkle up as he stretches his long arms out to me and calls me Blondie before folding me up inside them. He's the person who makes me feel the best in the whole world. He watches films with me and reads poems to me and takes me to the library. He smells of shaving cream and sometimes whisky and these are the reasons I love him. Aunty Liz makes me feel worried in my tummy, like a hard nut's in it.

Maybe it is best that Aunty Liz has died; at least then Jehovah might bring her back, in the new system.

Aunty Liz was really clever, actually, to slip out of her skin like a snake might. I think how she was always in the hospital and maybe she just wanted to be at home. I think of her baby and the pump she used to take the milk out of her and how sometimes I would see my cousin in Aunty Liz's arms sucking the milk from her and it made me feel strange, like I was far away and not properly in myself.

I sit looking out the car window thinking all of these things until they are stacked on top of each other and happening all at the same time, and now it is like time doesn't make sense.

I feel myself going away, like I am a glove with the fingers not properly pushed to their ends. I feel blurry. When I am big, I decide, if I feel sad I will make myself go away too. I'm pleased I know this trick now.

Buckle up, Mummy says.

When we get to Granny's house I am smaller than everyone else there, and no one notices when I slip through their legs and their arms, which are all winding around each other, and take the two flights to the attic full of the oil paintings no one wants to hang anywhere anymore.

AND THEN THE END WILL COME

1987

OCTOBER IS FULL OF SHADOWS and mist, as it always is in the countryside. The rain makes long tracks as it drips down the window of the school bus. I try to guess which drip will race to the bottom first, as they get heavier and faster on their way down the glass.

I want to go to Aunty Liz's funeral, but Mummy says I can't.

I want to ask her why I can't go but I can't make my tongue into the right shape. So the words don't come; instead they stay inside me and make me hot. I lie in bed and look at the glow in the dark stars on my ceiling that don't glow very well anymore and wonder if I'm not allowed to go because it is a pagan funeral in a church or because I am too little.

I tell Mummy I'm sad about Aunty Liz and she says, She's only sleeping, we'll see her again in the new system soon. Now I worry about sleeping, because I don't want to be dead. I try to keep my eyes open for as long as I can at night, but sleep comes anyway. Just as I am falling into its blackness I worry this is how dying feels. I don't want to feel it, not yet.

The next time I say I'm sad about Aunty Liz Mummy says, She was my sister; why don't you think about that?

The aunties in the Kingdom Hall tell me I am to be big and brave for my mummy. They say I need to look after her and I start trying to learn how to cook the dinner and dry the dishes but when I do cook dinner Mummy says I have made more of a mess than anything else. She asks if I know that the cooker has more than one setting when I make very sticky Chinese beef.

The day they bury Aunty Liz in the churchyard just next to Granny and Grampa's church, I go to Nina's house. Nina is the daughter of Mummy's study. She lives in a house that smells of peat and beeswax and the hard salt of the sea. They use different words in her house, words like 'anchovies' and 'olives' and 'capers', and things taste bitter and sour and salty and sweet, and I would never leave there if that were possible.

When I tell Mummy Nina is my best friend she says, She can be your second best friend. You must remember Jehovah your Heavenly Father is your best friend. I don't tell her she's wrong because you can't play wartime rationing games under an oak kitchen table with Jehovah.

I am at Nina's house a lot after Aunty Liz dies. I wish I was there all cosy and warm the day the storm comes.

They say it's coming on the radio, but things take a long time to get here. The wind whips its way up from London, where it pulled over trees in Kew Gardens.

I leave for school and the wind lifts me for a second off my feet. I think it's Jehovah. I think this is the end. Slates are ripped from roofs and crash to the ground. Everything is too loud and echoes too much. I stand there with the wind pushing me so hard I can't walk forwards or back. It makes me feel small, and everything else big. I am too little for the rest of the world. I am too small for the strength of it.

Mummy comes running out into the street and the wind steals her words so I can only see the shape her mouth is making. Once she's close to me she points to the house and takes my hand, and we bend our heads and shoulders against the wind and walk back towards the house. All I can think is that this is the voice of Jehovah who lives in the windstorm. He is coming to rescue us, but first, the end must come.

I don't want the end to come. I like the world and the things in it. I don't want to wake up to empty houses and streets. I don't want roofs ripped off and cars tipped over and pavements split into wide-open holes. I don't want to see the earth's insides. I don't want to see bodies in the street. I don't want power lines to come down or trees to block the roads. I don't want cars and aeroplanes to stop. I know I am a bad little girl because these not-wants are also sinful yearning for the world.

Inside the house Mummy strips my clothes off and tells me to sit next to the heating vents. Hot air blows out at me but doesn't get under my skin to my bones. She brings me a change of clothes and dries my hair and makes me hot chocolate even though I don't like it. I blow on the surface where the milk is getting a skin already and watch it ripple.

The rain hits the window so hard I think it might be trying to come in, like Cathy always was in the book Mummy read me. Zoe and Mummy and I sit on the couch watching the empty street and the things the weather does to it. Granny phones to tell us the power might come down, and we should go to her. I think of her coal fire and the way it spits when she heaps wood on it, the warm, red and yellow glow of it. I think of the smell of her roast beef fresh from the oven and her Yorkshire puddings with their heavy bottoms always ready to soak up all the gravy, and I hope Mummy will say we can go, but instead I hear her say it's too dangerous to travel.

All that long day and the day after the wind howls, the sound stuck in my ears. At bedtime on the second day, I pull the duvet up over my head and burrow down into my bed to try to shut it out.

When I wake in the night, my ears are finally empty.

I lie in bed with the new silence wrapping itself around me like a ghost might. Something is wrong. Nothing moves, there are no shadows on the wall from the outside. Everything is still. I know this means the end has come.

I open my curtains and the street looks just the same, but there are no lights at the windows because all the people in the houses are dead.

The street is empty. I'm pleased the end came with a storm; at least then the bodies are at home. The sky is a thousand different colours of ink, all of them swirling. Dark clouds move fast, and I watch as a fat tear lands on the windowsill.

I wipe my face dry.

I am not allowed to cry about this. By morning I will need to have a happy face and we will all sing a song of salvation together because Jehovah has saved us.

I know now this is why we didn't go to Granny's house. Jehovah was protecting us from seeing their bodies.

Angry red sky begins to break near the sea. This is not the colour I would have expected for the first morning of the new system. A car drives down the street and stops two doors down. Our neighbour gets out, goes up his path and into the house.

I'm confused. Did Jehovah save him? It would be a surprise if he did since Zoe says he castrates cats in his shed.

Am I wrong? Did Jehovah change His mind? I pull the covers up around me and try to close my eyes. I turn over and over and over so many times, I am like a dog trying to get comfortable. I try to switch my light on, but it doesn't work, I open my curtains so I can see enough to read.

When Mummy finds me she tells me the storm has passed. I wait for her to tell me about the end, but instead she tells me we're going to Granny's house to warm up. This is how I realise that it's not come yet, and we are still in the Last Days.

2. TREE OF KNOWLEDGE

'But as for the tree of the knowledge of good
and bad, you must not eat from it, for in the day
you eat from it you will certainly die.'

Gen. 2:17 NWT

FROM AMONG YOU WILL
ARISE FALSE PROPHETS

1988

I'M EIGHT AND SITTING WITH an open mouth in front of Grampa's television. My orange juice threatens to tip onto Granny's new carpet. Axminster, she calls it, like that means anything to me.

On the TV men with white beards are waving flags. One of them holds a book up high and sets it on fire. They're honking car horns and making a lot of noise. The camera cuts back to a half-bald little man who's caused all this fuss. They talk about his book, about *The Satanic Verses*, and when they say the title, I check Mummy isn't sitting behind me. There's no way we'd be allowed to sing a song to Satan.

Grampa is staring at the screen when Granny

pushes the door open and comes in with afternoon tea on the cake stand. What is it dear? she says. Grampa points to the television, his voice sounding like it's stuck in his throat when he tries to talk. Burning books, Louise, he says. It won't end well. She shakes her head as she pulls a table from the nest, with her chin wobbling from side to side.

I love books. I don't know why anyone would want to burn one. But it's exciting to think a book can cause this much fuss. Mum taught me to read when I was only three. I'd been crying because her and Zoe had been talking about *Little Women* and I didn't know who the little women they were talking about were. I was so cross when Mum said they were book people: I felt I was being shut out of a whole world. She sat me on her knee one afternoon and showed me how to turn the shapes into sounds. After that life felt more fun. I could escape at nursery when I didn't like being there. I sat in the house corner and read books about dark, dark streets and Meg and Mog and all the things I shouldn't have, and this is how I knew that books could be both good things and bad things.

Every night after dinner we read the Bible aloud to each other. I normally don't like reading the Bible; only people who haven't read it would think to call it the Good Book. There's an incredible amount of bad stuff in it. But I do like reading it aloud; I do all different voices and always try to read more than I'm supposed to, and then Zoe reads in her mouse-quiet voice and Mum reads in her voice that doesn't go up or down. I want to shake them to make them read in a more fun way.

The Bible has very thin pages, it would burn fast.

When I was little, my favourite days were when I was ill and Mum would put me on her knee and read to me. I'd hear her heart in her chest as Peggotty's buttons popped off and Jane was screaming in the red-room – my dreams were red and reddening for weeks after that – and Estella was shouting for Pip; these days were the best days. Jehovah and His litera-ture went away on these days; I was safe and warm and I'd sit cuddled into her wanting and not wanting to hear the sound of her heart thudding and thump-ing under her jumper, trying not to wonder if one day I'd hear it stop. I wish those days had lasted for longer, the days I sat cosy and curled up; the days I didn't need to learn about Jehovah; the days I didn't need to worry about hiding Him from people at school; the days I could forget the end of days was nearly here. Those safe good days feel far away now.

I'm transfixed by the blazing book onscreen. One book, and so many people care about it. Afterwards, when I'm tucked up in the blue bedroom at Granny and Grampa's house, because that is one of the places I am a lot of the time now Aunty Liz is dead, I can't stop thinking about the book. I think and think and think about it and try to find it on their shelves, just in case any have escaped the burning, but the most exciting things I can find are Dick Francis and Frederick Forsyth.

*

My seditious little heart; I knew then, didn't I, that one day you'd want to burn my book too.

VOW OF POVERTY

1988

SISTER RYDER SITS WITH HER tongue between her teeth, a bright lamp to the side of her illuminating the china rabbit in her hands. She makes repeated strokes with a paintbrush to build the colour up on the rabbit. Mum watches every careful movement.

I sit in the room that's just a tiny bit too cold, thinking about two days ago at school when we made our family tree. It's difficult for me to make mine since I don't know anything about my dad's side of the family. I took a long time colouring in leaves and cutting them out when I did Mum's side of the tree. The next day, I had a sore tummy and didn't need to go to school; instead I stayed in bed thinking about the family tree. At first, I thought about my dad and not knowing anything about him. To stop myself feeling bad about that I started to think about how the congregation is like a tree.

The Governing Body in Brooklyn would be the trunk; then all the central leaves would be the elders and their wives and children; the circuit overseer would be there too. We'd be one of the outside leaves, the way all the single mums and their children are. People like to help Mum, although sometimes I think they do it because they want to feel better about themselves. I need to remember I can't discern people's heart condition, it is for Jehovah to decide.

Mum likes being helped. She is very good at being helpless. That's why I do my best to help all the time. Often after dinner Mum gets the bound volumes of magazines down from the shelves and the society's subject index. She looks up subjects like CHILDREN HELPING or SINGLE MOTHERS and reads us extracts from the magazines so I know she's not asking us to help, she's giving us Jehovah's instructions.

How does it work? Mum asks Sister Ryder. Sister Ryder tells her how for every 20 rabbits she paints well she gets a few pounds, but if she doesn't do them well she doesn't get paid.

Mum nods and acts all interested.

Recently, Mum's started to worry even more about money and how poor we are. I sit in my room and try to think up business ideas, but I'm not very enterprising. This is a problem. A nice elder tries to help Mum with her problem of being poor. He suggests she could start her own business. Most of the brothers work for themselves as window cleaners and office cleaners. There aren't many offices here and Brother Llewelyn cleans most of the windows in the village. Most of the sisters stay at home looking after their families. The elder says Mum could sell silk flowers to offices and doctors' surgeries and then she could charge to go back and clean the flowers. He says she can buy the flowers from him for cost price.

Sister Ryder puts the rabbit on the side to dry with other identical rabbits. Wait a minute, she says to me as she leaves the room. She comes back in with a large Safeway plastic bag, rummages around inside it, and pulls out a tiny little painted cottage. It's beautiful, with latticework on the roof and roses climbing the side of the front door. Here, she says, that's for you, it's one of the rejects. Then she tells us that even though she doesn't get paid for the ones that aren't perfect, the company still sells them on. Sometimes, she says, I keep the ones I know they won't pay me for.

I look at the cottage. I think about how it would look on a shelf in my bedroom. I think I could collect them. I like the idea of collecting things. I like the idea of having enough money to properly collect anything. I don't think we can accept, Mum says; I'm not sure it's honest to keep something that isn't strictly yours.

Mum looks at me and I hand the cottage back. I smile at Sister Ryder. On the way home Mum says, It sounds a lot like a pyramid scheme to me. It's amazing, she says, how gullible some people can be.

FOR A WITNESS
IN ALL THE EARTH

1989

I SWALLOW. MY TUMMY HURTS AGAIN. I look down at the page, where my lines are, but I can't read them. Everything blurs and blacks. I grip the orange microphone more tightly, take a deep breath like Mum has told me to do, and then I begin.

This is a big moment for me. I'm giving my first talk at the Kingdom Hall. Baptised brothers and sisters give talks and so do unbaptised publishers. I've just become an unbaptised publisher, which means I am working towards baptism. Mum says it means she's doing something right. It also means that every month I write down on a report slip how many hours I've done on the ministry, and how many magazines I've placed and how many return visits I have. I put a 0 in the column for Bible studies. I'm not allowed to lead a Bible study until I'm older.

The numbers get added up and sent away to the society to be kept on my record. It is important to have a good accounting with Jehovah when the end comes. I like measuring myself in numbers. It is a good way of telling if I'm doing enough to please Jehovah and his earthly representatives.

The sisters who give the talks make them look so easy. Just like mini plays. I like plays; I listen to the afternoon play on Radio 4 every day until something inappropriate happens in it and we have to switch it off. I discover it's hard to write a talk and to make it sound convincing. I've spent three weeks writing this, after I got my assignment slip from the service overseer. I wanted it to be realistic but everything I wrote sounded wrong. Mum said she could help me but Jehovah would know I'd had help, and then what value would my talk have if I'd cheated writing it?

As I speak I feel as though I'm out of my body, watching myself. I hear as I talk about the rebellious students in Tiananmen Square who were foolish enough to think they could challenge leaders put in place by Satan. I don't say that I am sometimes confused about this part because we are also told that Jehovah is engineering world events. I know this means I am rebellious too and deserve to die. I know it means I am a hypocrite as I tell the audience that soon Jehovah will bring peace when he destroys the wicked.

They clap as I stand up to leave the platform. Mum looks flushed as I sit next to her, she smiles at me and squeezes my knee. I wonder if she's proud of me, but then I remember pride is a sin.

The ministry school overseer gets onto the platform to give me my counsel. Well, he says, thank you young Sister Millar. I think I can go lightly on you since it's your first talk. He laughs. The audience laugh a little bit too. Next time, he says, you will work on sense, stress and modulation, since you did talk very quickly. Then he explains how next time I need to work on slowing down and controlling my voice.

After the meeting, the ministry school overseer asks to talk to me in the second school. I sit in the shadowy room as he tells me about the next topic I need to work on, explaining how I will either pass or will have to work on it again. He tells me about dress and grooming, pitch, pace and power: all these things are to help me become a better public speaker. He explains how it's impossible to ever actually finish the course because you can never be a perfect speaker. It's a lifelong process, he says, smiling at me.

I want to ask him why elders don't give talks on the ministry school, and why they give the long public talks instead and always get to lead but I don't. I know he would say it is because they are the head of the congregation, just as the man is the head of the household. There is no man to be the head of our household, so sometimes the elders tell Mum what to do and give her extra advice they don't give to the other sisters in the hall. Mum says she is so blessed to have people who care so deeply for her spiritual welfare.

On the drive home, headlights light up the back seat. I like when Mum gets to borrow Grampa's car, otherwise we have to wait for Brother Llewelyn to give us a lift home. Zoe hates Brother Llewelyn. She says he's a creep. Mum used to tell her off when she said this, but now she just gives her a hug. Grown-ups and teenagers really are weird. I turn round to memorise the number plate of the car behind. It's important to do this, so I do it all the time. Soon the Great Tribulation such as no man has seen before is coming and they tell us you never know what small detail might save your life.

In bed I pull the covers up over my head as the Bible story tapes play me to sleep. I get nightmares and no one knows why. The doctor said story tapes might help, so I listen to the tapes about Jesus's return and the Nephilim who were born after sinful angels came to earth and raped women. When the Great Tribulation comes it will be worse than anything that's ever come before, including the Holocaust where thousands of faithful brothers and some sisters perished. We have chosen hiding places in the house. I am going to hide under my bed because it's got a kind of concealed place. I worry that I'm getting too big to fit in it, so I like to pinch my skin to check there's not too much fat there.

I fall asleep knowing how well looked after I am, as the story about Job doubting Jehovah plays into the dark.

MEN WILL GO FROM
BAD TO WORSE

1990

AFTER AUNTY LIZ DIES I'M at Granny's house a lot, and at Nina's beautiful house too, and I also fly to Ireland to stay with friends with a big sign around my neck saying UNACCOMPANIED MINOR. I like going places on my own. But suddenly Mum decides she wants me back. I'm not sure why. I'm not sure I want to go.

Meanwhile, there's a new brother at the Kingdom Hall. He's called Ritch. We all say hello to him and have him up for dinner and go on the ministry with him. He is very friendly to Mum and very nice to Zoe. Mum says, It's nice to meet someone who's so good with at least one of the children.

Ritch lives in a caravan that is quite far from our

house. It takes a long time to get there. To begin with we go at weekends and then we go during the week, and then we are there so often it feels like it might be our caravan too.

When we visit, he comes to collect us in his old beige Escort with slippery leather seats that me and Zoe slide across. I see him looking in his rear-view mirror at us. When he does, he's smiling and some-times winking. I can't wink yet. My eyes don't work when I try. His caravan is on a patch of mud, next to a building site with a half-built house on it. Every time we go the house looks just the same, it never gets more built. I suspect it might be Ritch's new house and that is why he lives in a caravan.

When I step out the car, I can hear the sea in the distance and the air smells of the thick stink of it, and sometimes of seaweed too, when the tide is high. Where he lives doesn't have a name because there are no other houses or even buildings there.

Ritch doesn't have a good face. He is thin with a hooked nose and a crooked smile and wears a gold necklace under his shirt. Mum and Zoe say he looks like Sean Penn, but I don't know. I think because we see him a lot he's going to marry Mum. How it works is if a man and a woman see each other often they're courting. The Bible says you're only allowed to court someone if you want to marry them. So Mum must be going to marry Ritch. Then she can be happy because she won't be poor and on her own all the time.

Ritch is rich. I know this because when we go to

his caravan, he cooks spaghetti bolognaise using bought sauce, which is something we don't get at home. When he cooks the caravan smells of animal fat before he empties a huge jar of sauce into the pan to cover the mince. At home we only have tinned tomatoes, because bought sauce costs a lot.

Ritch is also rich because he is a mechanic, I'm not sure what that means except that he has dirty hands a lot of the time.

Once Ritch's house on the building site is built, I imagine we'll all live in it together, when Mum marries him. The caravan always smells of propane gas. I know this is what it smells of because there is a blue canister of it that sits at the bottom of the wobbly metal step I use to get into the caravan: on the canister it says in big letters: FLAMMABLE PROPANE GAS. The gas comes out through a tube that hisses like a snake every time Ritch lights the stove or the portable gas heater.

The caravan also smells like grated cheese from a cardboard tube. This is not a good smell. After the sauce has spat from the pan onto the floor, Ritch puts the food on big plates and sprinkles what he says is parmesan onto it. It makes everywhere smell like sick, but the spaghetti tastes sweet from the bought sauce and slides down my throat easily.

We stay at the caravan until it is late, and afterwards he drives us home in the dark.

Suddenly Ritch doesn't live in his caravan anymore. He has a house. It isn't the house I thought it would be, it's a farm cottage with only two bedrooms and a tiny cold bathroom with a glass window in the door and a lock that doesn't work. The kitchen is tacked on to the side of the cottage and has a sloping roof. On rainy days tiny splashes of water come through the roof and spread yellow patches across the ceiling. Nothing some paint can't fix, Mum says.

In the narrow back garden the grass is overgrown. It's so long it's not green anymore, but dried brown. I lie in it on my belly and watch the insects play in their tiny world as the sun warms my back. Inside the house the grown-ups are painting, drinking cups of tea, and eating cake. I like it best out here. I like the dried-out smell of the grass in my nose and I don't mind the way it makes me sneeze.

A dark-haired girl lives in the big farmhouse up the dusty dried-mud track. She only lives there half the time, the rest of her life she lives in France with her dad. When she tells me that I shrug my shoulders like I totally understand what she's talking about and say, Yeah, it's like that for me, my dad lives in South Africa. I look up and see swallows who've come from there sitting on the overhead wires. How easy things are for them, with their wings.

As we walk down to the abandoned quarry, we kick stones. She shows me how to split them in two. She makes it look easy as she throws them against other rocks, and they open to show their seam, but when I try, I can't make them do it. She teaches me to run at electric fences and jump over them without

my feet touching the wire. The times we don't manage to clear them properly we throw our heads back
and laugh at the bright blue sky as we roll around the
field squealing. I like it when my feet get stuck on
them for the tiniest of moments, and the current runs
up my body and makes me feel alive in a new way.
Like I'm glowing.

I like the daytime at Ritch's house. I'm not sure
about the evenings. There are lots of films Mum's told
me we are not allowed to watch. But suddenly she
and Ritch and Zoe are watching films that have bad
things in them, like sex and blood and knives and
people being murdered and rabbits being boiled. To
escape, I go to sleep. When I wake up the three of
them have empty cans of beer at their feet. Ritch
drives us home in the dark. I know this means it's very
late, because in summer it only gets dark in the middle of the night.

Sometimes when I look at the clock it's two in the
morning. I'm not sure why we're still there and not
tucked up in bed at home. I also don't know why
Ritch hasn't married Mum yet. Sometimes there are
other people at Ritch's house too. This is called Christian Association. Once when I opened my eyes during
the prayer he was winking at a young sister. I shut my
eyes tight and pretended I didn't see. Another time I
ran in from the garden to the bedroom and he was
holding hands with a different young sister. I ran
quickly into the garden and waited for Mum to get
back from the shop where she was buying more paint.

Suddenly we don't go to Ritch's house anymore. I don't know why. Instead, Mum and Zoe are at the Kingdom Hall all the time; they're both tired in the mornings. I used to think being 15 looked like a lot of fun, but now I'm not so sure.

I go to Nina's at the weekends and play with her Barbie house and get to eat ice lollies in bed and we stay up late into the night and it's much more fun than being at home. Most of the time I don't miss being at Ritch's house. What I miss is thinking that Mum was going to get married, that we'd have money and feel safe.

One Thursday Brother Marshall gets up on the platform and says, Brother Ritch Jones is no longer one of Jehovah's Witnesses. I look along the row where Mum and Zoe both sit looking at the elder, their faces not moving. I want to turn round and look at Ritch, but I know from now on I am not even allowed to smile at him. Disfellowshipped people can't be associated with: this is part of Jehovah's loving discipline to return them to their spiritual senses.

No one tells me exactly what Ritch has done. I hear Mum talk about divine justice and Jehovah's bounteous blessings, and how we need to have faith that the elders are right, even if at times it looks like they're not. They're only men, she says to me and Zoe one night after dinner when we sit with candles on for a treat with the smell of roast chicken in the air. She explains how it might look like they'd got it wrong letting Ritch back into the congregation, knowing as they did that he'd seduced lots of young girls in the past before he moved here. Sometimes men make mistakes, she says, but Jehovah never does. Zoe nods and looks like she believes her, even though later I hear her telling her friend how stupid and blind Mum can be.

I spend a lot of time listening to Mum's grown-up conversations when she thinks I'm reading the Laura books. I hear her tell Nina's mum how hurt she is that Ritch was doing all these immoral things with so many people and yet he never tried to put a finger on her. Then she starts crying as she talks about wasted time.

Next summer, after a week in London, as Granny drives us across the border where English flags hang tattered and limp, Mum says, I finally feel like I've woken up. I can hardly remember anything from last year. It felt for such a long time as if I was sleepwalking in the day. Every morning when I woke up, I wanted to close my eyes again, I wanted to be sick or sleep. I never could choose which. It was like after – and then she lowers her voice – *he left*.

I know she's talking about my dad; she never says his name. I'm pretty sure waking up and wanting to go back to sleep doesn't sound right. We're told from the platform that we have the best life ever, but sometimes it really doesn't feel like it.

CONDEMNED BY DOUBT

1991

THE FAKE RED FLAMES FLICKER across the back of the electric fire. They used to fascinate me, until I realised it was the heat from the coloured lightbulb below the plastic coals that pushed a circular fan above it to make the flames. It hurt my head to discover that. Like when I realised the sea wasn't actually blue, and parts of the world seemed to break off, becoming less magical and more knowable.

Outside it's getting dark. Soon Mum will come out the kitchen and shut the curtains. They'll rattle along the wooden pole and she'll pat them to settle them in place. Covering the dark outside but not inside. She'll put on a lamp and switch the big light off, but all this will do is make a pocket of light in the wider darkness.

The room is quiet and still. Zoe is upstairs listening to music. Because Jehovah doesn't like loud music, she keeps the volume low. Mum's making dinner behind the kitchen door. I'm the only one who's not doing anything. I should be doing something. I should be helping or I should be tidying up or I should be reading the new magazines. But I'm not. I'm just sitting in the room, watching the flames that aren't flames moving in their steady rhythm. They're almost more mesmerising than real flames because they're so predictable. Transfixed, I watch them. The edges of the room become less certain: it's in the process of disappearing. Mum's sewing machine in the corner begins to melt down into the sewing table, the piles of fabric on it slide and shift becoming mercury, separating before joining back together as they slip to the floor. The threads on the thread stand begin to glow from where they're tightly wrapped on their bobbins, blood red, lemons sour and fresh from the tree, clashing greens of a wet walk in the woods. Outside, the street-lamp pulses sulphur orange, as if it wants in. I think it wants to light the room up fully, to make the dark go away. It wants to take me with it, it wants to take me to a new home, it wants to bring me magic, it wants to make the sea blue again, it wants to make the winter disappear. The fake flames keep going on and on and on in their repeating rhythm and will do until the plug is pulled. They never change, just like Mum says God doesn't change, everything will always be the same and the same and the same until the end of all time. I need the streetlamp to pick me up and take me away. I need it to steal me. I begin rocking back and forwards and forwards and back without meaning to. I rock and rock and rock because nothing else is happening, no one is lifting me up, no one is taking me away, no one is stealing me. Thick fat heavy tears well up in my eyes and I want to keep them in but they begin to spill out and tip down my face. The red bulb below the fire burns my eyes I've been staring at it for so long. I close my eyes and colours flash across them, pink and purple and black tinged with bright blue. Mum shouts from the kitchen. I can hear her and not hear her at the same time. I'm there and also not there. She is closer when she says my name again, more quietly this time. I don't open my eyes. I cannot talk. I will not talk. I do not want to know what is true. I am mute or muted or mutating. All I know is I am crying in front of the fire until the tears are done and the room settles, taking on its familiar shape.

Mum sits next to me. What's wrong? she says. Where did you go? What happened? I blink and pull my sleeve over my hand and use it to wipe my face. I say, I don't know, because it is the easiest thing to say.

I have done this before. When it happens, it's as if I'm broken. When they ask me about it I say, I can hear but it's as though I'm not properly inside myself. I don't say, I don't want to talk. I don't know if I can talk when it happens. I think I might be able to, I might be making myself do this. But I'm not sure. I am just there, and not there. It doesn't make sense, which means I mustn't make sense. It's easier to think there is something wrong with my workings – maybe the electrical impulses are confused – than to think I'm crying or stopped because I'm sad. Sometimes my head even feels too hot. I don't tell them about this either. I don't tell them that sometimes I just want to sit in a dark room and cry. Sometimes nothing feels more appealing than that. Sometimes there isn't anything else to do. There's only the Bible and all its horrible stories. Armageddon sounds so terrible I don't know if I want to survive it. I don't know if playing with lions and pandas would be enough to make me forget what it was like to clear the dead from the streets or to see all the signs of the end – famine, wars, earthquakes, diseases, financial crashes – and to know what's coming and then to live through it all. I'm not sure I'll feel all that joyful when the end comes. I hate that I'm this way. I hate that there's something wrong with me.

Mum says Jehovah has chosen me, but she's got it wrong. He chose her, and I came as part of the deal. Me and Zoe both. He didn't choose me. Why would He? All I think are bad things. All I want to do is to escape Him and all His rules. I am not even grateful for being saved. I'd rather sit crying in a room than go ice skating with other brothers and sisters. I'd rather read all about the Russian revolution and write silly poems than warn people about the end. I'm rotten. Of course I cry. I course I say I'm blacking out. It's the only way I can escape.

The doctors refer me to specialists in Edinburgh where they put jelly on my head and attach wires to it. Then a machine draws a graph of what's happening inside my brain. It's strange to see all my insides mapped like that. They still don't know what's wrong. Stress, they say, the same as the doctor did with my tummy aches. Mum is suspicious again. She says, I think they could be some sort of migraine. Mum gets migraines a lot. She gets them so badly she has a special sort of experimental medicine in a pen with a needle at the end that she fires into her thigh. When her migraines are bad, she needs to go to bed. Zoe follows her to her room, shouting at her and telling her she can't go, she needs her to be here. Mum closes the door and Zoe pounds on it, more and more insistently. Mum never opens it. I would like it if I could make myself disappear just so I didn't have to hear Mum crying, asking Zoe to go away. Just so I didn't need to hear Zoe banging on the door. Just so I wasn't here.

The doctors don't discover anything. Afterwards, we walk along the hospital's rubber-floored corridors to a window deep in the building where Mum fills in a form saying how far we've travelled. A woman slides the window open, gets her calculator out and types a calculation into it to work out the mileage, and then she counts money out for Mum, sliding it across the wooden counter marked with deep knots and scratches into Mum's waiting hand.

Then we walk across the meadows to my favourite

cafe and get chocolate cake and apple juice and look at the crystals and incense. Mum says, Of course the crystals don't work because magic isn't real, but I'm allowed to look at them. I hold them in my hands and feel the energy come off them. I want to close my eyes and make a wish but I don't. I do the same thing at night-time when I try to escape my body. I found a book in the school library about astral projection. I keep trying to do it. Sometimes I think I'm managing and other times I think maybe I just went to sleep and had a wild dream. I don't know how these things work but I do want to find out. That's why I read my horoscope in the magazine Zoe buys and hides from Mum because it has the position of the week in it, which is interesting mostly because I'm not sure how people make their bodies into those shapes.

When it is time to go home the bottom falls out my tummy. I love Edinburgh. I love how it smells of beer. I love Arthur's Seat and the sea shimmering in the distance. I even love the tramps and their frayed sleeping bags and huge dogs with hungry eyes. When we get to the top of the hill leading out the city I look back and wait to be turned into a pillar of salt.

WARS AND REPORTS OF WAR

1991

WHEN I'M NEARLY II, MUM goes away to Greece for a whole month, leaving me and Zoe with Granny and Grampa.

On the news the oil wells in Iraq blaze against the black sky. I look at the map, notice how close the countries are. When Mum phones, I remember how much I miss her and sit on the stair afterwards with my tummy feeling hollow.

We watch *EastEnders*, *Coronation Street* and *Neighbours* after school. We're allowed sweets and to go swimming at the weekends. There is no ministry. There is supposed to be a sister who takes us to the meeting in her car, but Granny says, If you don't want to go that's OK. It's OK to say you don't like it.

Sometimes I hope Mum won't come home. Maybe she'll stay there, and I'll get to stay here.

I like feeling normal.

Then she comes back. Best time of my life, she says. I could live in Greece if ... and her voice trails off. She cooks Greek food. She talks about Greek men. She tells me she'll take me there some day. But I don't know how many days there are left now the whole of the Middle East is beginning to look a lot like the Great Tribulation is on its way.

YOU MUST NOT EAT THE
BLOOD OF ANY SORT OF FLESH

1992

M Y TUMMY HAS STARTED HURTING. It's never really not hurt, but recently it doesn't know how to behave and balls itself into knots more days than it doesn't. My throat hurts a lot too.

Mum's taken me to the doctor for years for both things. I used to sit in the waiting room and read *HELLO!* magazine. It's much better than the *Watchtower* and *AWAKE!* Princess Diana is always in it, off having adventures with her pretty clothes and strange hair. I love all the famous people I've never heard of showing off their babies swaddled in white shawls in impossibly big houses. When the doctor came in he'd call my long name and I would forget to stand up because it was the only place I was ever called it. I sat in the doctor's office; Mum would shake her head when he said, Stress, maybe. Afterwards we'd climb the hill to the Co-op to buy Heinz tomato soup and hot dogs as an extra-special treat, and at home I'd watch as she poured the soup into the pan and half-filled the empty tin with milk, sloshing it around to get all the last bits of soup. It would bubble and pop over the hob as it heated and I'd look at the fat veins on Mum's long, skinny hands and worry they might do the same, imagining her blood spilling out and making the floor a big, red, sticky mess.

I have always been scared of blood. Especially spilt blood. Sacred blood. Wasted blood.

I know my life force is in my blood, and it is a sin to take blood in any form into my body. Now I'm about to have an operation, it's really important that I don't forget this. Mum says, It's a matter of life and eternal death. The elders help me strengthen my faith by reading a brochure to me about the faithful young Witnesses who refused blood transfusions and died. But it's OK, we'll see them again in the new system, they say. They help me practise what to say to doctors so I can prove how strong my faith is.

I keep getting tonsillitis. It's pretty grotty. My tonsils get red and swollen. Pus seeps out of them and tastes like I imagine rotting mushrooms might. I start to miss too much school. Now I'm at high school I can't miss as much as I used to.

I like the days I have tonsillitis. I like the banana taste of the yellow medicine they make from a powder in the pharmacy. I like sitting up in bed doing the jigsaw of Europe, slotting in all the capital cities when I finish it. I like looking through old photo albums at pictures of me when I was a baby. Sometimes there are white rectangles where photos are missing. I like curling up on the couch and pulling my covers tightly around me and closing my eyes and falling asleep to the theme tune of *The Archers*. I like the Shipping Forecast. I love the sound of all the faraway places that aren't land masses but instead are parts of the sea: Dogger, Fisher, German Bight. On those days I wake to the sound of Mum's sewing machine: she will have been going too fast and have hit a pin buried deep in the fabric, so the needle flies off. Then the tip needs to be found, and the needle replaced. I lie listening to these nearly imperceptible sounds.

Now I'm 12 and about to get my tonsils removed, I'm old enough to tell the doctor my feelings about blood transfusions.

I shift from side to side on the chair in the sweaty heat of the doctor's office, the leather sticking to my bottom. I hear it squeak when I move. I'm worried this might put me off saying what I rehearsed. I look around the room, at the slanted white blinds drawn half shut so the room is more shadow than light, the long bed I've had my tummy poked and prodded on, his wide desk with a big black swivel chair behind it and pictures of his wife and children on holiday in sunnier places, their faces squinting as they smile at the camera.

I like doctors even though I know Mum's suspicious of them. My granny is a doctor, and my dad too. Maybe that's why she doesn't trust them. I think they're clever even though the elders say knowledge is vanity.

I hope the chair stops squeaking soon. I have been practising this part for what feels like my whole life. This is my chance to prove my loyalty. This is my chance to earn my salvation. This is my starring moment, but knowing this doesn't stop me feeling sick or the blood rising in my cheeks when the doctor comes into the room.

I need to work harder to strengthen my faith.

My chest feels tight and I can't breathe in properly, the way it feels when my asthma is bad. I bite my lip, swallow the sick taste in my mouth and try to remember what I have to say. I try to tell myself the peace of Jehovah is all around me. It's strange to call it peace when my insides feel churned up. I would like to be on the beach now with Granny and the wind and the salt whipping our hair round our faces and drying out our lips; there, not here.

I lick my lips and stand up to shake the doctor's large hand as he comes into the room. I worry I'll hold out the wrong one, like David Copperfield did.

I look over at the elder who is in the room with us to give me strength. He nods at me. He said beforehand I didn't need to worry. He is there to help me remember what to say and to make sure I tell the doctor what I believe. I can't mess this up. I don't want him to have a wasted trip.

The doctor smiles at me. He asks me to tell him what I'd like to happen if something goes wrong. He explains that although a tonsillectomy is a common operation, it isn't without its risks. Then he lists them.

I dig my nails into the fat parts of my palms. I don't want to think about what could happen. I leave tiny half-moons on my hands, little scratches, not deep enough to draw blood. I'm 12 and grown-up now, some of my friends are getting baptised, I need to convey my superior Bible-based knowledge to the doctor. It felt so fixed and clear before, but in this room where science seems too much in evidence – the poster of the skeletal system, the doctor's kit laid on the table – I'm suddenly not sure that what I think I know is something I really know at all.

This is the wrong time to waver.

The magazines warned me this might happen. I need to stop Satan getting hold of me. I need to remember a blood transfusion would be like rape. Mum's helped me learn this; I even did a demonstration explaining this at the Kingdom Hall, so the rest of the congregation know too.

The doctor smiles at me as if he's trying to make things OK. I try to stop thinking how much I'd like to become a doctor if the end wasn't coming.

The doctor leans forward, with his hands on the desk, until it feels like there are only the two of us in the room. I wonder if he remembers the time I brought my toy stethoscope here with the squeaky bear on the end of it and he let me pretend to listen to his chest and then said, Looks like you'll be a doctor just like your granny. Mum kept looking at the floor.

I think of blood on white sheets. I think of its metallic taste in my mouth. At some point, does it begin to taste like something normal? Will I wake with it gurgling and choking me? Will I have time to spit it out since swallowing it would be a sin, like the time I licked a cut and Mum said, Stop! You can't eat your blood.

Mum would be sad if I died. She'd also be proud if I died doing Jehovah's will.

I know that, if something goes wrong and I need a blood transfusion, the doctors will try to get a court order. The courts are less likely to intervene if I've said I don't want blood. That's why it's important I speak now. But someone has stolen my voice. I want to disappear. The doctor looks at me. I know he expects me to at least look at him too. I raise my eyes to meet his. I open them wide and stare at him so he knows I mean it when I say, I don't want a blood transfusion.

The elder smiles, and I'm sure Mum does too.

Why? the doctor asks. I recite the scripture in Leviticus, telling him we're bound by it. He says, I thought Jesus did away with the Mosaic Law. I don't know what I'm meant to say now. The elder steps in. He says, As true Christians we're bound by both the Old and New Testaments. I nod. The doctor raises one eyebrow. I wish I knew how to do that. Then he sits back in his chair and looks at me like he's never seen me before. You'll have to sign these forms, he says, pushing them over to me. I sign with the signature I've practised, and Mum does too. The elder doesn't sign.

When we get up to leave, the elder reaches out to shake the doctor's hand as if he's done some kind of deal, but the doctor moves his away and gestures to the door. As we walk down the corridor Mum puts her hand on the back of my neck and sort of steers me along the way she does sometimes. I think maybe she's trying to tell me I've done very well.

Three months later I go to Edinburgh for the operation. We stay with a schoolfriend of Mum's. I love her and her husband, who's a cradle Catholic, which is what all Catholics are really, Mum says. I have no idea what she means although I do know Catholics are terrible because they sin, then go to mass and confess to the priest in a tiny box to ask for forgiveness. This means they think they can do anything they want, Mum says. I think this sounds like a brilliant idea, even if they are part of Babylon the Great and will all burn soon. They aren't as bad as Jews, Mum says. At least they didn't kill Jesus.

When we're there, Victor the cradle Catholic makes me his spaghetti bolognaise, which is better than anyone else's. The grown-ups drink red wine with dinner. It stains their lips. Victor makes a salad dressing from white wine vinegar, salt and sugar and pours it over ripped-up iceberg lettuce. Hardly a salad, Mum says later, but I know city people eat differently.

Victor tells me to taste the dressing to check it's seasoned properly, telling me to grind black pepper into it. He teaches me to squeeze a lemon with only my hands. I like him. Every time I see him, he makes a big fuss and pretends to be surprised that I'm more grown up and more beautiful than I was the last time I saw him. His wife has a fancy career and wears expensive suits and leaves her children with a nanny who does all the cleaning and half the cooking for them. I like her too. She talks about Grampa and how he taught her so much when he was her head teacher, and how he let her see that a life other than the one her parents had was possible and that she didn't have to stay in the same village forever. I sit thinking how strange it is that he didn't make Mum realise that too.

I like it in their house.

I like the fat carpet my feet sink into. I go to bed in their spare room, bigger than any of the rooms in our house. As I pull the eiderdown duvet around me, I let myself wonder what it would be like to be their child and how it must feel to have a confession box to go into and a priest to talk to; but I am too full of bolognaise to think for long and soon sleep comes and eats me up before morning arrives.

Saying no to blood means I'm classified as a high-risk patient, so I'm being treated at the adult hospital. Remember how loving Jehovah is, Mum says as we wait on grey plastic chairs lining the blue-painted corridor. In the kids' hospital the walls are painted with Disney characters and the ceilings aren't high like these ones. Here even the doctors seem bigger. Everything dwarfs me.

When I go into the room to change, I feel like I might fall over. It's OK, Mum says to me, you've got new pants, you'll be fine. I take my clothes off and fold them carefully and stack them on top of each other. This means I won't bleed badly. I put the backless gown on. In the mirror I watch Mum tie it. If I'm tied into this properly, I won't die. I flick my index finger against the top of my thumb to stop myself thinking too much. She opens the door and we go back into the corridor.

I want to suck my thumb, but I'm too big for that now.

I'll come back after it's done, Mum says. I love you. The chair's cold under my bare legs as she walks away, her feet making a sucking sound on the linoleum.

I watch her back leaving.

A nurse comes and says my name with a smile on her face. Hop onto this, she says, pushing a wheelchair towards me. You'll be just fine, she says, they do this all the time. She wheels me down the corridor and we go through two automatic steel doors.

The room we emerge into is full of doctors in blue scrubs, like some kind of disaster pandemic movie I'd be too scared to watch. One of them tells me a joke and I start to laugh. I'm laughing as they put the plastic mask over my face. I'm laughing as the ceiling comes for me; it takes my hand as I count down from 20. As the numbers get smaller and smaller, I walk away from my stupid body that's kept me in it for so long. This is a new feeling I want again and maybe have wanted my whole life. My body laughs as I walk away from it. It's so funny to see the two parts of me laughing at each other that I laugh and laugh because nothing matters anymore, they can do what they like to the outside of me because I am running away with my insides, I am running off with the ceiling, jumping over the moon long before I get to zero.

I open my eyes in a small, cramped room. For a single moment I don't know where I am or what's happened, then I feel the fire in my throat. It's as if I've rubbed sandpaper all over my tongue and over the back of my throat. I try to speak but my voice comes out in a croak. When I try to lick my lips my mouth is too dry, there's nothing left to lick with.

A nurse comes in. She's awake, she says. Let's get you sitting up. I sit up and can't understand how the pain in such a small part of me spreads to the rest of my body so quickly. Here, the nurse says as she hands me a bowl, spit into this. It's made from pulped-up paper, and the rim feels rough and strange. When I spit, blood comes out.

I look at her and she rubs my arm. It's OK, she says, it's just left over from the operation, absolutely nothing to worry about. I smile even though I'm not that convinced she's right. Tell you what, she says, I'll phone your mum to let her know you're awake.

I hear Mum's feet in the hallway before she swooshes the curtains open. She smiles a huge smile at me. Her eyes are damp, so I know it was hard for her too, wherever it was she went.

Before I can leave the hospital, I have to prove the pain isn't too bad, but it is. I spit blood. I drink soluble painkillers, which make me feel spaced out, although not as much as the anaesthetic did. I'd like some more of it, to be absolutely gone from my body again, if only for a little while.

I need to eat a whole slice of toast to show the pain is manageable, but it hurts too much and for days I can't manage it. I want to go home, I don't want to be stuck in hospital forever. On the fifth day when the toast arrives, I wait until the curtains are drawn around my bed and get up and put it in the bin. I'm careful to push it right to the bottom and cover it with paper towels. When the nurse comes, she marks that I've eaten on the sheet fixed to the end of the bed. She smiles with all of her teeth as she says in her sing-song voice, It looks like you'll be able to go home today.

We leave the hospital on a November afternoon; the gloaming wraps itself around us as the city's lights disappear in the wing mirror. Snow flurries against the windscreen. At first it's easy for the wipers to flick it away, but before long they're creaking under its weight. When we get to the big hill that leads down into the valley next to ours, Mum slows right down. The snow is lying thick and fat and treacherous on the tarmac. She inches the car forward as larger vehicles leave the road. The heating's up too high, making me sweat. I want to open the window or, better, the door. The medicine is still mixing itself into my blood so in my mind I'm half in the car and half in the cool relief of the snow. I'd like to lie down in it, I'd like to make snow angels and lie looking at the sky watching it fall, I'd like to watch it cover me, and I would hover, far above my frozen body.

Hours later, at home Mum gives me cranberry juice so vicious it tries to strip away the thin new flesh at the back of my throat. She puts the medicine I'm shaking for at the side of the bed. I watch the giant pill tip and float as it dissolves, getting smaller and smaller as the bubbles fizz, rise and burst.

YOU MUST NOT
COMMIT ADULTERY

1992

HIGH SCHOOL IS THE BEST thing. There are more people there. People who don't know me, people who I can pretend to be someone else with. I like this. I like feeling free of God and rules and expectations and the weight of the end of the world that pressed on my head all the fucking time like a pile of heavy books put there to make me stand up tall and proud when really all I wanted to do was to sink into the background and be just the same as everyone else. Even though that is sinful. All I do is think sinful things, all the time. All I like are sinful things. High school makes sinning much easier. And much more fun. Another thing that makes being bad easier is that Mum is preoccupied with Zoe.

Zoe is engaged to a guy called Dave. He's from a congregation down south, and they met when he sat in front of us at the meeting when he was visiting friends. He turned round and smiled at Zoe. Zoe was 15 and he was 17. They started seeing each other – chaperoned, of course, the way you have to be in the truth. I like Dave, he's funny. He has a big friendly grin on him, and brown hair he's always pushing out of his eyes. I like the idea of having a big brother. They got engaged and Mum was fine with it all, until suddenly Zoe's dad appeared and fucked everything right up.

Zoe told me that when she first met her dad, Andy, he collected her from the station and asked if she wanted to go for steak and red wine, even though it was only ten in the morning. When she told me this, I immediately liked him. It's London though, Zoe said, as if suddenly she knew all about how they do things there. He's a journalist, she added with a flick of her hair, they're all practically alcoholics.

He doesn't want Zoe to get married, because she's only 18. And now Mum has also started saying Zoe's too young, even though she didn't think that before. The first time Andy comes to visit, I watch from the sitting-room window as he gets out his shiny new Astra and walks up the path Mum has cleared specially for the occasion. He's smaller than I expected, smaller than any man I've ever seen. Looks like Rod Stewart, Zoe said. I get where she's coming from, but I'm not sure why she was so excited about it.

He sits on the carpet, flicking through records and

prowling round the sitting room running his fingers over the bookshelves, like he's trying to work it all out. He drinks his black coffee fast, slams the cup down on the carpet so hard that tiny drops splash out. I watch them getting bigger and bigger. I know I should get a cloth but I also worry that would be rude. Come on, he says, let's go for ice cream. He shouts through to Mum in the kitchen, We're going for a drive. She comes through into the sitting room and smiles as she picks up his coffee cup. She doesn't notice the brown marks seeping their way into the wool.

His car has that brand-new smell, the same as Granny's does. I press the button and watch the window roll down, press it the other way to make it go back up again. You like it? he asks. Yeah, I say, it's cool.

It's just a company car, he says. I get a new one every year. My real car's an MG. I'll take you out in it, you'll love it.

As he drives, he rolls his window down and puts his arm on the door, barely holding the steering wheel. He talks all the way to the shop, about how he's always loved Mum and he only left because Grampa told him to, and, talking of Grampa, what could he do to convince him he'd come back for the right reasons? I have no idea what he's on about. I just want ice cream.

He tells me about his two ex-wives and the soon-to-be third. The last one's a real bitch, he says, taking me to the cleaners. I look out the window and think of the launderette with washing machines stacked on top of each other and the dryers that spin round and round while people wait in long rows for their clothes to be dried. Although I know it has nothing to do with those kind of cleaners, and has everything to do with money, I'm not sure exactly what he is saying. I'm not going to ask; I don't want to sound stupid.

In the ice-cream shop Andy says, We should get tubs – breakfast of kings, and asks the woman wearing a red pointed cap behind the counter if he can have one tub of strawberry, one of rum-and-raisin and then he turns to me and asks what I want. Mint-choc-chip, please, I say, because it's the fanciest ice cream I know. He drives home taking the corners so fast that I fall across the handbrake. This and his terrible country music make me laugh so hard that by the time we get home my tummy hurts from laughing so much. My knees are cold from balancing the ice-cream tubs on them.

I need to check in at the office, he says. Is it OK if I use the phone? Mum nods as she licks her spoon. Of course, she says, even though when I ask if I can use the phone, she asks me why I need to phone my friends when I talk to them all day at school. From the hallway I hear him talking quickly, then pausing to listen to the person on the other end. When he comes back in, he tells me the news never stops. He tells me all about Fleet Street and how he'll take me there one day. And he does, later that summer. He's right, the news never does stop. It's a rolling cycle of big screens and phones ringing and people running everywhere to deliver copy in time for that evening's press. The whole of the world rolls through the newsroom and the back rooms of pubs he takes me to. I love this fast world, it makes me wonder how many other possible worlds there are out there, just waiting for me.

I love this part of him. I love this world he shows me. But I don't love the other world him and Mum show me. I'd like that part to go away. I don't love when Mum comes home with her buttons done up wrongly and her cheeks flushed and her lipstick sticking to her teeth. As if I'm meant to not know what's happening.

I start to notice that Andy smells of nearly-stale whisky, and his teeth are squint and yellow and he's always on the phone or popping out to buy an extra bottle of red, just in case. He drives us over to Glasgow where he takes us for lunch with some of his old colleagues in the back room of an old men's pub that has the lingering stench of sweat and fags and bleach. He drinks so much that Mum has to drive us home during rush hour, her knuckles turning white as she navigates the unfamiliar four-lane motorway.

He's always talking about giving up drinking and smoking until it becomes an endless refrain and he's imminent abstinence personified. Soon, soon, soon, he says, all future tense, and Mum smiles at him until she looks like a fish. She tells me she loves him and he loves her and we all stand there the day Zoe gets married, Mum with her arms behind her back holding his hand. I'm supposed to not notice any of this, the same way as I'm not meant to notice her dress hanging off her or her jutting hipbones as the wedding line-up squints into the sun and Grampa's flashbulbs wipe us out to kingdom come; the pair of them are trapped together after that, each swearing to give up their demons, but entwined, always, each with the other.

In the end, Zoe's wedding is fun. I love her husband. He makes everyone laugh. Even Zoe, and that's quite a challenge. Zoe takes life seriously, and likes everyone to know it. Whereas I do too, but I also like to make people laugh. I like people to think I'm a bit stupid, then they don't expect too much from me.

Mum loves Dave too. She says, Oh, he's like the son I never had. You know, you were meant to be a boy. Your dad was certain you would be one. She has told me that so often that I'm sick of hearing it.

I'm Zoe's flower girl. I wear a ridiculous dress and an even worse headdress, made of silk roses. I make a fuss in the wedding car about it looking like horns. Mum says, Don't be ridiculous, each time I rip it off my head, but it does look like horns. I look like the devil. Or a goat. I'm allowed to dance to Bryan Adams at the wedding, and a boy from the congregation tells me I'm beautiful afterwards. That's quite special.

When Andy comes up in the October holidays he says, Wouldn't it be nice to go to Colonsay? I'm not really sure what I'm supposed to say. We went there the summer after Aunty Liz died, and the whole tiny island is full of how it felt to still be alive after she was dead. I learnt to swim in the sea there and remember how warm and beautiful it was. But that was July, and this is October and nowhere in Scotland is a good idea in October. I think of Andy's newsroom in London and how much better it would be to go there, but I don't say it.

On the way we stop off at the uni where he and Mum met. I want to scream, It's not fucking 1972 anymore, but they're inhaling nostalgia like it's glue. When they suggest it might be a nice idea to stay the night there, I look at the damp fallen leaves turning to mulch already outside the breeze-block dormitories that look like they belong in Soviet Russia, not here.

In the middle of the night I wake in the room I'm supposed to be sharing with Mum. I'm alone. She's not allowed to be in his room, the elders would say that was sinful. I have to pretend I don't know what they're doing. I lie in the dark, telling myself it's not happening. The blackness tries to eat me up, it tries to get down my throat, it begins to sit on my chest. I sit up to get it off but it's a heavy sort of dark, the sort I know too well.

I scream.

The walls trap the sound in.

I'm scared because I know exactly what Mum's doing. I know she's not meant to be doing it. She's meant to be with me and instead she's away with him. She's chosen him over me. She's chosen him over God. God will kill her now He knows what she's doing, and He'll kill me too when he brings His judgment. I scream until my lungs hurt and I am empty.

As dawn makes its way through the thin curtains at

the window she pushes the creaking door open. It falls back into place on its heavy hinges. I shut my eyes tightly and try to breathe steadily, like I'm sleeping.

Three nights and I stay awake for each of them to check she's always gone. I drink Coke to try to stay awake, but it doesn't work. I doze in the back seat and hear Andy suggest I might be depressed because I sleep so much. Probably the Coke, Mum says. She's drinking an awful lot of it. I want to ask them exactly how fucking stupid they are. I let my mouth fall open and do a couple of fake snores.

When we arrive the island's full of mist, a mist that doesn't lift the whole time we're there. Not that it matters, there's nothing to see.

The hotel doesn't have any spare rooms, but we have dinner there anyway. The only thing on the menu is venison. Andy pulls a piece of shot from his mouth and puts it on his plate. I stare at it and then I stare at Mum. She doesn't say anything. The open fire crackles and hisses and spits a piece of coal onto the carpet. It blazes bright red before turning black.

I have another Coke and try to choke down the dead deer in its thick brown sauce, as they drink wine and make noises about how good it all is.

They're the same noises they both make later in the B&B with the blue wallpaper. The B&B only has one room left. It's OK to share, isn't it? Mum says, flashing her lipsticked teeth at the reception desk. Sure, I say, as I shrug. I'm trying to keep my sentences short.

The sound of their giggling and squelching wakes me. They don't try to keep the noise down. I feel sorry for the poor woman who runs the place. The walls don't seem too thick. I keep my eyes shut. I try to sleep but I want to be sick. I want to run away. I want to be at home.

We drive to the causeway the next day and get cut off by the tide. An awfully big adventure, they call it; I don't bother to change my face. There are no animals here and no plants and everywhere is only different shades of brown. The sea leaves salt in my hair, the mist makes it dark all day long and there are no streetlights to cut through it when night arrives.

On the last day, we go to the beach. They stay up in the dunes. I walk down to where the angry Atlantic licks its way up the sand. I walk into it. I let it soak my boots and don't care if the water ruins the leather. I like the lines it leaves on them. I wonder how it would feel to keep walking. I want to try.

Mum's laughter floats to me on the wind. I turn back and walk up the rough seagrass, struggling as the sand slips beneath my feet, and find them lying on top of each other, laughing. He takes his hand out of her top. She doesn't even blush anymore.

I know that God's going to be after me now. Not that I was on the safest of ground with him, but now he'll kill me for sure. Just great.

We get the late ferry home. In the bar, they sit toasting each other and their first successful holiday together. They don't hear me say I'm going onto the deck. I want to look at the stars but when I get up, the clouds have eaten those too.

I lean over the guard rail to try to find the dividing line between the dark sky and the obsidian sea. The rail stands out bright white against the darkness.

I think how they'll always be fucking in the same room or the next room. They'll fuck and fuck and fuck and fuck and I'll have to keep drinking Coke day after day after day and my teeth will rot and my legs will get fat. I think about disappearing. It wouldn't be so hard. It wouldn't take long at all.

I climb the rail.

Ordinarily, I hate climbing. But this feels OK, seeing as it has a purpose to it.

Near the top, I put my feet together. It wouldn't be hard to let go. It would be easy to fall, or to be pulled. I think it might feel like going home; Granny always says the sea's in our blood.

I look at the boat's wake and the scudding water broken up by the force of the engine. The waves make such an alluring pattern as they gather. It would be so easy.

The clouds clear, leaving wisps across the moon. I either want to be in the sea or be the sea; I'm not sure which.

Suddenly, I see Grampa's face, and the way his eyes water, and how he doesn't get out of bed easily in the mornings. Not since Liz. How he holds his arms out to me, how he smells, how he makes me feel safe.

I climb down the rail.

I feel my feet on the rolling deck.

I'll save it for later, when I really need to leave.

They're still in the bar when I go back down, holding hands and looking at each other. I wander over to the jukebox, put on a song I know Mum wouldn't let me choose. It's not like she's listening anyway.

Four weeks later and we're at Andy's house when he gets pissed one time too many. They've been to the pub and Mum starts to have a go at him for the state he's in, then he starts shouting at her. She doesn't do fighting, she thinks she's above that. She walks away and takes me up to the bedroom that's going to be mine after they get married. There are bags with rolls of Sanderson wallpaper stacked in the corner, my new curtains already hanging at the windows. He's going to murder us, Mum says. I think of all the expensive Japanese knives he keeps in the kitchen and how he showed me how to hit the exact right spot on a lobster's head to kill it immediately.

Listen, she whimpers, can't you hear him? I hear him opening drawers in the kitchen. The trick, he said, as he taught me to slice an onion fast, is to keep your knives sharp.

We'll be dead by morning, Mum says as she closes her eyes.

I hear her snoring in my single bed. I sit with my back against the door all night long, just in case he tries to come in. The next day the train lilts and tilts as it carries us home. I feel sick. Granny collects us from the station. I hear something about 'poor dear' from the front seat and know we're back where we always are.

Winter beds in, and three elders come to the house. I put the kettle on for them and arrange biscuits on one of the best plates before Mum tells me to go to my room. I sit for hours reading books I've smuggled home from the school library. Sitting there, I remember the elders doing the same when I was very little and my dad came back for a few days. I'd gone into the bathroom and he was in the bath with the water right up to his chin. Don't drown, Daddy, I shouted and he laughed, bubbles dripping from his elbow. Then the elders came, and he wasn't there anymore.

The elders leave, and Mum hugs me too tightly. After that she's all meetings and field service and association again and I tuck myself into the dark parts of me, and never tell her about the things I heard.

After that it's harder to care about God. I'll die at the end of days anyway now Mum's sinned. There's no point in trying to be good all the time.

LOVERS OF PLEASURES RATHER
THAN LOVERS OF GOD

1993

AND RUN. FEET SLIP ON the muddy banking. I scream, Where's my bracelet? before sliding down its sheer face.

Lola and Sarah are at the bottom of the gully. They're less pissed than me, which might explain how they found an easier way down. We start scrambling around for my bracelet, trying to think of ways of climbing back up the hill. Finding it becomes a point of urgency, because Granny gave me it as a present when she came home from Mexico. If Mum asks where it is, I'm really fucked. So we have to find it. But Lola and Sarah don't care about it as much as they care about getting more drunk. 'Mon, Sarah says, let's get to the Co-op before it shuts. We can find yur daft bracelet in the mornin'.

What also matters is that after we're pissed enough we find some boys to get off with. This is the second most important aim of the evening.

We aren't sure exactly what 'get off with' means. Lola says it's snogging someone, Sarah says it's snogging and getting fingered. She knows because she's done it but also because Jodie told her. Everyone knows that Jodie's done everything. She gets called the village bike. It took me ages to get the joke, but I laughed at the time anyway.

If we're going with Lola's definition, then I've got off with a few boys. The first time I snogged a boy in the first term of first year, it was a fright. I tried to remember what they do in films, how they tilt their faces to the side, and I was concerned that my nose might get in the way even though mine is pretty small. I was thinking all of this when suddenly his tongue was in my mouth, pushing its way around my teeth and right down the back of my throat until I was gagging and running back through the school doors where Lola and Sarah were desperate to know what it had been like. So desperate you'd think maybe they hadn't done what they said they had.

We're camping in Sarah's garden tonight so her mum and dad won't see us pissed, although she says they don't care about that anyway. Cool, she calls them. Mum's visiting friends in Glasgow and I'm staying with Granny. At least, that's what Mum thinks. Granny said I

114

could stay with Sarah. It'll be nice for you, Granny said, to spend some time with normal people your age.

I'm good at covering up all the things I don't want Mum to find out about.

By the time we get to the Co-op my head's beginning to feel a bit weird. Like I have a migraine coming on. It's after nine, but it's still light. It won't get dark for ages yet, if at all. Earlier, the light felt piercing and bright, as though it had been turned up somehow, and I felt fast like I'd been sped up. I like that feeling. We'd been on the swings in the park and some boys, Big Gaz and Baz and Daz and Chubs who's really called Ian, had come up to us with a big Coke bottle but it didn't have Coke in it. It had something else. It was all cloudy and kind of yellow.

What's that, I asked. Now this, Baz or Daz said, is special. We made it for you girls.

I swung a bit more on the swing, pretending I wasn't interested.

Yeah right, Lola said, from the swing next to me.

That's just crap from yer maw's booze cupboard, Sarah shouted as she jumped from the swing, gliding perfectly through the air.

From behind us, Jodie came striding across the grass. Man, she said, will you stop tryin' to shag the wee lassies, they're in first year for fuck's sake.

Like that ever put you off, said Chubs.

All the boys are called something else, just to be cool.

Ah, fuck off, said Jodie, as she came across to the

swings and leant against the rusting metal frame, pulling a packet of cigarettes from her shorts. You want wan? she said, holding it out to me. Sure, I said and then I tried to jump from the swing, but I couldn't do it like Sarah did. Dusting my knees, I leant into Jodie as she lit the cigarette. I tried to remember how this worked: breathe in but don't breathe in so much that it hits my lungs and makes me cough. I walked over to the boys like I didn't care, my cigarette between my fingers.

What is it then? I said, holding out my hand for the bottle.

Well, said one of them, it's a cocktail.

Fancy, said Lola from my side.

Totally, he said, pure fancy, like. It's Southern Comfort, vodka, an' Malibu, topped up wi' a wee bit o' Newcastle Broon.

Fucking rank, said Jodie, ye cannae expect them to drink tha'.

Here, let me try, I said.

You'll like it, said another one of the boys, yur fancy.

I do sometimes steal some of my granny's G&T, I said.

They all fell around laughing, clutching their sides.

God, yer priceless, said Big Gaz, the oldest one.

Lola and Sarah had told me about him and how fit he was, but he just looked sort of large to me, his Fred Perry T-shirt stretched across his chest like it was too small for him.

I took the bottle. There was no way this would taste

good. We've been drinking cans of Newcastle Brown for weeks on the banks of the river. I hate the taste of beer, but I love the feel of it. I don't know why Mum lets me go to Lola's house, I think it's got something to do with Zoe and how difficult she was when she still lived at home. Mum found her drinking cider in her room once. Zoe was daft – she always got caught. I think because I'm good at home Mum thinks I'm good all the time: I hear her telling people how easy I am.

I sniffed the bottle. It smelt like it might rip my throat out. Big Gaz stared at me as I swigged a mouth-ful looking right at him. It was the worst thing I'd ever tasted. It was fire in my mouth and rage in my throat. I can still feel it corroding in my belly.

Not too bad, I said and took another mouthful. It was easier that time.

Don't hog it, said Sarah holding out her hand.

I gave it to her. She took a mouthful then spat it out, spray glinting in the sun.

Aw, man, she said, that's bad. Then she took another mouthful and screwed her face up as she swallowed it, still grimacing as she patted herself on the chest. Wheefffff, she said, that's amazin'.

Lola indicated she was next by pointing at herself with her two index fingers. Will youse hurry up, she said.

Sarah gave her the bottle and Lola took a great big gulp of it. Her face didn't flinch.

S'awright, ah suppose, she said after she swallowed.

It was my turn again. I made sure to take a big drink since I knew Lola has an appetite like mine. We

117

passed the bottle between us as the boys eyed us like hawks. Then we told them we were off to the Co-op to get more supplies.

There's a guy outside the Co-op who Sarah knows. She tells me to go up to him because I look the oldest. Just say you want some Diamond White, she says, an' tell hum yer seventeen. Jus' so you don't sound too young, like. OK, I say, taking the money from her. As I walk away she shouts after me, Tae bottles, awright?

I put my shoulders back and make my hips try to move from side to side as I walk. I know this makes me look older. I try to look like I don't care. I go up to the guy and smile at him. Hiya, he says, smiling at me.

I don't suppose you might be able to get me two bottles of Diamond White? I say to him.

Aye, right, he says, laughing.

I have the money, I say, holding out the fiver.

It's no the money that's the problem, he says. How auld are yea?

I'm six—seventeen, I say.

Eh, which is it? he says. Sixteen or seventeen?

Seventeen, I say, it's just been my birthday. I keep forgetting. And then I laugh to make him know it's funny.

Awright, he says, gie us the money.

I hand the note over.

Jus' wait roond the cornur fur me, he says before disappearing in the shop. After forever he comes round the corner with two bottles in a Co-op bag. Thank you, I say.

You need any'hing else? he says.

No, I don't think so, I say.

Aye, you sure aboot tha'? he says as I walk away back to where Sarah and Lola are.

Fuckin' yas, Lola says, as I wave the bag in the air.

Come on, let's get mortal, Sarah says.

We link arms as we walk back to the park with the sun setting behind us.

I wake with the desert in my mouth, my tongue so parched it can hardly move. The morning sun comes in through the stretched cheap canvas of the tent, turning the air red. Sarah and Lola are still sleeping, the steady rhythm of their breathing filling the tent.

I need something to drink. I need to puke. I need to pee.

As I unzip the tent the sunlight burns my eyes. I put my arm up to shield my face and stumble to Sarah's back door. I try to open it, but it's locked. I bang and bang and bang on it until Sarah's dad opens it. He's wearing a vest that used to be white and shiny football shorts, his face covered in stubble. He looks surprised to see me.

I need some juice, I say, I'm really thirsty.

Aye, he says, shure.

Inside, he opens the fridge, the blue light inside blinking on. Here, he says, huv a mouthfu' o thus. I take the glass bottle of Irn-Bru from him. Thank you, I say. He's not given me a glass, so I drink from the bottle, keeping my eye on him to see if he gives me any sign this might be the wrong thing to do. He doesn't. The sharp metallic taste of it brings bile into my mouth. I hand the bottle back to him. Huv mare, he says. I shake my head. I'm fine, thank you, I say.

Afterwards, I crawl back into the tent, the light hurting my eyes. I blink it away as parts of last night float back into focus. There's laughter and spinning and the river flowing past and suddenly a field and Big Gaz standing over me and I'm on my back and my jeans are open and he's standing up and undoing his and I'm saying, No, not this time, and he's saying something like 'slag' or 'tease' and then he's saying, I can still poke you again, can't I? and I'm nodding and he's on me. He tastes of gum that's been chewed for too long and the grass itches under my skin and he puts his hands in my pants and takes 'poke' too literally, and I'm thinking I can't come back here because I need to give Big Gaz what he wants next time and I don't want him, didn't want him, but somehow ended up looking like I wanted him.

I open my eyes to be back in the morning. I think of Mum and how she'll be home by now and how Granny will pick me up in a few hours and she'll take my bag and ask if I had a nice time as she walks me to the car. I'll smile at her and tell her it was lovely and hope she doesn't smell any of it on me.

It is too dangerous to keep doing this.

BAD ASSOCIATIONS
SPOIL USEFUL HABITS

1993

NOW SHE'S BACK WITH GOD for good, Mum battens down the hatches. He's all she needs. He is her purity, her light, her guidance, her everything. For a while, this doesn't extend to me, and then suddenly, I'm no longer allowed to stay with worldly friends. This means I can't drink or smoke or be touched. Lola and Sarah and everyone else think I no longer like them. I can't tell them the truth, so I let them think what they like. When the bullying starts, I let that happen too. Mum says bullying is to be expected: it's a sign of the end, after all. Elders give talks saying young faithful brothers and sisters should be thankful and proud if they're bullied, because it shows they're doing something right.

There are ways of bringing the outside in. I am good at this.

I bring music and books I shouldn't into the house. I need to be careful about this, so that Mum doesn't know what I'm doing.

I try not to think about how the bad things I've done mean that I'll die when the end comes. But I become obsessed with working out how Jehovah is going to kill me. This means I start reading the magazines and books a lot. It also means Mum thinks I'm going through a spiritual phase. She likes this. She says, No one knows for sure how the end is going to come. This sounds like a cop-out to me. It won't be a flood, because he's already done that, she says, and the rainbow was a promise to Noah that the Flood wouldn't happen again. Other than that, we need to trust in Jehovah and realise his ways are mysterious.

The pictures in the literature terrify me. I hate the ones of pavements cracking and buildings falling and balls of fire flying through the streets as women in high heels and short skirts try to run away from them. They give me nightmares.

I hate sleeping now, because of these dreams. Most nights I lie awake listening to John Peel's burred voice in my headphones as he talks about music I've never heard of. When he plays a song, a door opens into somewhere else.

I hardly ever feel calm, or settled. Most of the time it's as if I'm watching myself from somewhere else.

That's the problem with pretending to be two people; I'm never fully either of them.

There's also always the fear of being watched. According to Mum, I am being observed all the time. She says, Jehovah's always watching. What a show I put on for Him.

The only time I feel like myself now is when I'm listening to music. When I do, it feels like I am finally stepping inside my skin. Uncle Richard sends me mixtapes. I still call him Uncle, even though he's not really my uncle now Aunty Liz is dead. I love his tapes; he packs them full of Joy Division, the Velvet Underground, Patti Smith, Blondie and the Undertones. I listen to them late at night, letting one side play itself out before flipping the tape over and falling asleep to the music. I write to tell him I like Joy Division the best. He sends back their full albums, and a letter telling me about going to see them. One time he sends an actual vinyl album. Mum even lets me keep it, so long as I don't play it.

Mum finds the box of the Joy Division tapes one day. You'll end up like Ian Curtis if you keep listening to them, she says. She said the same thing when I started reading Sylvia Plath. I don't tell her that I'm fine working on my own extinction without either of them.

Mum thinks I should get rid of it all. Something about the devil and music like that. Worldly influence, she says. I learn that if I put a different label on top, she doesn't ask any questions. This is what I do when I bring Nirvana home, *Nevermind* on one side of the tape, *In Utero* on the other. It says, EVENING SESSION MIX on it.

I spend days lying on my bed that summer listening to music when I should be doing something better. I lie there with stacks of books and the tapes turned up loud on my personal stereo. I lie there thinking about the people who wrote the music I love. I like how none of them sound like they belong. It's as if they're all on the outside of something. Somehow that makes me feel better. Maybe it's OK to feel like I don't belong. Maybe one day I'll do something useful with the feeling.

WHOEVER INCREASES
KNOWLEDGE INCREASES PAIN

1993

I'M HARDLY ALLOWED OUT AT the weekends. This means I read a lot. Although the house is full of books, I'm bored of the Bible and I'm sick of the classics.

Mum keeps trying to make me read more Dickens, but I don't need 16 fucking pages to describe the sunset. Zoe loves Jane Austen; I don't find fans and balls and who's going to marry who very intriguing. I do discover *The Rainbow* by D.H. Lawrence and quickly realise it's not about rainbows, which is good. I'm not sure why we still have it, the same with *Women in Love* and *The Go-Between*. I keep them hidden, just in case Mum remembers what's in them.

The school library's shit, it mostly only has Point

Horror books. I tore through them last year. I was scared Mum would look in my bag, so I'd read each as quickly as I could before returning it to school the next day to get another out. Still, weird to think they aren't half as gruesome or terrifying as some of the shit in the Old Testament. It's properly fucked up. It's so full of vengeance and bloodshed and rape it makes it really hard to like God. He was forced into it, Mum said, Those Israelites were always sinning. Hardly the best excuse, I think but don't say.

In the middle of the summer, I find a thin book with a silver cover. When I first find it, I think it's *The Satanic Verses*, because the name is worn from the spine. I've never seen *The Satanic Verses*, I've just always wanted to, ever since seeing it being burned on TV. But it's not, it's *The Catcher in the Rye*. Mum notices it on my bed. Oh, she says, I couldn't read that after John Lennon. I don't know what she's on about. I read it in one night with the windows open to the summer rain and the smell of the warm ground as the rain hits it, with *Unknown Pleasures* turned up so loud my ears hurt, as flashes of lightning light up the cobalt night.

Holden hates everyone; so do I.

I write in my diary that if I ever have a kid, and it's a big IF, I'll call it Holden. Or Curtis. Or Kurt. Or River. When he died, I couldn't tell Mum why I was so upset. I couldn't tell her about watching *My Own Private Idaho* on repeat in other people's houses, watching him and Keanu Reeves's skin glistening as they moved over each other.

After that, I run out of books to read. At Granny's I discover the attic is the place to find the best books. That's where I find really interesting biographies of Lenin and Stalin and Mussolini, and *The Communist Manifesto,* which helps to contextualise things a bit. When I talk to Mum about communism she says, It was a good enough idea, but humans always spoil everything, don't they. Like communism would be possible without them.

The magazines are always saying it's important to have a hobby. I manage to spin learning the guitar into one. I play classical guitar to Mum, and she's impressed by all the fancy Spanish finger-picking stuff. In my room I practise Nirvana chords. Then I move on to Hole. I play as quietly as I can, because if Mum heard me playing worldly music, she'd sit me down with the *Young People Ask* book and we'd have to look at the section about worldly entertainment. After that, there would be no more guitar playing for me. Sometimes I wonder what it must be like to be a kid who doesn't have to hide things all the time. It must feel weird to not have to pretend to be someone else; still, I'd like to try it once or twice.

I become obsessed with Mum's collection of sewing patterns, especially the ones from the sixties, with either really long skirts or really short ones. Both immodest, in their own ways. For some reason Mum lets me use one of the patterns to make a green crushed-velvet babydoll dress. Just make sure you make it a bit longer than the pattern, she says. I accidentally forget about that bit.

Lots of evenings I stand in front of my dressing-table mirror wearing the dress and playing my guitar, the sound of children playing outside spilling through the window along with the hot smell of cut grass. I like how I look then. Almost like Courtney Love.

And I like how carrying my guitar at school makes me feel. I wear the Doc Martens that Mum let me get because they're practical, and walk around with my guitar. I don't care that I'm not friends with Lola and Sarah and all their hangers-on anymore. I don't need them. I just need books and music. One day I'll have a house full of books I want to read and music I want to listen to and there will be nothing Mum can say about any of it. What I try not to think about is what having a house like that will mean I'll have to give up.

ENTICED BY MY OWN DESIRE

1994

ALTHOUGH MUM DOES A GOOD job of making the world go away, I'm skilled at bringing it back. It's like I have a nose for sin, I can sniff it out anywhere I go. I can even find it at the meetings.

It's Thursday night and Simon runs his hands through his hair in the Kingdom Hall.

I've known him all my life. He's wild. He used to dare me to do stuff when I was little and I kind of loved him then. He told me to ride his BMX down a hill, and I did it for him, even though it didn't have brakes and I fell off at the bottom. He dared me to climb a tree and I did it, even though I didn't know how to get down. He dared me to break the glass slides for my microscope, just to see what happened, and I did.

Sitting in the Kingdom Hall, with its windows boarded up so we aren't distracted by what's happening outside, he looks different to me now. I didn't notice him changing. His chin-length thick auburn hair is something I want to reach out and touch. His green eyes could be something to fall into. The sharp jut of his chin something I could hold in my hands, his back something I could run my fingers down. On the platform the elder says something about sinful desires or the end coming or the importance of the preaching work or deadening, therefore, our body members. It doesn't matter, it's only noise.

He reaches up and runs his fingers through his hair again, brushing it out his eyes. I swallow.

That's the beginning of it.

He isn't a good association because he doesn't answer much at the meetings and he never looks interested. His hair is too long and he makes it quite obvious he isn't into it and is only there because his parents make him go. He was, at least, baptised a couple of years ago, when he was 12, so he has that in his favour. Mum lets me hang out at his house with him and his sister and says things like, It's nice you've got friends in the truth now. I smile and don't tell her how most of the time I'm there I'm watching Simon.

He moves like water. His body makes itself into lithe shapes as he walks, skates, surfs, bangs the taut skins of his dad's drums. The sinews in his arms stretch and tense, his long fingers are never still.

I want to touch him. I don't know how to

communicate this; instead we talk. We laugh a lot. We talk about music and how sick we are of living in a small town, how stupid our parents are, how boring they've let themselves become, how it'll never happen to us.

Kurt Cobain is dead when we teach each other how to fuck.

We're on his bed and it's dark. Mum only lets me stay over at his house because I'm friends with his sister. Maybe it's two in the morning, maybe we should both be sleeping, maybe we shouldn't be listening to Nirvana, maybe we shouldn't be so close to each other, maybe we shouldn't be kissing as Kurt screams into the darkness. Not so much kissing as eating each other. We're both so hungry. He claws at my buttons. I pull his zip down. My heart hammers hard as I feel him inside his trousers. I'm worried I'm doing it wrong, I don't know how to touch him, but I keep going, my skin exploring his, the long veins on his hard cock. It is interesting to feel him like this. And to be sober while doing it. Sweat beads on his brow. We breathe faster. It's like discovering a place beyond words, where language dissipates, where thinking isn't needed anymore. It's just me and him, my skin, his skin, and our sweat-slicked bodies. It's not clumsy or awkward or dirty fumbles like it has been with other boys. It is like being filled with something lighter than air.

Sharp click. The tape stops. Simon sits up, his bare chest glistening in the light from the uncurtained window. He lets out a long exhale. I lick my salt-sweet lips. He says, We should probably stop before . . . Yeah, I say, we don't want to wake anyone up. He laughs. That's not what I meant, he says.

When I'm not with him, I become slow and lethargic with the weight of wanting him. I close my eyes and see him there. I lie in bed feeling him on me, tracing where his fingers were. I can't eat or sleep or think. I just want him all the time. I want the new ways of forgetting he brings. I want the new ways of tunnelling into a different kind of absence.

DOUBLE LIFE

1996

FOR YEARS, I KEEP HIM secret from Mum. When he totally stops going to the meetings, I worry that she'll stop me from seeing him. Now that I'm 16, Mum's busier than she used to be. I don't count as a child in the government's eyes anymore, so she doesn't get money for me like she used to, which means she has to work for it now. I almost feel bad about growing up because of it. She always did some work, but never so much that it would take her over the 16 hours allowed by the government before her benefits would stop. The house was full of material that she'd make into elaborate wedding dresses, and sometimes she'd fix other people's clothes. It's funny, farmer's wives and landowners, they all look so wealthy with their Land Rovers and big houses, but they'd come to

Mum and ask to get the sleeves on their cuffs turned and their pyjamas darned, and it was an insight into another kind of subsidised life: all the money for crops and cattle, but hardly enough to scrape together a fiver to pay Mum on time. She used to cry a lot before I turned 16, and it was hard to understand, because it wasn't like she didn't know how to do anything. Not like she hadn't been to uni, or hadn't worked when Zoe was little. It all changed when she had me, she said. Difficult to tell, I suppose, if it was having me or becoming a Witness, since the two things happened at the same time. But she'd been out of work for so long that she worried she didn't have the skills to get back into teaching.

She went to evening classes this past winter, even though the elders advised her against it, and now she's back teaching, at a college this time. She teaches people how to look after children, which is so hilarious when I stop to think about it that I want to cry.

I want Simon when I'm on the school bus and I want him in French class; I want him when the paint squeezes through the silk screens in art; I want him when the rhythm rises in my headphones; I want him when I'm meant to be thinking about preparing myself for the end.

The want does things to me, it makes me forget who I'm meant to be or what I'm meant to believe.

Mum's warned me, Boys only want one thing. She might be wrong about it only being boys.

All the weekends I can manage, I go to his house. I

want him to have all of me. He makes me laugh. He makes me scared because I'm not used to wanting something and getting it. I am not used to wanting a person and getting them: everyone goes away eventually. I try to remember he only wants me for what he can get from me, but I don't care about that. We both take what we want and what we need. For a few hours late on Saturday nights with the music on loud to drown our noise, our needs and wants line up.

I usually hate the winter, with its heavy days and skies, when the lights outside only seem to compound the darkness within, but this year it's different. I'm warm and safe enough and even school is better. I started at a new school in the autumn, a private one. In the summer I'd sweated through the scholarship exam and was so convinced I'd messed it up that I had to read the admissions letter twice when I was offered a place. Better class of girl, Mum said would be there. Really, what she should've said was, Better class of drugs.

Simon and I are always watching *The X-Files* and listening to music and touching each other, until it gets to spring, and I hit a problem.

The problem is, I haven't really thought through what Mum not knowing anything about the other part of my life might mean. I turn 16, and she tells me I'm old enough for a boyfriend. I can't tell her I'm totally happy with Simon; no, that would be a problem. When she tells me about a boy who's also called Simon and is from a different congregation, who said he thought I looked beautiful at the assembly, all I can do is smile at her.

He writes to me and sends me a mixtape, and it's difficult because he has really good taste in music. Better even than Original Simon who's started listen to metal. Simon Two is more into Smashing Pumpkins and Silver Jews. He plays guitar and takes really nice photos, with a real camera. The problem is, he's really shy. I actually think he's better on paper. I go to visit him a few times and he's really lovely. Too lovely. He doesn't try to do anything inappropriate with me. He doesn't try to touch me. He's too wholesome.

But Mum calls him my boyfriend. Then I have to too. He doesn't know anything about him being an imitation. I see Original Simon less and I'm not sure he isn't up to stuff with a girl from school, because she starts talking about him with a sly smile on her face that makes her look a bit like a fox. Simon Two and I go and see Smashing Pumpkins in Glasgow, pressed against the safety barrier at the front of the concert with Billy Corgan lit up from behind, the metallic ZERO on his T-shirt changing to different colours as the light show plays around him. Mum is waiting outside in the car. I've played her some of their softer stuff so she thinks we're going to a nice quiet show. Simon Two has his arm round my waist. I like him, even though I still like Original Simon. The weird thing is, they sort of merge together in my mind until it's almost like I'm seeing a single person.

Original Simon and I go to the beach one weekend.

His stupid dog runs away over rocks and stones right onto the next peninsula. The water's freezing, like the North Sea always is, when we wade in to get him. It quickly soaks through my Converse shoes and starts to make its way up my jeans. We scramble over rocks to get to the dog, who's barking frantically now, and that's when we notice that the tide is coming in and coming in fast, and that it's not a peninsula at all, but rocks that soon will be covered by the sea. Seaweed slips from under our feet as we half clamber, half swim to where the dog is. We stand on the rocks and laugh at the sea as it comes towards us, spitting its grey foam. We jump off and run back to safety just in time, Simon with the dog on his shoulders.

Afterwards, I sit in his bath with my knees pulled into my chest and watch the sand wash off me and settle at the bottom of the green water. I am consumed by how much I need him. In this pause I realise what we've been doing: how I'm cheating on him and on the other Simon, and I'm cheating on Mum and I'm cheating on Jehovah. I don't think that maybe I'm being cheated, or that I'm cheating myself.

I need to learn how to behave. I need to discover ways of making the world simpler, inside and outside my head before it all comes crashing in. The thing I need to learn the most is how to get rid of all my desires. This awful hunger I have for the world, I need to tame it, soon.

NO ONE KNOWS
THE WASTE YOU ARE

1996

I NEED TO STOP WANTING EVERYTHING. The first thing I teach myself to say no to is food.

Learning not to want began quietly, like most things do.

I'd been trying it out for a while. I didn't know if I'd be any good at it, seeing as I was always hungry and Mum says I give up on everything I try. You never stick at anything, she's always saying. I didn't want her to know about it, not until I knew I wouldn't fail.

On one damp weekend in February, I started throwing up. The week before, Mum had been away at work. The college she works at is in a town quite far away, and snow was forecast, so she'd sent me to stay at Granny and Grampa's. She stayed in the other town, with a sister she knows. Granny let me visit friends, so I went to visit Xander. Xander is one of the good guys, even though he was expelled from his last school for dealing drugs and didn't stop when he got to my school. A few of us went to his house and lay on his bedroom floor silently as the snow began to fall outside. I got stoned for the first time. I liked it.

Maybe that's why the next week felt so dismal, back at home in our dark sitting room.

Sometimes I think the hills eat the sunlight. Then things get muddled. The outside becomes darker than the inside and the inside becomes as dark as the outside, and on it goes, getting darker and darker.

Christmas cards are lies. They have their pictures of crisp white snow and red-bellied robins and green holly. They don't have slush and robins attacking other birds and piles of dead leaves. Which is probably a good thing, since they wouldn't sell. But still. I have never seen winter days like that here.

Here, it's either rain or sleet. When it does snow the boys ball it up and pack it hard together with a stone in the middle just for fun, and throw it at the bus window as we drive past. Sometimes the window shatters and the bus driver stops to swear at the kids and then the wind whistles in all the way home.

I hated the old school bus. I'd sit on it staring at the grey floor, wet from footprints trudging to the back seat. I made up rules about the bus so I felt safe on it: don't look up when the older kids or the cooler kids walk past; don't turn round when they shout your name on repeat or launch tiny balled-up bits of paper at the back of your head; stay sitting until they all get off; don't sit down the front or up the back. The trick was to try to be as small and as still as possible for as long as possible.

The new school bus is better. There are fewer girls on it. At the new school I learn to dye my hair and put make-up on so it looks like I'm not wearing any. I like making myself up. It feels like being free.

At the new school I tell them my dad's a doctor and my mum's a teacher. Both true at some point. I tell them they're divorced now and my dad lives in South Africa. It's really cool, I say, when I go and see him. They tell me their dads are farmers and pilots and lawyers and lecturers. Here I don't need to try to remember to talk like the rest of the kids – I can use my real voice, so that bit's easier – but I have to make sure no one finds out how poor we are. Wherever I am, I still have something to hide.

That weekend in February, I couldn't stop throwing up. I was sick for a whole week, until I couldn't even manage to throw up green bile. I'd never felt so clean.

In the bathroom I stood in front of the mirrored tiles I used to hate. I didn't look like I had the week before. I ran my fingers over my hipbones, counted every rib. I liked it. I liked taking up less space. I thought, If I can last a week without food, then I can do it for longer. Mum seemed to think I was the same as I'd been before. She kept wanting to feed me. She'd say, You must be so hungry, and she tried to give me Heinz soup like I was still a kid. I'd shake my head and say, No, no, I'm fine. When I went back to school the girls all told me how great I looked, the boys wolf-whistled. Best of all, Stephen, the fittest boy in Upper Sixth, started to talk to me, like I'd been waiting for him to for months.

Weird thing is, now I don't eat much, it's all I can think about. I'm always thinking of what I'll eat next – not that I want to eat. I have to plan ahead otherwise Mum will ambush me and try to make me eat something that isn't safe. I even dream about food.

I've discovered things about food I didn't know before. There are good foods and bad foods. The more you learn about food, the more you discover most foods are bad and very few are good. They all do something to you. Red meat will give me cancer, bacon will too; too much fruit is basically just sugar; even carrots will turn me orange. The thought of food inside me making me fatter or clogging my arteries or making me diabetic makes me feel so disgusted that it's safer not to eat very much. The thought of food being made in factories also makes me feel ill. Thinking of eating food that has travelled through tubes or down conveyor belts is just disgusting. Why would anyone want to do that to themselves?

When I say to Mum, I wish I could just take a pill and get all my vitamins from that, she looks at me with her eyes wide and says, Where would you get any pleasure from then? I don't tell her about boys' tongues and wrapping my legs around their shoulders or that first hit from a joint as your body begins to bleed itself into your surroundings. How can any apple ever compare to that?

Both Simons tell me I look great. I begin to notice

Simon Two is also a bit strange around food; he doesn't eat all that much and pushes his food around the plate at mealtimes. I worry about him sometimes. He looks heavy behind his eyes, and seems far away when I'm talking to him. I worry that he's too much like me. He's funny, and knows how to laugh, but I think he knows about feeling like an outsider in a deeply dark way. I want to ask him about it, but I also don't because I'm scared about what he might say. I discover that if I keep thinking about food I stop worrying about him. When I think about food there isn't space for other thoughts. This is a very good thing.

The bad thing is that people are beginning to say I'm too thin. This means they know what I'm doing. It also means they might try to fix me. And fixing me means making me fat. I don't want to be fat. I don't want them to think I'm a broken thing that needs fixed. I'm not broken: I'm making all the uncomfortable things go away. I've never felt so invincible. I've never felt so free. I've never felt so much like I'm flying. All the trees and flowers are so bright all the time, everything smells like it never has, life bursts from everywhere. If they take this away, it will go back to how it was before. I will have to close doors and pack desires into boxes and make the world grey and the sun dark, and God will raise his head and say, I am your God, your flesh is My flesh. He takes my body back. I will not have this happen, not now my body is mine and I am finding new ways to master it.

Whenever Mum asks if I've eaten I tell her I have, and hope she doesn't ask what. I don't think this is particularly deceitful. It's certainly less deceitful than I've been for years.

I tell myself I've got six months to disappear. I like deadlines.

At lunchtime I sit with the other girls in the hospital-green refectory on long wooden pews left over from the days our school was a convent, and fold my ready salted crisp packet over and over on itself. I hear the squall of boys outside chasing rugby balls; inside, all I hear is my heart drumming under my shirt, faster and faster the way it's started to do.

I turn my crisp packet into a fan. This means nothing bad will happen. I've been making these kinds of bargains my whole life. I used to do them with God, when I was still young enough to think he would bargain with someone like me. I'd say, If I eat my dinner then Mummy won't be sad, or if I am a good girl for seven days in a row then Mummy will have more money. God never answered: maybe it's safer to depend on myself.

I put the fan inside my empty Diet Coke can: this means I will be safe. I stand and walk across the room; I lift the lid of the metal bin and hear the can drop down deep into it. I have learnt to move my hips from side to side as I walk, to check my legs, stomach, bottom, don't move.

On the way home I sit at the back of the bus, sharing Xander's earphones, Billy Corgan or Eddie Vedder or Courtney Love singing us home. When the bus

143

drops me at the bottom of the hill I stand on the pavement for a while, making it look like I'm about to go into one of the nice houses. Once the bus moves out of sight I turn round and walk up the hill. Halfway there, I put the rest of my lunch into the bin next to the church. There's a stone carved owl over the door. Every time we go to the meeting, I have to look at the owl. This means we won't crash the car. I've been doing it since I was little, and Mum's still never noticed how I crane my neck and look backwards at the same point every week like Lot's wife.

I look round to check no one's watching as I push my lunch further and further into the bin. This means Mum won't know what I'm doing. I take my lunch to school so the food's gone from the house, and make sure it doesn't come back.

Mum's still at work when I get home most days. I drink a large glass of water, the same as I do every morning for breakfast, and then I start to make her dinner in the quiet, still house. I like making food for her. I put all the things I am scared of into it. This means I'm not really scared of them. I can touch meat and butter and cream; I watch as she eats. I read cookery books and dream of food, but I don't want to eat it. I am not hungry: all my hunger has just gone.

Every evening I shut myself in my room and exercise for 30 minutes, never less and never more. I do the same every morning.

I chew every mouthful 60 times, never less and never more.

When I do have to eat, I eat at 12.15 exactly. I watch the giant clockface in the refectory or the small clock reflected in the glass of the pine dresser, and as soon as the long arm clunks into place on the 3, I put my food onto my fork. I need to be finished by 12.25, otherwise I've eaten too much. If I eat dinner, I eat at 5.30, and need to have finished by 5.45.

These are my new rituals. Mum has hers, so why can't I have mine?

I like dividing the day into parts and doing the right thing at the right time. I like the way I am beginning to feel nothing.

Original Simon finds out about Simon Two and I find a way of feeling nothing at all about either of them. I don't need them. All my life I've felt too much all the time, and now I am numb.

Original Simon takes his surfboard to Cornwall. He phones me, his voice cracking as it travels down the line. Something about breaking his heart. I sit in the hallway with my back to the wall and stretch my legs out long, watching my toes as I move them away from me and then towards me, feeling the stretch travel up the whole length of the back of my legs. My legs are so thin. When I stay silent for too long, he repeats the part about me breaking his heart. The sun streams in through the open front door and catches on dust fairies dancing in the air. Yeah, I say. Sorry, it was complicated.

I don't feel sad, just relieved it's easier to be pure now. I am free of the weight of wanting him, free of the need for him.

KNOWLEDGE IS A GREAT VANITY

1996

THE CAREERS ADVISOR'S OFFICE IS hot. We've all been given a 15-minute time slot to talk about what we want to do with the rest of our lives. I haven't told Mum we're doing this. I know she'll say what she always says when I try to talk about the future. She'll say, The only thing I want for you is that you serve Jehovah, that's all that matters.

But this isn't really an answer. It doesn't give me anything to do. Mum talks about how lucky we are to have a purpose in life when everyone else has none: she tells me our purpose is to serve Jehovah, but I think it doesn't sound quite specific enough. I nod, though, knowing one day I'll believe it too. She doesn't let up in her campaign to inculcate me in the ways of the truth. This is what the organisation call it. They say, Children are not indoctrinated, they are inculcated, learning to love the truth since infancy. Every week we still prepare for Sunday's *Watchtower* study together, reading the paragraphs, underlining the answers to the questions at the bottom of the page. We also prepare for the theocratic ministry school, and for the book study on a Tuesday evening and for the ministry on a Saturday, and we do the Bible reading. It never changes, just the same as Mum says Jehovah never changes. When we're told to believe something new from the platform she says, That isn't Jehovah changing, it's new light. Still, it doesn't mean it's not boring having to sit there studying all this stuff I already know, but Mum says, The truth about Jehovah is infinite, it'll take the whole of eternity to learn. I don't want to tell her that her phrasing is a little dubious. Or that she's contradicting herself, because when I ask her questions about Him she says, The truth is very simple. Don't complicate it by asking questions.

My head hurts every time we read the society's literature. Just like it hurt this morning when we read the day's text and Mum said I had to read it twice so I could memorise it for today. The day's text is a protection when I'm at school. I'm meant to remember it when I come under trial. I think Mum thinks the careers office might be a trial.

The careers advisor smiles when she opens the door and Verity ducks out clutching a bunch of paper. Come on in, she says. I follow her into the small room. Sweet Williams, stuffed into a white vase on her desk, nod in the breeze from the window.

Whew, it's hot, she says as she pulls at the strap on her camisole. Let's get started, shall we?

I put my hands together on my knee and nod at her. She's sort of how I imagine a fortune teller might be, but less mystical. The future feels like a strange thing to me. When my schoolfriends talk about the future it sounds exciting and full of possibilities, whereas when I think of it, it is a closed, small and certain thing full of everything I already know: ministry, study, prayer, Jehovah, eternal blessings.

Now, I'm going to ask you a few questions about yourself, she says, and then I'll put the answers into the computer and we'll see what it comes up with. Does that sound good?

Yes, I say, even though it doesn't sound quite right. Surely a computer can't know what I should do with the rest of my life. Mum would probably say there's something Satanic about it.

It's difficult to answer her questions, especially when she asks me what I do outside of school. I can't tell her how many hours a week I spend at the meetings or on the ministry or studying. I'm not even sure what I do like doing. I tell her I like reading. I tell her I like writing even though I don't write poems as often as I used to, and my diary entries are beginning to make less and less sense. I tell her I like acting because I'm really good at drama. I pause and she's still sitting nodding at me, which I think means I'm to keep talking so I start scraping the barrel. I say I love horseriding, even though I've not been to the stables for years. She nods again. This is getting tricky. I tell her I like riding my bike and worry she'll suggest the Tour de France. She gives me a smile and nods really enthusiastically. Anything a little more academic? she says. She could've been more specific the first time.

Oh, I say, well, English lit, of course.

All the girls love English lit; it would be some sort of aberration not to love it.

History too, I say, I'm really good at it – trying to forget that I just wrote an essay blaming Chamberlain for World War Two, even though my history teacher had told me to ease off a bit. And German, I love it, I say. *Sprechen Sie Deutsch?*

She laughs. That'll do, she says. I think we've got plenty to be getting on with here.

She taps the keyboard. I try to think of something funny to say. I can't so I begin to play with my blazer cuff. She looks up, stares at my fingers fiddling with the buttons. I stop.

Well, she says, quite an eclectic selection of suggestions. I'll just print them off.

The printer hisses as it moves slowly across the page, depositing traces of letters that build with each traverse. Finally, the page is free.

Now, remember these are only suggestions, she says, nothing's fixed. She laughs. Under each suggestion is a description of the job and some entry routes are signposted.

I frown.

Entry routes, I say.

Yes, she says, someone with your academic calibre will be obviously be thinking about university. Have you given some thought to where you want to go?

I'm confused. I think of how the other girls throw around words like 'York' and 'Durham', and lately 'sixth form college', but these are words for other people. Mum's never once mentioned university to me. Or college. I'm just not going. There was enough of a fuss when Zoe stayed on at school at 16. The elders came to the house to tell Mum it was a bad idea. They said all the extra learning was unnecessary and would only take Zoe away from the truth. Mum had had to fight hard for them to listen to her. When they left she said, Would they have done this if I was a man, I wonder. That was the only time I've ever heard her say anything against the organisation.

I say, Moray House, maybe.

That's where Mum went. It's the only place I know – that and St Andrews, where Granny went, so I say that too.

You know Moray House is only for teaching, she says, and that's not suggested for you. Do you want to know what is?

Yes, I say, please. My hands are sweaty. My mouth dry. It feels really daring to even pretend there's a different future out there for me.

OK, she says, really interesting. First choice: actress. Wow. Well, you won't want to be doing that, now, will you. (She laughs again.) Job security. And second choice, well, that's also a bit off the wall: writer. (Prolonged laughter.) First time I've had that suggested. Let's skip to the third ... Historian. Excellent, great match.

She smiles, and somehow her teeth look larger than they did before.

Back in class the girls ask me what my results were. Actress, I tell them, as they crowd round. No fucking way, Angie says. You jammy cow, Kirsty says. She gave me vet. Like I want to spend my life with my arm up a cow's arse.

I laugh.

Some people don't have a single fucking clue how lucky they are.

DESIRES OF THE FLESH

1996

BRANCHES SNAP HARD UNDER HIS feet as he runs through the woods. It's dark but it's hot still, the heat making the smell of the damp ground escape. I'm on his back with my arms around his neck and I'm slipping down until I'm nearly off him. He stops for a moment to hoist me back up. Behind us we hear laughter so we keep running on, deeper and deeper into the shelter of the trees where he stops and puts me on the ground and we double over laughing as he pulls a packet of cigarettes from his pocket, puts one in my mouth and the lighter flares as it sparks, making our faces glow, just for a moment.

Everything spins. This is the second time today I've been pissed. Earlier, which may as well have been days before, Angie and her friends and I had vodka from a

Coke bottle in the park. It didn't take long until we were on the swings, going higher and higher with our heads tipped right back shouting at the clear blue sky. Mothers pulled their kids away from us. It was all so funny, and it got funnier and funnier, until everything was hilarious. Then we were back at Angie's house drinking Hooch and getting changed for the school ball.

I'd saved up my babysitting money for ages for new clothes. I bought a white top with silver angel wings on the back that move with my shoulder blades. It makes me look even thinner than I am, which is fine with me. I couldn't find a skirt that fitted my tiny waist, so I made one from white lace. It's short. I told Mum the length was a mistake, that I messed up when I made it. I love it; it fits with the angelic theme.

I got changed, and brushed out my new highlights at the front of my hair. Mum loves it when my hair's blonde, because it reminds her of when I was little. Now I'm older, it's faded to a kind of dull straw colour. I can get away with it being bleached; she doesn't mind if it makes me look like I did when I was small and innocent.

We passed round vodka and lip gloss, loading our mouths with both until they were sweet and sticky and heavy. We sprayed our hair into rigid, well-behaved sheets, and then we were a pack, out into the lengthening shadows where the heat had pooled and stuck, as over the sea the gulls swooped and screamed at each other. We stormed up cobbled streets, and pushed open the double doors of the pub. Everyone knows we're too young – we don't even pretend to have fake IDs – but no one cares. We sidled up to people who are always happy to get the drinks in, and what I drank I don't really know, something brightly coloured in a glass bottle. Clutching its neck, I poured it down my throat. It burned my mouth. I didn't care. I'd started to level out, so I needed something to get me pissed quickly again.

I was really thirsty and didn't know why. I drank as fast as I could but it didn't help. I drank and drank but all that happened was I got thirstier and thirstier, and then I was in the toilets and I was crying my eyes out, shouting for Mum. Throwing up, doubled over, and saying, I'll never do this again, even though all I wanted was more to drink. I worried I might die, and what would Mum think of me if I died on the floor of the Brown Bear's toilets?

After it passed, things didn't feel so bad. I put my head under the tap, rinsed my mouth, dried my eyes. In the bar I ordered another drink. I forgot about the vows I'd just made. The minibus came to drive us down dusk-eaten roads to school where we stormed the ball and I found the chemistry teacher who's been giving me the eye and fags all year, and then we were out and into the woods, and now I am slipping down his back and asking him if he has anything else and he thinks I mean something I don't. I have to spell it out for him, telling him, I'm not talking about protection, I don't want to fuck you. He's at least 22, properly ancient. The rumour is he sometimes brings drugs to school, and I thought he might have some pills, but it seems he doesn't, or not if I'm not doing what he wants me to.

Give me another fag at least, I say. We smoke as we walk out the woods. The ball is winding down and everyone is being thrown out into the night. I walk over to a crowd of people spilling out the school hall, the chemistry teacher disappears into the shadows. Stephen, who's in the sixth form and is so fucking hot, takes my hand and pulls me towards the minibus, saying, You're going back to Xander's, yeah? He's got some shit-hot stuff. I wave goodbye to Angie, shouting, I'll see you in the morning! I need to be back at hers by the morning when Mum's picking me up for the meeting, and now I'm sitting on Stephen's knee seeing as there aren't enough seats in the bus, and we are off and screeching round corners, flying down country lanes through the dark.

Then I'm drunk for the third time and finally stoned enough to leave my body and the room is loud with laughter, thick with smoke and bodies.

In the corner of the room Stephen and I start to kiss. I've wanted this for so long, it feels like we burn together. I need the toilet.

I walk into the bathroom and another sixth-form boy is there, just sitting, his back to the wall. I'm sorry, I say. He looks at me and then I don't know, somehow we are skin, we are sweat, we are slick, and I lick slowly, lower, taste salt, sweat drips into my eyes. The hard porcelain sink cold beneath me. He bites me, I am bruised fruit. I bite back. He says, Ouch. Sorry, too much? I ask, knowing.

It's all too much, too much desire, I desire too much, there is too much to desire.

That was some leaving present, he says. You know I've wanted you all term. Then he opens the door, brings laughter in from elsewhere. It shuts.

Shit, he was Claire's boyfriend. Still is. Shit. I hate her though. She thinks she's so superior with her sixth-form boyfriend. Well, well.

There are cracked tiles on the floor. White on black. Dirty grout, stained, staining, greying grey.

I blink. Wipe my mouth. Back in the bedroom Stephen's sleeping, and I settle myself against his bare torso. He makes a noise in his sleep. I like how he smells.

When I wake my tongue feels unfamiliar in my mouth. My eyes are red and hot. I move Stephen's arm from over me, pick my way through people on the floor. I'm wearing someone else's shirt. I don't know where my own T-shirt is. Back in the bathroom, I look like a stranger in the mirror, but one I like. I'm looking at this new version of myself when fuck! it hits me: it's light in here, which means it's morning and I don't even really know where Xander's house is compared to Angie's. How am I meant to get from here to there? I run up the stairs, step on fingers, arms, toes, not caring who I wake, shake Stephen, he sits, rubs his eyes, looks surprised, I hope he remembers who I am. I tell him I need to be back at Angie's. It's cool, he says, chill, we can get back there later. I can't tell him. I can't tell him that it's literally a matter of life and death. If I don't get back to Angie's before Mum arrives, I am beyond screwed. I'm utterly fucked. In fact, I'm more than fucked. I'm dead, I'm . . . I can't even think what I am. I tell him, No, I need to get back now. There's nothing I can say that even sounds sane, so I say, I totally forgot but I'm going away this morning. If I don't get to Angie's then I'll miss my flight. I'm going to my dad's in South Africa.

Fuck, he says, leaping up, you're going to feel awful on the plane. Yeah, I say, I know, but can we please go?

He wakes Johnny, who has a van, and we pile into it with birds screaming morning. None of us know where we're going but Johnny is inspired. He says, Angie lives near the sea: if we drive towards the sun we'll get there, so we drive. It all seems to be going OK until the van splutters and shakes and stops right there in the middle of the single-track road, just stuck.

Fuck! I shout. Can't you just fix it?

The boys laugh. It's OK, they say, this happens all the time. They get out and look at the engine for a minute like they know what's wrong. Then they jump back in and turn the key and after a few times repeating this, rumblings coming from deep inside the van. The engine starts.

As we drive, the van lurches wildly from one side to the other, flinging me all over the back seats. This doesn't help with the nausea I'm beginning to feel, but there isn't time to stop to puke. Finally roads start to look familiar, we're not lost any more. At Angie's house, I leap out and they keep the engine running because they're too scared to shut it off in case it doesn't start again. Stephen rolls the window down. See you next term, yeah? he shouts as I run up the drive waving them goodbye.

Angie's house is still locked up, everyone's in bed. I tiptoe round the back of the house, think about throwing stones at Angie's window, but that only works in films, not in the cold light of the morning. I sit down on her front step and think maybe I can wait here for Mum. I begin to shiver as the alcohol and weed ebb from my blood. I'm returning to myself faster than feels comfortable. Suddenly, Angie's mum opens the door behind me and is all smiles as she says, Come in, come in.

She doesn't ask where I've been, just if I'd like a cup of tea. I nod. As the kettle boils on the Aga I brush last night from my teeth, wash other people's sweat from my face.

Mum collects me and the sun lights up the road as we arrive at the Kingdom Hall. In the car park everything seems to shimmer slightly as if it might be moving and the tarmac might be melting, although it's too early surely for it to be that hot. I am loose and loosening.

Inside the Kingdom Hall it feels cool first but

suddenly becomes too cold. I run to the toilet where I sit, shivering and full of dread. Last night loops in my mind like a disjointed film. Some people say when they're hung-over they can't remember anything, but I remember it all. It's a gift. Or a curse. I rub my arms to try to make the goosebumps go away. My teeth begin to chatter. My heart does what my heart is always doing now, beating so fast I think it's trying to break out of my body. I can't do this again. But if I can't do it then how else am I meant to escape?

★

There was never any possibility of escaping God.

He was the weekly refrain. God was the rhythm and the routine. God was the shadows and the light. God was in my dreams and my nightmares. God was the news on the radio. God was the weather. God was the after-dinner Bible reading. God was my other parent. God was the thing I wanted to escape from, but God was the impossibility and the certainty. God was the hills that fenced me in, God was the future, God was the limits of my imagination, God was the beginning and the end, God was the Word and the Word was God and God was the walls and the secrets behind them and God was the only truth, stretching into eternity.

God was the whole world, and I was his puppet.

NEW GODS

1996

FLAMES DANCE HIGHER AND HIGHER in the real fire we have now. They are worth watching. I am 5 stone of bone wrapped in stretched yellowing skin and the doctor is talking but I'm not listening.

It's winter.

What has been has been. I have lived my last summer. I have learnt to un-need everything. I'm finally close to transcending the confines of my own body. Soon, I will float.

Tell me about your father, the new doctor says. I keep staring at the fire. I don't trust him. He looks suspiciously normal. He doesn't look like he was bullied at school like the other doctors they gave me did. He doesn't listen when I try to bring the conversation back to food. That doesn't mean I don't try.

I think I'm fat, I say.

What about your father? he repeats. This doctor is such a fucking cliché.

We sit, silently, in our war of attrition. I bet he'll crack first. It hurts when I speak now, it makes me breathless. My voice is quieter than it used to be. Hoarser too. So many things happen when you starve yourself, things they don't warn you about. There's not a manual. Maybe there should be, instead of the crappy leaflets they gave me when they first diagnosed me. For a moment the Latin name felt important, until I began to think that now it had a name, was I problem they would try to fix? And worse, would they try to take it away from me? Would they try to make me into the person I was before I discovered this slow way of escaping?

Mum liked the leaflet. It gave her certainty. It told her how sneaky and manipulative I am, now I'm just another anorexic.

Being good at starvation has certain side effects, significant and noticeable weight loss being not the worst of them, but the one everyone notices. The side effect I hate the most is now that I'm eating my organs it makes it hard to think. It also makes it hard for my heart to beat.

Last week, I scared myself. My heart became strange. Mum says I nearly died. I don't know if she's right or not. What I do know is I was sitting there and I felt all strange and lightheaded. I thought, Finally, I'm leaving my body. Mum asked if I was OK and I couldn't speak to answer her. She picked me up, put me on her knee and I rested my head on her, like I used to when I was younger. Everything was slowing down, apart from my heart, which tried to jump through my skin. I could see it under its taut surface, beating faster and faster as I felt further and further away from my body. There weren't lights so much as different colours and shapes. I couldn't make my fingers or toes move. I couldn't speak. I almost couldn't breathe. For a few seconds, it was the most beautiful thing to know I was nearly free of it all. And so painlessly too. But then Mum started screaming, carrying me to the back door and opening it to get the cold on my face. She pulled the wooden door open and the cold cracked around my jaw, like a slap. I smelt the wood smoke, saw the first stars over the farmhouse on the hill. I was back, for now.

She got in the way, and this is why I have not left yet. A miracle, she said afterwards, Jehovah brought you back to me. So much rejoicing on her part, before she said, Don't tell the doctors, they'll put you in the hospital, and then how are you meant to get better? That night we watched *Poirot* as a treat. I tried to eat a banana for supper. But eating is difficult now it's no longer an instinct.

I look at my hands. They're nearly transparent, the light shines through them, pink and red. It is a beautiful thing to be so thin, even if everyone else says I'm ugly now. Even if they point and laugh from cars on the high street. Even if Mum's friend tried to shove a sausage roll in my mouth. This is a beauty they've never known, so full of need as they are. Feasting on it. When the elders tell me I'm sinful because I don't partake of Jehovah's bounteous blessings – meaning food – I don't call them gluttons. I also don't tell them I am a new god of my own making. My hipbones are two posts of bone, my pants slung tight across them. When I stand in the shower and look down, all I see are my blue feet. How can they think this is a sin? How can they not understand the art I'm making myself into? Carving closer and closer to bone.

I am free. I am purified of need. Two plums two months ago were too much to need. I needed to rid myself of my excess. Now I eat one pot of yogurt a day. Less than 50 calories. I am washed clean. I need no sugar, fat or dairy. I need no blood of the Lamb. I am my own salvation and deliverance.

In the late summer, when I came back from London, just after we moved to the farm to be closer to Mum's work and the goddamn countryside, Granny held scones out to me. I shook my head. She looked at me like I had slapped her. I smiled. All these years, she had it coming. Finally, I have found my own way to say no. Original Simon saw when he came back from Cornwall. He phoned me to say he was home, that he'd forgiven me and did I want to come and see him. I sat shivering on the edge of his bed as he stroked my skin and called me too thin before asking if I was OK. No one else has asked me that. I nodded and kissed him to stop him talking, feeling him run his hand up and under my skirt.

I don't need him like I used to. He's nothing compared to this. I have no need for boys' eyes or hands or skin. I only need myself and nothing else. See, I am shouting, I am cannibal. You can keep your God and your Bible and your saviour and your eternity. I will leave it all for this. This will eat me and I don't care. I will be consumed by it. I will have it with me always, even until the end of the world.

Are you cold? the doctor asks. You're shivering. I nod.

Can I get you a tissue? he says. I put my hand up to my face. It's wet. I don't know how that happened. I nod. He holds the box out to me. I pull a tissue from it. I blow my nose.

London. That's when the balance tipped. I was staying with Mum's friends, having been sent to the assembly there to meet nice brothers, young men to court and to marry. London was the best place for it, Zoe said. But days before the assembly, I fainted on a trip to the zoo. I woke on the black tarmac with someone cradling my head, and in the end everyone went to the assembly without me, urging me to eat as they pulled the front door shut behind them. I put a boiled egg and some couscous on my plate, but they grew there when I looked down. The egg became two eggs, four eggs, eight, the couscous a mountain. I couldn't lift my fork. I shook under the weight of trying. I took the food out to the garden. I dug a hole and tipped it in, packing the earth hard over the top of it. Safer than the bin. How could I be sure they wouldn't check there? Everyone watching, all the time still.

Or maybe it was Edinburgh when things changed. That time, it was work experience at a theatre. Mum said it was OK because I was staying with my cousin. I watched actors rehearse their lines, and they often sent me to the shop with fivers to buy fags and then let me steal one. For food, I'd eat half a tin of custard every night. Sometimes it was half a tin; mostly it was a quarter every second night. That's when the fuzz on my arms began to grow longer. That's when I couldn't keep myself warm. That's when something stopped working inside me and I couldn't eat even if I wanted to. I stopped ever being hungry.

Now that I am in my own gone-away world, I'm peaceful most of the time. In the middle of the night sometimes it's different, and I try to think my way out of it, but if I know anything, it's that nothing makes sense in the dark.

If only this doctor would stop trying to save me.

I know you don't want to talk, he says.

But could you write it down for me? he asks. If it's easier that way, we can try that.

He leaves, and I keep looking at the fire. I get out the purple pen Zoe gave me on my first day of high school. It has a purple plastic spring at the top that pushes the nib down. I try to write in my notebook but some words, no matter how short they are, are hard to write. How am I supposed to write about my dad when I don't know anything about him? It's easier to focus on how difficult it is to breathe. How fast my heart beats. These physical things are good ways to distract me from everything in my head.

I will not do what the doctor wants me to do.

He thinks it's so simple. He thinks I could put a word after a word and it would be like I was speaking to him. How beautiful his world must be if he thinks this is any sort of a solution.

I hate him for what he wants me to do.

The page glares back at me. It's too white.

I write my name. It seems like a good place to begin. Especially since my dad gave it to me and it is an impossible thing to escape from. I write: 'My dad is a doctor and he lives in South Africa.' Then I cross that bit out. I don't know where he lives anymore. I write: 'My dad doesn't live with me.' But that looks too much like the truth. I score it out until my pen rips the page.

I can't do it. I put the page in the fire and watch as the flames lick their way up it. I will not do what he wants. I will not do what Mum wants. All I need now are my own acts of salvation.

REPENTED OF MY SINS

1997

IT'S JULY. SOME DAYS ARE warm, some days rain comes. It's been a year since I was at school.

I am in recovery. This is what they call it, even though I am hardly any heavier than I was.

To begin with I wanted to die, then I wasn't so sure. It felt too final. It didn't seem like the right time. I wanted the end of days. I wanted the last tide. I wanted the Four Horsemen. But I still want my own pure, raw-edged hunger. I hide the want and let them think I'm getting better. I trick them into thinking this by eating tiny pots of jelly and meal replacements. I lie on my bed in just my pants and crop-top, looking at the way my stomach dips between my hipbones, and the only carnal thing I desire is to eat myself, to stay forever beyond the need of anything other than my own flesh.

I hide that want. I become an object of fascination to the doctors as they map my diminishing contours when I carry on losing weight. I eat more and more but still get smaller. Hypermetabolic the doctors call it. My body can't stop eating itself and everything I put in it. I have starved myself for so long that my body is on fire, consuming everything that comes near it with a zeal I didn't know I could possess.

The desire to keep starving myself is as strong as it was. It talks to me in the dark now it is hooked into me, and me and it have become a new, merged form, never to be without each other again. I cannot free myself from it. I do not know where I end and it begins. I do not know if I am doing this to myself or if it is doing it to me. From the outside, the answer seems too simple. All I need to do is eat. But it isn't like that at all. I am terrified of food. I am scared of losing the control I have. I like the distraction this causes. I like life being paused. I like how it makes everything else go away. I like how it is my friend and I am never alone and maybe what I like the most and am the least able to admit is that being ill like this feels like I am little again. It feels like the days when Mum read to me and fed me Heinz soup and it feels like rejecting those and recreating them all at the same time. When Mum says, This illness really doesn't make sense, I want to scream at her and ask her if it doesn't make sense to her then how does she think it feels to me? But I don't. I stick to my meal plans and therapy and weekly weigh-ins and blood tests and everyone thinks

I want to get better and I have tricked them in the same way I always have.

The thing about thinking I was paused was that maybe *I* was, but time wasn't. Grampa got older, had more strokes, was less and less able to speak until he became someone I didn't recognise. As though who he'd been was replaced by an old man, one I didn't know.

One evening as the sun sets, Grampa holds my hand. Instead of speaking, he holds the bones of my hand tight as tears run down his elephant-creased cheeks. I want to snatch mine away from his. I want to be away from this stupid old man who's making my nose twitch like I might be about to cry. I stare out the conservatory at the sun dipping purple behind the hills with birds clamouring as they sing the day to sleep. I want him to stop. I don't want to bring feeling back.

Over the winter, I sought out Jesus. I read about him and I liked him. He was never that appealing before and I still find God difficult, but Jesus, He actually sounds really nice. Really compassionate. He cared about people, He wanted to save people. He even wanted to feed people, although I like to skip that bit. For the first time, I like the idea of right and wrong. I like the thought of certainties being true.

When I told Mum I was ready to get baptised, I had to prove to the elders I was really was. I made pages and pages of notes as I studied the baptism questions. The elders visited me three nights in a row to quiz me all about what we believe. I got all the answers right. Mum said, Best not to tell your doctor, best not to tell

Granny and Grampa. As Grampa sits squeezing my hand, I think how next time I see him I'll be one of Jehovah's baptised Witnesses. I think it's strange that I'm supposed to warn everyone about Armageddon coming and yet I'm not to talk about it with my family. Mum says this is because it would upset Granny, and it makes me wonder if Mum knows about being two people too. How much of herself does she hide from her mother?

Two days later, I stand in a freezing-cold football stadium in Perth at the District Assembly. It's packed full of brothers and sisters gathered together from all over Scotland. At the beginning of the convention, the chairman told us it was the most important event in our annual calendar. The speaker has just given a talk about how important baptism is, and how Jesus set the example for true followers. Now it's time for me and the rest of the baptism candidates standing in the same section of the stadium to answer the Baptism Questions. The speaker has asked us to do this in a loud, clear voice.

He asks the first question:

Have you repented of your sins, dedicated yourself to Jehovah, and accepted his way of salvation through Jesus Christ?

YES, we all say in unison.

Do you understand that your baptism identifies you as one of Jehovah's Witnesses in association with Jehovah's organisation?

YES.

My teeth begin to chatter. South of here, 358 miles

away, Grampa's brain begins to bleed for one final, disastrous time.

All afternoon my uncle will try to call the stadium to tell us to leave, to come back quickly. The rest of the family gather at Grampa's bedside. Meanwhile I pull a loose white T-shirt on over the top of my swimming costume to protect my modesty. Uncle Andrew presses REDIAL: the receptionist tells him we are all away witnessing. I wade into a cordoned-off area of the local swimming pool as the public swim up and down the other lane. Mum and Zoe watch me. Granny takes Grampa's hand in hers. I walk towards two brothers I don't know. Grampa's eyes flutter open. The brothers hold me in their arms and try to dunk me under the water. I splutter. The door opens, Granny's sister carries a Styrofoam cup of coffee into the room. The brothers explain to me they'll have to try again. I take a deep breath. They hold me under. Uncle Andrew, impatient now, tries a different number. I rise to the surface. No one answers the phone.

All 32 kilograms left of me are washed clean in the blood of the Lamb. I am dead to my former self. My sins are forgiven. I am made new.

Mum gives me a ring. Remember, she says, when you were little, and I explained Jehovah to you with a ring. How he goes on and on and on.

I rub the back of the ring and can feel a tiny lump where it's been soldered together. I can't find eternity in it. Thank you, I say, it's beautiful.

The next day we return home. I can hear the house

phone ringing outside the cottage as I open the car door, the first tiny stars suspended over the hills in the distance. Mum looks at me. I wonder, she says, who that could be.

Mum pushes the door open, picks up the phone. I stand watching as she lets out the sound of an animal in pain. It is a sound unlike anything I've ever heard. It makes the hairs on my arms stand up. It is the sound of pure loss. Then she swallows, and it is over. OK, thank you, she says.

She doesn't need to say anything to me, because I heard Uncle Andrew on the other end. I heard him say Grampa wasn't dead yet, but nearly was, and we were too far away to get there in time. My grampa, my grampa who I'd wanted to convince myself was a stupid old man; my grampa who took me to the library and who tucked my poems between the pages of Wordsworth and Longfellow, winking at me as he told me that's where they belonged. Grampa whose last moments my love for Jesus had taken from me.

Mum looks at me. Just as well we didn't hear yesterday, she says. Jehovah was keeping you safe on your special day.

I swallow. I think I'd like to sit down, I say.

It is now I realise I am dead to all that I was. I am now to remain forever safe in the confines of the Christian congregation as Satan roams around outside like a roaring lion, seeking to devour the weak, and I am to remain steadfast, unwavering, forever and ever. Time stretches, long and certain, ahead of me.

SHE TOOK FROM ITS
FRUIT AND ATE

1998

THERE IS HISSING FROM THE gas fire in the tiny dining room. Blue flame jumping. It's April but it's still cold.

I have weighed my Bran Flakes into a bowl. I have cut one small Braeburn apple into tiny chunks and scattered it over the cereal, and now I will pour 150ml of skimmed milk over the top. The trick is to get the milk in before the apple begins to brown otherwise I can taste it decaying and my breakfast is spoilt and I can't eat it.

There's a card on the table. Today is my 18th birthday. Normally on birthdays nothing happens, because nothing is allowed to happen. So the card is strange. From across the table Mum smiles. It's not a birthday card, she says. Inside it says: 'Bring your wellies and your passport, we're going on an adventure.' It is hard to talk and eat so I take another mouthful of breakfast. I can't let the cereal go soft otherwise I can't eat it. Wow, I say, where are we going? Mum starts to laugh and looks really excited. I was going to wait, she says, until we got to the boat but it's too exciting. We're going to Amsterdam!

After breakfast I pack a suitcase with lots of warm clothes. It might be cold there and it might not be, but because I am always cold now I pack layers and layers of thin jumpers like I've been wearing all winter and all autumn and for most of the summer before that too.

It *is* cold on the boat, and the whole vessel feels flimsy, as if the walls are made from paper. I am not a big fan of ferries. They capsize and they sink. This one is full of people going from Newcastle to Amsterdam for the weekend and most of them are drunk and Mum says, They are only going to Amsterdam for drugs and prostitutes and not culture like we are.

In the cabin I pull a jumper over my pyjamas, tug and tuck the covers up round my neck and try not to listen to the sound of people in the corridors, stumbling into the thin walls as the boat lilts and pitches in response to the sea beneath it.

Amsterdam is cold too. Grey stones slicked wet, red-brick buildings turned redder by lowering slate-coloured rain-heavy clouds. Mum says we must be careful to avoid the red-light district. Women stand in windows, she says, with no clothes on. I try not to think how it must feel to sell your body. Some part of me thinks it sounds like a good idea. I'm used to the idea of using your body as a form of protest. I don't say anything.

Mum thinks that because I've started eating again I'm happy about it, but this isn't true. She doesn't know about the horror. How every mouthful goes against my gut instinct, which is to get smaller. To never need anything ever again. Anorexia is a thing I am able to hide inside, to rest inside. I can do it in secret. The better they think I am, the less likely they are to take it away from me. I eat enough for it to look like I'm happy eating. Mum never thinks to ask if it's hard for me. We both are complicit in this fiction of recovery. As soon as lunch is over I am thinking of dinner. I need to plan ahead. I keep a running tally of calories in my head. I curse myself for my lack of bravery because I don't say, I do not want to eat or I am not ready to eat or I am not ready to live or I am not able to keep living. Chew, swallow, don't spit. Easy things. Impossible things.

That evening we walk to find somewhere to eat. I find the streets scary. I'm scared of spotting a stray prostitute or junkie or drunk or any of the people Mum's warned me about. But we don't. We find a basement restaurant that's open. Inside we sit with giant menus obscuring our faces. Mum orders a glass of wine, I ask for water. There's nothing on the menu I can eat. It's all meat and cheese and butter and milk. My legs feel twitchy and fast. There's too much saliva in my mouth. Sounds delicious, Mum says as she scans the menu. I can't tell if she means it.

The waiter comes to take our order. What's the soup? I ask.

French onion, he says.

Does it have cream in? I say.

No, he says, it's mostly just onions.

This sounds safe enough. There are 28 calories in an onion. There can't be more than three onions in a soup. This means the soup won't have too many calories in it. This means I will be safe.

I'll have the soup then, I say. Mum orders pasta.

We wait. I play with the red-and-white-checked tablecloth that looks almost like fabric but when you touch it, it isn't. Easier to wipe clean I suppose.

My soup arrives. It is not soup. It is something in a bowl partly obscured by two huge croutons covered with melted cheese, so fresh from the grill it's still bubbling. I used to love cheese on toast. I used to love waiting for the perfect moment to take it out from the grill but I don't eat cheese now. I have not eaten cheese for a long time. I cannot eat cheese. I cannot let it sit in my arteries. I look at Mum. She does a sort of smile that might be a grimace. I think I could take the croutons out and put them on the side plate. I put my soup spoon under one and lift it up. Brown stock drips from it. It would make the plate wet. The table too. I lower the crouton back down and notice tiny golden globules on the surface of the soup. Butter. Congealing. Immiscible particles. I stare at them. They multiply.

Mum, the waiter, the tables, the other diners – all disappear. The whole world is me and this bowl of impossible soup.

I want to throw it at the wall.

I want to launch it at Mum.

I want to hurl it through the window.

I want to let myself fall into the oil-slicked petrol-black sea. I want it to close over me.

I have made a mistake in swapping one kind of emptiness for another. I have been empty in so many ways for so long that I don't know how to fill myself up.

I don't do any of the things I want to.

Instead I put my teeth together in my mouth. I hear the right-hand side of my jaw click. I smile. I pick up my spoon. I put my spoon down. I pick up my spoon. I put my spoon into the soup. I put the spoon in my mouth.

The taste: butter, crisp apple from cider, waking some latent muscle memory, sweet onions cooked slow and long in too much butter, stirred and stirred so they never brown, so much care, so much attention, under it all the warm, heavy musky beef stock, waiting like a bass note. I swallow this mouthful, feel the thinly sliced onions slip and slide their way down my throat and settle deep in my stomach. I do it again and again, faster and faster, ploughing the spoon into the thick stock-soaked flesh of the crouton. I take it into my mouth and feel the flavours spill themselves over my tastebuds, flooding me, filling me, making me hungry.

It's the best soup; it's the worst soup. The room comes back. I take a napkin and wipe my chin. Mum's voice sounds harsh and raspy as she says, I didn't think you'd eat it. Well done.

I'd like a drink now. I'd like an actual cider. I remember how the first hit of it used to feel. I remember how the dry-mouthed dawns felt. I remember how legs, arms, insides of mouths felt. Tasted. I remember how wanting felt, the insistent drum of it. The way it filled me up.

Wanting becomes a wave. I think it might be too powerful for me to resist its force.

I close my eyes.

From now on, I will keep my mouth tight shut.

BOOK TWO: EXODUS

1. RETREAT AND RETURN

'Where you go, I shall go, and where you spend
the night, I shall spend the night. Your people will
become my people, and your God, my God.'

Ruth 1 v 16

INTO THE WILDERNESS

PARIS

1998

THE JULY SUNSHINE BOUNCES OFF the plane's bright white wing as below me Edinburgh gets smaller and smaller, a miniature toytown.

Then clouds swallow the plane and the city's gone. Mum's somewhere below, still in the airport, or back at the car maybe. I turn my Walkman up louder, let the music take my thoughts away.

This was the plan I came up with last summer when the doctor said, You really need something to live for. Mum said, You have forever to live for. She also said, for extra reassurance, Jehovah will resurrect you if you die.

Last summer, I ate and still lost weight. I was still hypermetabolic, still eating myself faster than I could replace myself. I couldn't sleep. I couldn't stand up. I couldn't shower with the door shut. Always watched, like always.

Mum said I was making my life boring now I wasn't doing things. The brothers in the congregation said I was being unfaithful by not eating Jehovah's bounteous blessings. Even the doctors said I was dragging this on for too long. But I know they only thought that because so many people don't like science. I like experiments. I was my own test subject. Black spots, dizziness, breathlessness, strange pains, easy bruising, inability to concentrate – the list of things that happened was long. If you've never starved yourself, not even a little bit, you've never let yourself explore your true potential. It's amazing what you can achieve when you put your mind to it.

This has taken me to the very edge of myself. I'm not the same now as I was. I don't know if Mum and Granny really get that. They seem to think I'll get better and things will rewind and I'll go back to who I was before. Mum says things like, This isn't really you, and, You're not really this skinny. She can't see this is my purest manifestation.

But the problem with going anywhere is that eventually you have to turn around and come back. That's what's happened when, the summer after Grampa died, I began to see I was losing things. I sat with the September sun highlighting the golden grain of the pine dining table, picking at my lunch as the doctor said, Have you ever thought you might be wasting the best years of your life?

I hadn't thought about it. I liked him by then, too. I had discovered that he was the only person I could really be myself with. He didn't expect anything of me or want me to tell him easy stuff. No, I said, there's loads of time.

After he left, I walked past the cows in the field to the crest of the hill, where in the distance I could see the Cheviots, the whole valley spread in front of me. Maybe he had a point.

I didn't want to risk him being right. I started doing my Highers by distance learning. Mum said, Don't expect me to help, I'm too busy with work. My doctor said, You'll never manage, you're too ill. Every time he wanted me to do something, he said I wouldn't manage to do it; he knew, somehow, that this would make me try to defy him. As for Mum, well, I was determined to show her.

Granny didn't seem to have an opinion either way, or perhaps she just kept them to herself. She showed her feelings in other ways: she took me to all my appointments and on drives all over the countryside, nowhere was ever too far. When we had lunch together, she didn't comment on what I could or couldn't eat. As we drove, I would listen to the stories she told me about her own granny, Aja, who'd lived in the big house in Tighnabruaich. Aja owned a whole country estate and never let her husband get his hands on a penny of it. Always have your own money, Granny said to me, that way no one will ever be able to control you. Then she told me how Grampa had

had a girlfriend when she met him. If you want something in life, she said, make sure you get it.

Sometimes after those drives, I'd wonder where Mum came from. They weren't at all similar, Granny and her.

As I started to remember what it had been like to feel, I started to want things again. Mostly to be away from the farm, to have new views.

In spring my doctor said, Have you thought about what you're doing after your Highers? Of course I hadn't. It's not like I can go to uni like other people, and there was nothing I wanted to do at college. I'd be an awful beautician; I'd have to touch people.

PARIS, I sort of shouted, remembering how much I loved visiting once, when I was little. He said, Paris? And I said, properly possessed by then, Yes, Paris. I'm going there.

I'd never thought of living there until that moment, but as soon as I said it, it became a good idea. All the boulevards, the wide streets, the long windows and cute metal balconies, and the accents too, my God, the fucking accents, I was thinking, just imagining all those Frenchmen. OK, he said, Paris it is then.

Yes, I said, Paris. And somehow that became that. At first, I didn't tell Mum. Thinking of leaving her alone on the farm made my stomach contort itself into harder, tighter shapes. I kept ideas and conversations around Paris strictly contained to Friday lunchtimes with my doctor. It wasn't like I was really going to do it.

Then my doctor started making diagrams. Weight goals to reach every month so that I'd be heavy enough to go. I had previously fantasised about hospital: white walls, white linen. All those tubes feeding me. I tried to replace those thoughts with pictures of Paris and everything I could do there. Sometimes it worked. Sometimes it didn't.

I liked the look of these charts. I liked how solid they were, how mathematical. I liked the cause and effect made manifest on the paper. Maybe, I began to think, I could, just for a while, a week or a month or a summer, go to Paris. The thought grew inside me and one day after the prayer for lunch, I said to Mum, I want to go to Paris. We spoke about it and she said, So long as you stay with a sister and go to all the meetings. I said, Yes, of course.

The plane banks sharply as it veers over towards the North Sea, a loud ping and the 'fasten seatbelt' signs switch off. I open my book.

At the Ecole Militaire I stand on the platform with my big orange suitcase. Mum said a bright one would come in handy at baggage reclaim. I've stuffed it full of clothes, forgetting that I'll need to carry it around the city on my own. They slapped an oversized label on it at check-in in Edinburgh, a big black incriminating thing I peeled off at Charles de Gaulle.

I stand with my goosebumped arms crossed in front of my chest as the arriving train throws black clouds of dust onto the platform. I'm wearing my blue marbled top, the same top I wore in the park two summers earlier, those days spent necking vodka with Angie. I don't know how to get the suitcase up the escalator. Suddenly, a guy comes up to me, he pushes his dark hair out his face and leans into mine, talking quickly. I understand every second word. Or every fifth. It feels like he's telling me I don't belong here, like he's saying I'm an idiot for thinking I could. French seems like a slippery thing, moving in the wrong direction away from me. Suddenly he grabs my suitcase and puts it on his shoulders. He runs up the escalator with it. He's stealing my suitcase. I've just arrived and this worldly guy is stealing all my stuff. I trot after him.

At the top the French sun hits my eyes. It's brighter, purer, more dazzling than Scottish sun. It pulses in a different way.

He puts my suitcase down, turns round and smiles at me. Has he changed his mind?

He begins to talk to me very slowly, asking me where to next. Maybe he's trying to help. I ask him if he's helping me. Of course, he says. I must look like such an idiot. But I don't know if I should give him my address. Maybe he's going to lure me somewhere.

Traffic roars by, horns blare, tabac signs flash. He walks fast, and I try to keep up. Outside the apartment he says he can help me up the stairs, but I say, *Non, non, merci beaucoup.* He wishes me *bonne chance* and then he is away, off to find someone else to rescue.

And here I am. Finally, in Paris. I am also warm, finally, in the hot July sun.

In fact, it's hot all the time, apart from first thing in the morning when I find myself in the rabbit warren of tunnels that take me out to Disney. That's the drawback. The only place I've managed to find a job here is at Disneyland Paris, working in Guest Relations. It is a suitably nebulous title for a pretty hellish job. Every day I have to get up at just about dawn and navigate my way through the Métro to the RER. When I arrive, I get the bus to the backstage area, which is really just a glorified locker room, though I suppose calling it 'backstage' gives it a certain air of glamour for the failed and aspiring actors who spend their summers working there, labouring under the weight of synthetic fur and polyester princess costumes. I get changed into my ankle-length wool skirt and matching jacket, both too loose, then I spend all day switching between English, French and German trying to keep visitors happy, which I do with varying degrees of success depending on my level of comprehension. I'm pretty sure the number of escalating arguments I seem to be privy to are caused by my linguistic ineptitude, but that doesn't matter. The rides are free. And I have Paris, which is what I'm really here for.

I want to think I belong here. I'm sharp-elbowed and opinionated. I'm thin. I don't say sorry when I push people out the way on the Métro. I'm good at blending in.

All my time off is spent walking. First thing in the morning I buy a baguette, a 2-litre bottle of Evian and a banana. These last me the whole day. I don't want company. I have a French translation of *The Picture of Dorian Gray* for that. I think I might understand it better if it were in English, but still, I feel it helps me fit in.

I put my guidebook in my bag before I leave the apartment, after memorising maps, directions and Métro stops, and I clatter down the circular staircase outside the apartment as if I have somewhere urgent to be. I've prowled round the Jewish quarter, ventured to the Parc Monceau, timidly tried to muster up strength to enter the Musée Nissim de Camondo. I've snuck into Rodin's garden, hoping no one would ask for student identification, and sat looking at the smooth contours of the sculptures, the shadow play of the leaves.

The Kingdom Hall is in the banlieue. I'm not interested in the people there. I only go because I have to. I want real Parisians. I want the granular detail of their lives, I want to know how to live like them.

One day I see a man in the market buying thistles and roses. The stall holder wraps twine around and around the stems before bundling them into brown paper. It feels like watching a story. I wonder what these flowers say. Sorry? I love you?

As it gets hotter, I sleep less. I spend long nights twisting the duvet around myself, my legs sliding and slipping. I eat undercooked chicken by mistake. Maybe I'm younger than I thought I was. One night, I drink cider until the room spins, and the Eiffel Tower glowers at me as I walk home. I cry as the hangover sets in.

There are celebrations all night on the Champs-Elysées after France wins the World Cup. I hear it through the open apartment windows. The whole city pulses but something is wrong with me. I can't access the joy that others feel. I want it so badly, but I am so scared to let it in. I think of Mum at home alone on the farm and I think of the hills and the countryside and the peace and I am so confused, because I'm split in two. I want both. I can only have one. If I stay here, I will become worldly, chasing after things I desire. I need to go home.

In London, waiting for the connecting flight home, I need something to distract me. A book maybe. I pick up *Enduring Love*. The first page pulls me in. I devour it during the flight, and have finished it by the next day. I'll go back to my safer ways of seeing the world. At least books won't lead me astray.

LONDON

1999

I STAND AT THE BOTTOM OF the escalator with people pushing past me. Everyone knows where to go, apart from me. I hate the tube.

I've tried my best to memorise directions. But I didn't think about the connections. I don't know if I need the train going west or east.

I take a leap and pick east, jump on the train, my stupid orange suitcase making people tut as they move out of its way. The carriage is full, so I sit on my suitcase and look up at the map. Shit. I wanted west.

I try to look casual when I get off at the next stop, heaving my suitcase over to the next platform to wait for the train I actually want. I count the stops to Turnham Green, then pull my suitcase past rows of stone-built Victorian houses, under a railway bridge where a flower seller stands, down the high street with cafes, estate agents and little boutique shops selling pretty things no one needs. I get to the flat and Rupert opens it, holding his arms out telling me that hey it's great to meet me and I can have Oli's room at the top of the stairs.

These are things Mum isn't to know. Things she must never find out.

I met Laura a few months ago, by accident at an interview. I go for interviews all the time and they offer me the job and then I find reasons for not taking it. Only this time, they didn't offer me the job. Maybe they knew my heart wasn't in a retail merchandising trainee scheme. My heart isn't in anything. I don't have a clue what to do with the rest of my life. Everything has the potential to infect me with the spirit of the world. The only way I can avoid it is to stay in my room. Although come to think of it, my books and music are probably contaminating enough. At the end of the assessment day Laura and I swapped numbers and addresses; we kept in touch.

A couple of months later a friend dragged me to a modelling competition that she wanted to enter. As she paraded up and down for the judges who were only looking for the next Kate or Amber, I found myself talking to some magazine people. They offered me their cards. When I next talked to Laura, she told me her mates had a room going and did I fancy coming to London for the summer. Yes, I told her. I phoned the number on the card one of the women had given me. She picked up and sounded like she remembered me. Sure, she said, there's plenty for you to do for the summer here, I'd love to have you help.

In London, I realise for the first time that it's only a matter of time until I can't keep being a Witness anymore. The thought doesn't quite come into full view, but it's there. Lurking.

I want to stay in London. I think about getting a permanent job at the magazine. I don't go to any of the Witness meetings. Then I think about France. I think maybe I'd like to go back there now I'm more confident. I find a job with a nice French family. When I phone Mum, she doesn't want to hear it. She tells me I'll change my mind, and when I tell her I won't she hangs up the phone.

It's Saturday, and I'm in the London flat alone when the door buzzes. I clatter down the stairs, fling the door open, and stand with my mouth slightly agape when I see a man and a woman smiling at me, each clutching a Bible. Our Bible. The woman smiles at me, and tilts her head to the side in a concerned fashion. Have you ever wondered, she says, what the purpose of life is? I shake my head. She holds out a magazine to me. Maybe you'd like this, it explains God's purpose in more detail. They both smile. I shake my head again, more rapidly this time, and close the door in their faces. I know they'll be used to that.

Beneath me the floor feels weak.

Through the frosted glass I see them walk back down the path. To them I'm just another teenager needing to be saved.

My teeth begin chatter. Why didn't I just tell them who I was? Why didn't I smile and say, So nice to see you? Why didn't I talk about the worldwide brotherhood? Why am I always trying to hide the thing I'm supposed to be the most proud of?

I realise Jehovah sent them. He's the only person who knows I'm staying here, in a worldly flat with boys. And I've just sent them packing. I've basically spat on His messengers. I sit on the floor, wait for it to open up. He will exact some vengeance on me really soon. Unless.

The next day I put on the most sensible skirt I have with me. I find the address of the local Kingdom Hall in the phone book and I set out to go to the meeting. But when I arrive, I find that I can't make myself go in.

Instead, I go back to the flat. I pack my bags. I leave a thank-you note for the boys. I phone the French family and tell them someone's died. These sorts of lies are OK if they are for God.

I leave London behind and get the train north, the smell of bonfires in the air.

RURAL SCOTLAND

1999

IT'S NEW YEAR'S EVE. The news is full of the Millennium Bug. The newspapers print words like 'Doomsday' and 'Armageddon' like they don't mean anything.

Mum says it will be OK. Mum says no man knows the day or the hour, which means the newspapers are false prophets and false prophets are always wrong. But I watch the clock anxiously upstairs at the Witness party I'm at. Mum said the party was OK because then we'd all be together, just in case. She said, It's not a New Year's Eve party, it's just a party on New Year's Eve. I take a sip from my warm beer and force myself to swallow it, even though I hate the taste and am worried it'll make me fat, but I want to look like the other young brothers and sisters who don't care so much about the rules. The clock turns to midnight. We don't cheer or hug or anything. The numbers flip round, and nothing happens. Whipping Boy keeps playing on the stereo. Someone cracks open a beer.

We drive home with the sleet hitting the windscreen, the headlights picking out the eyes of sheep huddled in the field. I put the radio on, just to check they're still broadcasting. The voice of the presenter fills up the car.

I breathe out.

At home my bedroom's full of boxes. I've been packing up my stuff to move to Edinburgh. I've found a job at a bank. I have no idea what I'll be doing there, but it'll give me enough money to live on until I get married. I don't know who I'm going to marry yet, but there are more brothers in the city, so I've got a better chance of finding a good, spiritual husband. I've found a flat to share with a sister I've met a couple of times, and Mum says everything will be OK if I trust in Jehovah.

I have my suspicions about Mum. I think she wants me to leave home. There's a brother in our congregation who she's been seeing. He says he's an artist but he never seems to sell anything. He paints and paints and paints until his flat is filled with pictures of hills and fields and stone walls. When he's not painting, he pushes trolleys around Tesco car park for his real job. Sometimes I see him do it when I go to get the food shopping when Mum's working, and I put my head down and hope he doesn't see me.

Mum says he won't marry her if I'm still living with her. I think she wants to swap me for him.

Mum often comes home late at night with a stubble rash I'm not supposed to notice on her chin. She giggles all the time. She drives me to the city to look at flats and says the first one I see is perfect. She buys cardboard boxes to put my things in. I'm all packed up and ready to leave in the middle of January, and two brothers drive a van full of my stuff down the motorway. Later, she waves goodbye to me outside my new flat. Before she goes she says, I'd best not see you for the next few weeks, it'll be easier for you to settle that way. I stand in the middle of the road with the night that falls early this time of year lit up all orange by the streetlamps with the stale smell of hops in the air and watch her tail lights make their way up the street.

She phones me the next month to tell me that she's marrying her boyfriend. It feels a lot like one out, one in, but I don't say that.

SIGNS AND WONDERS

EDINBURGH

2000

THEY'RE DANCING IN THE FRONT room. I helped
move the furniture earlier, pushing the sofas
against the walls. It's March 17th but this is absolutely
not a St Patrick's Day party. Marc has told everyone
this – it's his party in his flat. He likes telling people
things.

Marc is one of the brothers in the congregation
here. After I moved to the city, it was a shock to see
how different things were in the new congregation
from the old. I began to realise there were degrees of
Witnesses, just as Mum had always warned me. Some
are more serious than others. Here, all the young
people go out for drinks after the Thursday meeting,
and to lots of parties too. The first few I went to I felt
uncomfortable, since the parties I was used to looked

very different and were mostly people playing charades or games inspired by the Bible. Before long I learnt I didn't feel out of place after a couple of drinks.

City Witness parties are different to country ones – the rules seem more relaxed, even when the elders come towards the beginning, to make sure nothing bad happens. When they leave that's when the party gets properly started.

The dancing isn't the same as it would be in a club. Clubs are banned: dens of iniquity, the elders say, never once thinking that this might make them more alluring. This dancing isn't like worldly dancing: sisters dance with sisters and the brothers sort of edge themselves around the women's bodies, never getting too close, so things never become immoral. Or particularly appealing.

I don't dance. It makes me think of death. I don't tell anyone this because I'm pretty sure dancing is supposed to be something you enjoy. But in someone's front room with the lights turned down, it's a stretch. At Marc's party now, I leave them to it and go to the kitchen, where I find a bottle of vodka in the freezer. I don't know whose it is, so it's mine now. I'm still thinking about death, even though I'm not dancing. Moby's on the stereo. That doesn't help.

I lean against the sink, looking out the window at the garden below. There's a music promoter who lives in the flat beneath, he drives a crappy old car and has giant dogs. Marc says he's a gangster, like all people in music are. Whatever he is, he never cuts his grass, which winds up Marc and his flatmate, Brett. Brett's nice, he's from New Zealand and buys expensive bottles of wine for Witness parties, which he always shares with me. Marc's from Glasgow.

In the garden, there's nothing to see apart from shadows. The floorboards vibrate slightly from the music. The sound mixes with the noise of everyone laughing. I drink another shot. Everyone begins to sound far away.

Marc looked at me with wide eyes when I arrived, because I've made my own outfit. I'm pretty pleased with it. I've been sewing for a long while, but this is the first time I've designed something all on my own: a black top with elastic at the back holding each side together, lined with pink snakeskin satin. Technically, it's pretty clever. My trousers sit low on my hips, black and flared and open at the bottom where they're lined with the same pink snakeskin satin. I think I might have copied it from something Britney wore. Kerry, who's always saying things like how she wishes she was 20 again, and that she could only fit my jeans over her ankles, has already told me how worldly I look. Patricia tutted and asked if I'd like a cardigan since I might get a bit cold. I told them I was just fine, thank you. But now I am kind of cold. One of the elders looked at me askance when I arrived, but I just smiled at him. I like copying designs I see in magazines, even if maybe they end up looking more provocative than I mean them to. They make me fit in better at the pub when we all go out together at the weekend.

I see someone reflected in the window, moving around the room, looking for something. I hear them ask if that's mine, pointing at the vodka.

I turn round. Someone I haven't met yet is standing in front of me: his hair's a mess, his eyes are a deep watery blue, nearly green, and he smiles at me. His smile makes him look like he might know how to be bad. I like him immediately.

Yeah, it's mine, I say, hoping it's not actually his.

Can I have some? he says. I've run out.

Sure, I say. I pour him a tumbler. He laughs as he holds it up.

Quite big, he says.

Ah, I say, it's a cunning plan, though. If you're only allowed to drink three, then make sure they're big. No one ever asks about the size of the glass.

I don't know where the three drinks rule came from, something about more than three being binge drinking, but now we're only allowed to have three in a row; any more than that and the elders might need to get involved.

Smart thinking, he says. I'm Murray, by the way.

We drink, and we talk. He asks, as though it's the most normal thing in the world, if I fancy going to Paris on Monday. I tell him I really do. I ask what he does, and he says he's a postman, but he's going to be a photographer. That's why he's off to Paris. I tell him I used to live there, and we talk about travelling and don't say a single thing about God.

I don't go with him to Paris. We both know it's a

joke, something we couldn't do even if it's a thing we'd like to do. But I do start hanging out with him. I have a hypothesis that when you're drunk you're your true self. We drink Morgan's Spiced until I can't stand up. I cut his hair, we kiss, we keep our clothes on even though I want to take his off. I visit him in Glasgow, and we drive to Loch Lomond and spend the day drinking on its banks.

I really want to fuck him. I can't tell him I know how it feels. The wanting, and the fucking. This is a thing I've not wanted for a long time and now I'm so full of wanting I want to be sick. I want him so badly that I can't look at him properly because if I do, he'll know.

The night we go to Loch Lomond we drink too much, and I forget to catch the last bus. We dare each other to do stupid things. But we still don't fuck. We don't talk about God but he is there between us. Forbidding us access to each other's bodies.

Murray comes to Edinburgh, bringing Boots meal deals and a bottle of wine for lunch. We lie on our backs in Princes Street Gardens making shapes of the clouds, choosing our favourite buildings from the street. I tell him I like the modernist one, just to be provocative, but he agrees, says it would photograph well, the way it's all lines. He talks and talks and talks about photography and how it's a way of telling stories and I love that. I've never thought of photos like that before. I just thought it was a mechanical process. He tells me about standing on the sidelines of the football pitch trying to capture the pure joy in a footballer's face or at other times the despair. I've never met anyone who loves something so deeply before. Photography is like a calling to him.

I don't tell him about what I love. How can I tell him all I want is to be empty? How can I tell him I just want to be free of myself? How can I tell him I like eating my own heart, brain and lungs? How can I tell him how hard it is to make sure I don't look like I love it anymore? How can I tell him thinking about it stops me thinking about God? How can I tell him I like it? How can I tell anyone these things?

This means I don't have that much to say to him, which is maybe why I want to fuck him so badly. Maybe I want to consume his desire, his passion, in the hope I make it mine. But I do at least tell him about books I've read. I tell him the things I've loved in them and as I do I begin to feel like I'm less empty than I realised, though I need to read a lot more, and quickly if I'm to keep up with him.

I begin to think that maybe I could have a passion too. Something just for me. Maybe I could learn to *do* something. But there's a danger in this. I would need to go somewhere to learn. University. It's not that I don't know people who've been. Marc has been to university. He likes to talk about his having gone, and I'm impressed by how clever it means he must be. But he also says it meant his dad wasn't allowed to give talks at the assembly while he was there, and so in a way his family were punished for his choice.

Nevertheless, Marc is still a Witness, and his faith seems strong. It's less common for a woman to go to university: we're meant to get married or pioneer. We don't need to know things. The magazines warn against worldly wisdom and how it'll lead us away from Jehovah. We are meant to cultivate a submissive attitude, and education will get in the way of this. But still I am curious.

One hot June day, I begin flicking through prospectuses I have gathered in my flat. I've decided I need to study something that's nearly vocational – those kinds of courses are less frowned on. I am not allowed to study philosophy. We are explicitly warned about this. I'd like to do English literature or history. But English literature means I'd have to study worldly books, and a lot of them would contain sex or drugs or other immoral things, so that's out. History doesn't have a clear career path afterwards, so I couldn't justify it. Instead, I find textiles. It sounds useful, like it will lead to gainful employment. I already know how to sew, and have been making and designing my own clothes for ages. It doesn't sound too academic, so it's not going to make me think like a worldly person. It's perfect. I fold the page down. Soon I apply, without telling anyone.

Three weeks later I'm offered an unconditional place.

ACTS OF IMMOLATION

EDINBURGH

2000

THE ROOM IS LINED WITH mirrors. I see myself splintered by them, repeated in them. I stretch my legs under the table and lean back in my seat. Through the glass doors I can see a real fir tree, decorated for the season, coloured lights sparkling.

In the room everyone speaks quietly, but there are so many diners that the air still feels alive with noise. Marc sits opposite me, his face partly concealed by the large black menu he's holding. I wonder if this is how it feels to be grown up, but then my thong digs into me under my satin dress and I try to itch my back without anyone noticing. I like simple knickers, black ones that look like shorts, but lately I've started to wear fancier underwear. Marc likes it. Sometimes Marc and I do things the magazines tell us not to.

Heavy petting, they call it. Apparently everyone does it before they get married. Recently, I've started to realise how little I know about how things actually work in the truth. Lots of people have two faces: their meeting face and then their other one. There I was, thinking it was only me who felt split in half by my desires.

Marc has a very good meeting face. He helps people all the time and is lovely to the old sisters in the hall. Everyone says he's very charming, and most of the time they're right. I struggle to see people properly, I think: I expect too much from them, expect them to be perfect before the new system has arrived for them to be perfect in. I need to expect less from Marc; he can't be nice all the time, especially considering how difficult I am. Most of the time Marc takes me to fancy bars and restaurants and kisses me in pools of light in the street, and it's very romantic. At the beginning, when I chose him over Murray, I thought he was a good idea. I thought, because all I saw was his meeting side, that I wouldn't get into trouble with him, like I knew I'd get into trouble with Murray. Murray and I were too alike, both of us too drawn to the world and all the things in it. Although I suppose I am in trouble with Marc now too. I am always getting into so much trouble. I am always getting too carried away, just like Mum always said I was.

Sometimes I stupidly suggest the things Marc and I are doing are wrong, even though it's a bit late for that. But Marc reassures me that, because he's five years older, he's seen more of life than I have, and he's an urbanite whereas I'm a country Witness. He's right. He knows so much more than I do. He's been to university after all, and has a good job and works with intelligent and important people. I am blessed to have been chosen by him.

Marc puts down his menu. I think I'll have the salmon, he says. How about you? I don't tell him that the words on my menu were jumping around, that eating is still so difficult for me and that doing it in public feels doubly hard. Instead I drink the last of my gin, the ice hitting my top lip as I tip the glass back. I might try the langoustines, I say, I've not had them before. Really? he says. Oh, you must, you've not lived yet! I laugh. Under the table I play with the edges of the white tablecloth.

The waiter arrives, looks at me and then at Marc. I'll have the salmon, he says, and she'll have the langoustines. The waiter nods, but doesn't write anything down. And to drink, Marc continues, we'll have the Pouilly-Fumé . The waiter looks at me: Anything else? he asks, and I shake my head. He's hardly out of earshot when Marc says, I hate it when they don't write it down. He's going to get it wrong, isn't he. Marc leans forward, takes my hand in his. You look so good in black he says, with your blonde hair. Have you ever thought of going blonder? It would really suit you.

The waiter brings the wine back, I look to the side as he asks if we'd like to taste it first, Marc nods.

I haven't, I say. But he's right, it would look good. Blonde always stands out so well against black. Maybe I will, I say, before trying to shift the subject back to university. I tell him about getting an A in my exams, and drink, thirstily, from my glass.

Oh, well done, he says. It gets harder later on. First year is a doddle really. Don't let that trick you into thinking you're going to get a first. No one gets a first unless they're really bright. Although I suppose making clothes isn't that difficult.

I realise he's saying this because I sounded too proud. I was trying to boast. Boasting is wrong. I need to stop it. I turn the conversation instead to his work, and he speaks and speaks as I drink and watch the other diners.

I drain my second glass. Maybe we should order a second bottle, I say, it's a good wine.

Somewhere halfway through the second bottle Marc becomes background noise. I focus on the langoustines, pulling their heads off, cracking their shells to expose the sweet flesh below; I suck it into my mouth, the taste of the sea a reflexive memory, until I am eight years old again and swimming in the Atlantic on the west coast. The room becomes watery when I try to stand, and in the toilets I slick lip gloss across my mouth, check my teeth for food. Walking back to Marc I try to walk in a straight line: must remember to not look like I'm tipsy, or, more probably, drunk.

Are you up for a wee bit of dessert? he says. A cheeky crème brûlée?

I nod. I wonder if this is what being 45 feels like.

Dessert arrives. Marc uses his spoon to divide it exactly in half. Don't you be stealing any of mine, he says with a laugh. He breaks the thin shortbread on the side in half, pops it into his mouth. So buttery, he says. You need to try.

I think of Murray and our afternoon in Princes Street Gardens. We sat in the park all afternoon, lying back making shapes of the clouds scudding overhead, and then later used an empty wine bottle as a football, kicking it back and forth to each other. I had to keep stopping because he was making me laugh so much. How did I get from there to here? How fooled have I been by the lure of fancy places to eat? By expensive bottles of wine?

Nightcap? Marc smiles. Sure, I say, nodding.

The waiter brings a whisky for Marc, a Grand Marnier for me, coffee for both of us. Under the table Marc starts to run his foot up my leg, the soles of his leather shoes smooth against my tights. He rests his elbows on the table and leans as close as he can to me. I was thinking, he says, how about we get a room?

What, here? I ask.

Yes, he says, let's, you know ... celebrate.

We can't, I say. Can we?

But afterwards we are in the hotel room and Marc is sitting on the edge of the bed, telling me how we shouldn't have done that; he says we need to go back to our flats now so no one knows we're missing. I'm tired and I'm drunk and I want to stay, but I know he's right.

Outside, wet snow falls. Later the slush will stain my shoes. Back in my flat, I can't sleep, too much alcohol, sugar and caffeine in my veins. I shouldn't have done what I did. I shouldn't have drunk so much. I shouldn't have let myself be in such a vulnerable situation. Now I know why the magazines say you need a chaperone when you're dating. Now I know why we shouldn't be alone together.

I remember a sister who did the same thing I've done with Marc with her boyfriend, but eventually married someone else. She felt so guilty about what had happened with her first boyfriend that she told her husband and, because he loved her so much, he made sure she sought Jehovah's loving direction from the elders. She was disfellowshipped and has to sit at the back of the meetings. I'm not humble enough to do that. I need to make sure no one finds out about this.

Four months later, in London with friends for the weekend, Marc asks me to marry him. I say yes because I know no one else would want me if anyone knew what I'd done, but I know this secret is safe with the pair of us. I know too that I now need to learn to do Marc's will, as he will soon become my spiritual head.

EDINBURGH

2001

I SIT IN THE ROILING JULY heat that has pooled in the city streets, watching a bee move through the room's stagnant air as it collects pollen from lilies in a crystal glass. It drones on and on.

My ankles are crossed and my hands are clasped together in my lap. Marc's told me I need to look wholesome, and I hope this works.

Brother King is sitting opposite us on his floral chintz armchair, the open window bringing in the steady slow hum of more bees.

Brother King is here to interview us; he needs to do this to see if we are allowed to get married in the Kingdom Hall. I didn't know this happened. You wouldn't, Marc said, not being a third-generation Witness like me. So many things for you to learn.

Marc coached me on the way across the city, so I knew what to say. We've not been alone together without the door open, OK? he said, and I nodded. And the night at the hotel didn't happen either, he said. If we can't convince Brother King our courtship has been honourable, we won't be allowed to be married in Jehovah's house, and everyone will know what we've been up to. I need to be careful not to give anything away.

Marc's family are a big deal in the truth. Like West Coast Witness Mafia, he told me, although I was pretty sure that wasn't the best analogy. His brother was made an elder when he was very young. I'm heading the same way, he said. Imagine, you'll be an elder's wife soon. I try hard not to imagine this. I'm not sure I'm cut out for an eternity of baking cakes, hosting dinner parties and polishing silver. But Mum says Marc is nice – a stable prospect is what she calls him. He can look after you, she says. She's right. Marrying Marc means I'll finally be able to belong, at last, in the truth. I've never had any sort of status before. Now I will.

Brother King's wife elbows the sitting-room door open. She carries a huge tray with clattering teacups, a steaming teapot. The silver cake forks on the tray shake and slide into each other, the sound of them reverberating in the too-quiet room. The Kings' youngest son walks in carefully, clutching the edges of a huge plate, upon which a giant courgette cake is precariously balanced. Their other son brings up the rear with a carrot cake. It seems strange to add so much sugar to vegetables. I don't say anything, though. Marc already thinks I'm weird about food.

The King family are at the top of the congregation tree. He is the head of the congregation, and his wife is the leader of the elders' wives. She likes to wear grey shift dresses when she's on duty, and tank tops tucked into jeans when she's not. Her hair is cut like Princess Diana's was just before she died, and she favours a red lip. They have a Mercedes and a people carrier, and he has a motor bike, just for fun. They holiday in the South of France in the summer and go skiing in the winter. Play our cards right, Marc says, and we could be just like them.

I don't think Mum would like them, with all their flashy displays of wealth. In the countryside, Witnesses show how faithful they are by how much they are prepared to give up. In the city, it seems different; everyone looks up to the rich ones, and no one says anything about their money. It's as if it's OK because they've become rich by working for themselves, with cleaning businesses or property empires, not having to mix with worldly people. It's the worldly pursuit of things that seems to be the problem, so that's why my going to university is seen as evidence of my worldly attitude, when I could be cleaning houses for Brother King.

Earl Grey? she asks, turning to me as she puts the tray on the tiled coffee table. I nod. I'm trying to make myself like it, but it still tastes like cut grass to me.

Milk or lemon?

Lemon, please.

I don't ask what sort of a monster would put milk in fancy tea. Cake? she asks, and I shake my head, trying not to catch Marc's eye. He clears his throat; I refuse to look at him. She lifts a single eyebrow, artfully. I wonder if she's practised this in the mirror, the same as I sometimes do, although the movement of my own brows lacks her finesse.

Marc has expressive eyes; they say a lot that he would never say aloud. The first time I noticed this was last autumn, when my flatmate was moving out, and I had to find a new place to live. I looked up the classifieds in the paper that Thursday and found a flat quickly. A guy with long hair tied back off his face showed me a room with high ceilings and a paisley-printed shawl covering one wall. I liked it. I liked the communal kitchen with slated cupboard doors, and the smell of weed hanging in the air. I wondered how it would feel to fit in in a house like that, to be able to come home after a long day and sit smoking around the table and to talk to people with accents I couldn't place, with piercings high up their ears and hair dyed rainbow colours. These were people I knew I was supposed to be afraid of; they *are* people I'm afraid of. I don't know what I was thinking when I told him I would take the room. I realised I didn't mean it later, when Marc explained that I couldn't move in with worldly people: it would paint us both in a bad light. I really hadn't thought through the implications of living with sinful people and how it would tarnish my

own reputation. I also hadn't thought how my reputation wasn't the only thing at stake anymore: it had
implications for Marc and his family. I realised I needed
to do my part to preserve their good name. Instead,
Marc helpfully suggested I stayed with a sister who
was looking for a flatmate.

Now, I live in the flat we will share after we are
married, getting it ready for us both. I love being there
on my own. Somehow, when Marc visits, it feels like
he's in the way.

Now his eyes are telling me to eat the cake, but I
will not eat it. I couldn't eat it even if I wanted to,
because my appetite has been gone these last few
months.

Thank you, Brother King says to his wife as she
backs out the room, taking her children with her. He
smiles at both of us, licks his lips.

I'm so pleased you chose me to do your wedding
talk, he says. I smile and at the same time I curl my
toes up safe inside my shoes where no one can see
them, and with my right hand in my left palm, I dig
in my nails, like I used to do when I was little.

Marc said I was to leave him to do the talking. I
make my smile bigger, so that it stretches all the way
up to my eyes.

Brother King clears his throat and looks at the
floor. I just have to check, he says. Just housekeeping,
you know, just one of the things we have to, umm,
well, ask. I need to check there's no reason you can't
be married in the Kingdom Hall.

I feel a bit lightheaded, as if I'm a balloon a child has forgotten to hold on to tightly enough, and now I'm floating away over the rooftops.

Of course there isn't, Marc says, no reason at all. We'd be honoured to be married in Jehovah's house. Wouldn't we?

In the large armchair across from me, he sits with his legs crossed.

Yes, yes, yes, we would, I say. It would be ... it would be a privilege. It really would.

Brother King exhales with satisfaction. Good. That's settled then. Just a formality, really. I'm so pleased.

He calls his wife, and she trots back into the room with a smile on her face.

Everything OK? she asks brightly, her voice just a little too high-pitched.

Yup, all done, Brother King says, and she passes the cake round again. I shake my head a second time.

EDINBURGH

2001

M UM TROTS ME DOWN THE aisle, all eyes fixed
on me, her right arm linked into my left. When
we reach the end, Marc takes my right hand. For a
moment I am suspended between them both, but
then Mum takes her arm out of mine; this how she
gives me away.

I stand at the bottom of the steps that go up to the
platform, and I promise to honour and to obey Marc
until death do us part. Although I know we are never
going to die: the new system will be here soon, and so
I wed myself to him for the rest of eternity and then
we eat and we dance. I give a speech at the wedding
reception then listen as I am told that this isn't really
a wifely thing to do, especially not to give a speech
that's funnier than my husband's; this is how I know I

getting married is not a happy ending, but instead a beginning. Now I need to learn how to be a wife.

We sit in a circle in my sitting room, some of us cross-legged, some of us on cushions, all of us concentrating on the cloth squares made taut by the circular embroidery frames they're stretched on. We do this every Sunday afternoon, in the dead hours after the meeting and field service but before dinner. There are 12 of us in our sewing circle, like the apostles one of us once tried to joke, but the rest of us didn't laugh, since it was hard to tell if a joke like that was blasphemy or not.

We are the young wives of the congregation. Our husbands are elders or, if not elders, are ministerial servants working towards appointment as one. I don't want to become an elder's wife, but I don't say this. I see the other wives in the Kingdom Hall trying to heed the society's instructions to discipline their children and make sure they listen and answer and follow along at the meetings. They make it look so simple, they're professionals, almost, at reaching across the row and putting their hands on their children's knees or at widening their eyes to tell them to be quiet. They all keep perfect houses, unwrap homemade sandwiches with the crusts carefully removed on Sunday in the break between meetings and ministry, conduct Bible studies with newly interested people, and have the older sisters up for homemade afternoon tea, all without putting a hair out of place, and I know I am wrong to be so self-absorbed that I'm not giving up university now I'm married. I know I should realise that the time left is short and learning is vanity. I know I should be better at helping new members of the congregation and I know I should want Marc to become an elder and not see the hours a week that takes up as a sacrifice but rather a gift to Jehovah similar to a fattened offering on the altar. And yet I can't seem to make myself. Perhaps I see everything the wrong way.

I snip the red thread, pass it to the sister who wants it, ask another for the scissors. I ask if anyone needs a refill; mostly they shake their heads apart from Abeba, who jumps up as soon as I ask. I'd love a cup of tea, one sister says. Me too, says another. In the kitchen I fill up the kettle, taking care to wipe away the splashes from the tap. Marc likes the house to be tidy when he comes home.

I stand the kettle on its base, flick the switch. Outside, beyond the long sash and case window, white clouds ribbon across the darkening sky, the first stars beginning to blink. Abeba opens the fridge, and divides the remaining wine into our glasses. Cheers, she says then hurriedly apologises.

I keep forgetting we can't say cheers, she says. I tell her it's OK, she's new in the truth, there must be a lot for her to forget. There is, she says, and so much to learn too. I know, I say, there's so much I need to learn as well. She frowns. What about? she asks. Being a wife, I say, and she laughs. Oh, that – I know, she says, I have so much to learn too.

Abeba was married the month before me to a brother who grew up in the truth, so he knows what's expected of a husband, whereas Abeba is like me, she doesn't yet know how to be a wife. I never saw Mum with a partner (apart from Andy, who was more of an indiscretion than a partner), and she married after I left home. I haven't seen much of her at all since then. All I have to go on is Granny and Grampa's relationship, and they didn't set a very good scriptural example. No one told Granny what to do; she made all the choices, she earnt more than Grampa, she had the fancier car, she hired help to clean her house, she went back to work when her children were teenagers, she had a great career. In short, she was the opposite of the submissive wife I need to be.

I don't know how I'm supposed to behave. Fortunately, Marc keeps me right and tells me when I've behaved wrongly, or embarrassingly, in public. He tells me to smile if I'm crying, helps me choose the right clothes to wear so I look like a good, loyal sister. So that I know he loves me, he buys me flowers, takes me shopping for new underwear and to eat at all the best places in town. I know I'm so lucky to have him.

The switch on the kettle clicks. I take the lid off the clearly marked tea canister, which matches the sugar and flour ones – all part of our John Lewis wedding list – put two teabags into white bone-china cups, and pour the water on them.

I never know how strong to make it. Marc says my tea is awful.

I really don't understand tea, Abeba says. Wine's more my thing.

Mine too, I say, maybe a bit too much.

Shhh, she says, I won't tell if you don't. Plus, it helps with . . . you know. She winks at me.

But I don't know. I hate when someone expects me to know something and I don't have a clue what they mean.

Do I have to spell it out? she asks as I stir milk into the tea.

I nod, getting a fresh dishcloth from under the sink to wipe the countertop. It might help, I say.

With rendering my husband his dues, she says. The wine, it makes it easier.

Oh, I say, I get it. Then I turn away from her, put some biscuits on a plate on the tray and try not to think about what she's saying, or about any of the things that happen in bed. Some thoughts are best stopped. I am very good at stopping thoughts now. Nearly as good as I am at rendering my husband his dues. Obedience, it's a skill I'm improving. When I look at Abeba, she's staring into the middle distance, like she isn't fully in the room.

In the sitting room, I shut the curtains against the dark. You've got such a nice flat, a sister says. Thank you, I say, it really is.

Marc's so good to you, another says. What with all your baggage.

They laugh.

My baggage? I ask, hating again that I'm not sure what they're talking about.

Your anorexia. It's mad, you know, to starve yourself to close to death, she says.

And vain too, so self-obsessed, another one says.

And not really showing much appreciation for Jehovah's provisions, a third adds, showing me her teeth so I know we're still friends despite her needing to make this important scriptural point.

Guys, leave her alone, says Abeba. You know it's an illness, not some kind of indulgence.

If you say so, says the one who started it all, bending her head back to her sewing.

I pick up my own, but can't seem to bring the stitches into focus. As I breathe in, I press my arms against my ribs, feeling the safety of bone there. I rest my elbows on my hipbones and they make me safe too, have done ever since I was 15 and was first learning how to starve myself. I stood up to sing the song and realised I could feel my hipbones through the wool of my skirt. Ever since, I've made sure I can feel them; they are like a touchstone, they are my North Star, they are the thing that's always there when everything else feels uncertain. They are there right now. I can use them to make the room and the people in it feel further away.

When the sisters leave, I go into the sitting room and begin to tidy everything up. I have an hour before some dinner guests arrive for an informal Sunday supper. I'm not serving anything fancy, only monkfish wrapped in Parma ham, and for dessert a lemon tart I made earlier.

That evening, we all sit round the dining table, laughing and swapping stories about the weirdos we met on the ministry earlier that day. Marc has a new study, who came to the meeting earlier. He looks sort of homeless, and Marc had to give him a shirt for the meeting. We didn't realise his trousers were too loose and he was using a rope for a belt until he stood up and his trousers all but fell down. And his underpants, our friend says, her cheeks puffed out like she might be sick. You'd think he'd at least have put on a fresh pair.

I play with the crumbs filling the cracks in the table and try not to think about Marc's study and the things he told us about his life that have made him the way he is; I try not to think about him sitting crying as we left him alone in his flat with only a sofa in the sitting room. To try to make myself feel better about visiting him and not giving him any help other than the comfort offered in the Bible, I make soup every week for him, and every week he hands me back the empty Tupperware. I don't know if he eats it. I worry sometimes that he thinks he's supposed to eat it cold, straight from the tub. But then I stop myself thinking about him too.

Our guests leave and we clean the kitchen. Marc and I have a system. He's in charge of the dishes, because he's better at getting them properly clean, and I dry them, using a special cloth for the glasses, put them away, clean the work surfaces and the hob before sweeping the floor and putting the dishcloths in a bowl filled with bleach and boiling water. I'll put them in the washing machine with the white wash tomorrow.

Marc says he's tired, and needs to go to bed to get a good night's sleep before he leaves for work in the morning. It's nearly 11 when I sit down at the kitchen table to write an essay for university. This is really what I've wanted to do all day long. When I write the rest of the world falls away. Time stops. Nothing matters but the blinking cursor on the screen and the thoughts I line up into well-behaved words. I love uni for this. I know I shouldn't. I know learning is vanity. I know I shouldn't be so attached to knowledge. I know the world and all its desires are passing away and I know Armageddon is coming soon and I know I shouldn't want a career and I know I should be working for myself, and I know I am being enticed and drawn out by my own desires, but knowing all these things doesn't stop me from loving the late nights I spend working. I work then because I'm not allowed to let my studies get in the way of the truth: of meetings, field service, talks, personal study, family study, Bible-reading, prayer, association, my marriage. I make sure of the more important things first, as I'm told to do in the literature, and then I focus on my studies, and I know I am sinful for loving them as much as I do, but in the dim light of the kitchen with the hum of the fridge for company, I don't care.

EDINBURGH

2002

WINTER COMES AND BRINGS DEEP cold. It's dark in the mornings as I defrost the car and drive east, into the rising dawn, to university, the fields streaked with pink-hued sheep, frostbitten leaves lining the roads, hedges strung with glittered cobwebs.

Sometimes, I let myself think how it would feel to drive and drive and drive. I think how it would feel to drive to Granny's house and to sit and talk to her and to tell her how empty I feel, that the hole in me is getting bigger. I want to tell someone how there is no way to plug it, how my hunger is back, worse this time, my stomach an empty hollow, how the smaller I get the larger the void seems to grow.

But at the end of the day, I head west, into the

sunset, over the hills, back to the jaws of the city, where everything waits, wide-mouthed, for me.

Saturday mornings I want to stay in bed, but as usual it's up and out into the cold to preach. I try my trick of not pressing the doorbells, but I have to press every third one, otherwise my avoidance will become obvious. People my age come to the door, all sleep-warm and messy-haired and bleary-eyed, as if woken from a winter's hibernation, and I envy them, but Marc says, Imagine wasting your life like that. I don't tell him just how much I'd like to imagine it. I want to sleep all the time. The more I want it, though, the more it eludes me.

On Sunday afternoons, when Marc plays badminton, I walk and walk and walk to the fringes of the city, where the sea stops it from growing north. I stand looking at the waves edging up the beach. When I'm there I can see how unhappy I am. The sea lets me think of escape, always a new horizon waiting. I want to keep walking, away from everything. I want to become someone new. But I never do. I do what I'm expected to, because that's all I've ever done. I turn around and walk home, past lit-up pubs with people inside, past the launderette with the machines spinning eternally, past the off-licence. I push open my gate and walk up the path where I can see light escaping from the gap in the heavy curtains, and sometimes I wonder, until it's all I'm ever wondering: why I don't just turn round and leave?

WEST LOTHIAN

2002

WARM AIR BLASTS INTO THE car but under my coat I am still cold. The lights of Glasgow are behind us, and we drive into the darkness with the radio on. It's full of news of the Queen Mother's death. I never liked her, Marc says, total alcoholic.

Wouldn't you be too, I say, if you had to live like one of them?

I would, he concedes, I'd definitely be on the gin for breakfast.

Me too, I say as I try another station, but tonight all the music has stopped, death and nostalgia filling the airwaves.

I rest my head against the window, feel the engine vibrate beneath my skull. My feet ache from dancing all night at the wedding we've been to. I'm nearly sleeping when Marc switches the radio off, and silence fills the car.

I sit up. You know Charles and Kylie, don't you, he says.

I know who he means, but don't know them very well. I think they were at our wedding, but then there were a lot of people I didn't know well there. Marc paid for it, and because of that he got to decide who came. All his friends are my friends now, even though I forget it often, and feel strange around people he's known his whole life who I've only known for a year. I know this is because most of my family are worldly and strange and I'm not good at socialising or fitting in with people.

Yes, I say, I know them. I have to tell you something, he says. Did you see them laughing? I shake my head. They were laughing at you. I didn't like it, he says, but quite a few people were. Charles told me afterwards you looked really repulsive. That's the word he used, he was talking about your bones and the way you were showing them off with your halterneck.

I've become very thin since I married Marc. I'm not really eating again. I'm running at lunchtimes at uni and swimming and walking and going to the gym and pushing myself and it helps me feel like life is OK, stops me thinking about the parts of it that aren't OK. Losing weight is just a stupid side effect of all of that. I couldn't decide what to wear to the wedding, until I found a silk calf-length skirt and matching halterneck top. I took the skirt in, and Marc suggested

I wear a cardie to cover up my shoulder blades, and he was right, that was the best idea, but then I danced and got too warm and forgot, the way I'm always forgetting, and so I took the cardie off and made a show of myself and my thinness. I really should learn to listen more to Marc.

I'm so sorry, I say, I need to think more about how all of this affects you. I see him nod and I know for the sake of our family name I need to get bigger, just big enough so no one knows my days are full of counting calories and steps and measuring myself; all the silly tiny ways I push the world away, all the risky things I do to fool myself that I am safe.

EDINBURGH

2003

WE GIGGLE AS WE WALK along the street. Ash grips on to my arm, trying to stay upright.

We're not drunk, are we? she asks.

I laugh. Of course we aren't, we're just hungry.

That's it! she says. Shit, we didn't eat, did we?

Shhh, I say, not shit.

God, she says, I keep forgetting.

Not God either.

Crap, she says, I'm rubbish at this.

The streetlamps throw pools of light out into the Edinburgh night. It's only 6.30, but it's already been dark for hours. Around us the haar rolls and thickens, making it more and more difficult to see. We link arms and walk towards my flat.

Ash hasn't been a Witness for long. She told me she was drawn to us for our group psychology, whatever that means. She's studying mental-health nursing and is obsessed with everything to do with the mind, as well as herbs and plants and gender and critical analysis. She doesn't eat meat, Marc says this makes her a bit dubious. She mostly became a Witness because she was secretly going out with Alex, a brother who recently moved into the congregation. She says he's terrified of Armageddon, and the fear rubbed off on her. She has a thing about being pure, which is why she doesn't eat meat or sugar or dairy. I guess it's also why she likes the truth. It makes us all pure.

I like her. She's fun. She also knows about the world, and her knowing it makes me think I know it too. She called me bohemian once, which made me laugh a lot. She says Marc is with me because I make him feel better about himself. Which is a stretch, since he's always telling me what hard work I am, what with all my history.

We spent the afternoon drinking cocktails, our new MAC lipstick rubbing off on the ice-frosted glasses. We'd gone to Harvey Nicks, to the beauty counter where Ash's worldly friend had given us a makeover. Don't tell Marc, Ash had winked at me, and I'd smiled back.

We were in the newest bar in town, tucked down in the basement, all mahogany and polished concrete. The alcohol was beginning to hit my stomach, hard, just the way I like it, until the room began to blur just a little. We didn't care about the three drinks rule, or the gathering dusk, or that Marc would soon be home from work and wonder where his dinner was, until suddenly I realised how much I'd drunk and how late it was. But beside Ash I felt almost invincible.

You're so subversive, she says, not like a real wife. Like, I don't think I know any other Witnesses who would do this on a Friday afternoon with me.

Her breath makes white haloes around her mouth. I don't know what she means by 'subversive'. I don't know if it's a good thing or not.

Yeah, I say, I'm a bit crap at it. I don't know. (I pause.) All the time it feels like I live in the wrong house. Don't tell him. But I keep looking at his shoes and they don't look like they should be there. They look wrong in the hallway. I keep waiting for Mum's shoes and they're never there. Just his.

You're really young. It's going to be weird, she says.

Not, really, I say, I'm twenty-two. That's quite old.

No, it's not, she says, laughing, I don't know anyone your age who's even thinking about settling down. It's weird. I love Jehovah but I do find some of the other stuff a bit mad.

She's drunk, I think. Don't listen to her. She doesn't know what she's talking about. It's different for her. I need to remember my spiritual armour.

Maybe, I say, I guess in the truth we do things differently.

We walk, the haar dampening our hair. I shiver.

When we get back to mine, the sitting-room

curtains are open, and through them I can see the room is dark. Maybe he's not home from work, I say, turning my key in the lock. I push the door open but there's no sound from inside.

We look at each other and laugh. We could steal his whisky, she giggles. But I notice there is a small chink of light coming from beneath the kitchen door. I open it, and we both walk in. Marc is standing at the sink under the tall, narrow window. The blind is still open, letting in all the dark. He stands stock still, as if staring out the window, although there's nothing to see. Ash and I sit down at the table and both say 'hi' at the same time. He doesn't turn around. He stands for what seems like forever. Finally, he places a glass on the drainer with his right hand, and then runs the tap to free his hands of suds, washing each finger carefully, deliberately. Still he doesn't turn around. With his back straight, he reaches for a towel, dries his hands, each finger one by one, and only after that does he turn to face us.

He's angry. And rightly so. The elders talk a lot about righteous anger and now I see him like this, I know what they mean. I know they mean I have to try much, much harder to do what I'm told. I need to learn how to be submissive. I need to learn to be industrious. I need to be home to make dinner. I need to make a warm and comfortable home for my husband. I get everything wrong all the time.

I think this in the kitchen and I think this when I'm on the doorstep and don't know how I got there, and Ash is gone and I don't know where, and I bang on the door until Marc opens it and looks around and tells me to be quiet because he doesn't want the neighbours to hear. I fall into the hallway and say, I'm so sorry, I'll never be a disloyal wife again.

WHERE YOU GO I WILL GO

EDINBURGH

2003

EVERY FRIDAY NIGHT, I MAKE up my face, and we eat and drink, and we appear normal.

I look at my plate. The food on it feels impossible now. The thought of swallowing it feels like another wild ambition. I see the years stretch. Every Friday this; every Saturday ministry with the big food shop after and then good associations up for dinner; every Sunday the meeting. I see my life, a long line, stretching on and on and on. Until it stops. Or worse, it doesn't stop, it goes on into the new system, the line becoming an eternity.

I imagine how it must feel to be free. I want my life to feel like an adventure, and not one that's mapped out or half lived or waiting for the next life, the good, pure, true, forever life in the new system. I want to stop waiting for the end of days and to start living.

It's like this for everyone I know. When I let myself stop and think about it I see we are all trapped, all of us all trying to be better than each other, all trying to be holier, all trying to get the most hours in on the ministry, or be the first one to walk out the cinema when something not quite theocratic happens in a film, or when someone dares to voice doubts be the first to close them down. It doesn't matter how late you've been out the night before, you get up to go on the ministry first thing to show everyone how devout you are, until it isn't so much about saving lives but being seen to save them. We suck mints on a Sunday to clear the alcohol fumes from our breath before we give the right answers from the *Watchtower*, and everything is about trying to live forever without any of us ever stopping to wonder what it really means to be alive. We are all copies of each other, wearing what we're told, obsessed with the right haircuts, the right length of skirts, some of us shining lights through our dresses to check they aren't sheer and immoral, and others sitting down to make sure they're the right length. We live like this because the organisation tell us it's the best life possible; we are all one happy, loving brotherhood united in worship until the end of days.

AMSTERDAM

2003

I STRETCH MY LEGS OUT ON the long rubberwood table. My feet are tanned. I run my fingers around the top of my wine glass, gently rubbing away the condensation from its side. Sliding doors are open to the roof terrace, bringing in the sounds of the street in the early evening. The smell of weed floats up on the breeze, and I breathe in, remembering how it felt to be high. I lean back, turn the stereo up. I think about reading the book that's face-down on the table, but there's time enough for that.

It's beautiful here, I love it. I love the canals, and the markets and the tall beautiful Dutch people, but the thing I love the most, is that I did this. I got me here.

I am starting an internship soon. I need to, to complete my degree, but I didn't want to stay in Scotland.

I applied to a design company in Amsterdam in secret, and I didn't know how to tell Marc. I drank a couple of glasses of white wine before I met him after work one Friday, in the pub. That helped. I drank more and then spat out that I was thinking I should do my internship somewhere else. He said that it was impossible. We couldn't just up and go and live in another country, especially since he was the one with the good job. That was that. Or at least it was until the following week, when he came home. You'll never guess what, he said, Jehovah has made it possible for us to go to Amsterdam! A secondment has just come up. Now that Jehovah had spoken, that was that. I wasn't entirely sure that it was Jehovah guiding us, but the timing did seem fortuitous.

I've been here for seven days now; Marc will join me at the end of next week. As soon as I arrived I went for a walk, the smell of dank water in the canals mingling with the food in the market in the square round the corner from the apartment. I found a second-hand book stall. I know I shouldn't buy second-hand books because of the demons inside, but at the same time I'm not totally convinced those stories are true. I also know I'm not supposed to read Camus, but Ash does, so I bought *The Fall* and read it in one night. No demons so far. The bookshelves in the rented apartment are stuffed with books by people I've never even heard of: Burroughs and Ginsberg and Kerouac. I plan to get through as many of them as I can.

I even bought a notebook, and have started to

write things down. I've not done that for years, not since I married Marc. Life's so busy, I'm always making sure of the more important things, as the society tells us to do, and Marc reminds me that writing feels frivolous and pointless. This last week has been the first time I've been alone in two years; for the only time since I have been married, I feel like I am being who I am, and not who I'm expected to be.

Then Marc arrives, and most weekends visitors come so we can show them the amazing apartment and take them round the city. I'm cooking and cleaning, leaving for work at 6.30 and getting home late. It isn't long before Amsterdam feels the same as home, I've just swapped one location for another: the expectations of me remain the same.

The Kingdom Hall is different here, but we're in the English-speaking congregation. When we arrived, a brother explained to us that they are a mix of nationalities. Bit strange, he said, to have so many migrants and ex-pats in the same place, but it can't be helped.

The weekend Ash comes to visit, Marc is quiet. He takes himself on long bike rides into the countryside and hardly talks to either of us in the evenings. Ash asks if I'm OK as we drink cocktails alone on a roof terrace. Yes, I say, why?

It's just ... you don't seem right, she says. Are you happy?

Yes, I say, I love it here.

I meant with him, are you happy?

I take a drink. I'm not. I'm not happy. I try to write things in my notebook, imagining it's better to be creatively fulfilled than happy. I don't think I'm either.

I don't know, I say, it's like Edinburgh exists in another dimension somehow. I don't feel like the same person here. There's this . . .

I pause. Play with my straw.

Right, don't tell anyone. There's this guy at work.

She laughs.

You dark horse, she says.

It's not like that. I can hardly talk to him. But every time I'm at the water cooler he comes to talk to me. And he asked me to go for a drink. It's not like he doesn't know I'm married, I wear my rings.

Maybe he doesn't care, she says.

I suppose, he is worldly after all. They're all having affairs.

You do know it's not as exciting out there as they say it is, Ash says. The elders make it sound like everyone's shagging everyone else, but most of the time they just aren't.

Really? Damn.

We laugh. Then it's Ash's turn.

Can I tell you something? she asks.

Anything.

I think I'm going to have to leave.

Why? You've just got here.

No, I think I'm leaving the Witnesses. I don't know if I can keep doing it.

Time seems to slow, as it always does when something scares me.

Why? I hardly manage to ask.

She tells me it's complicated, that her parents hate the fact that she is a Witness. She tried to cut them off, but she misses them. Especially her mum.

I think about this. I think about how Mum was supposed to come to visit me last week, but she didn't. I went to collect her from the airport, as we had planned, and waited there for hours, but she never came. I called her when I got home. All distant and cracking down the line, she said, It's you or my marriage: I had to choose my marriage. Then she hung up and was gone. I knew her husband could be difficult, but I didn't know it was hard for her too. Maybe it's hard for everyone. It's not easy to be submissive and accept that men are heads of the family. Although it seems to be easy for men to behave like they are. I suppose it's our fault. I know, above all things, we have to choose our marriages. Even when men at the water cooler seem appealing. That's a temptation from Satan. I also can't imagine living without Mum, even when she's difficult.

OK, I say, I don't really get it, but I understand wanting your mum. But maybe it will pass. Maybe you just need to get used to missing her and then it'll get easier.

I go quiet. I think about how I'm not sure that Marc doesn't have doubts of his own. He's been keen to miss the meetings since we came over here; we

242

sleep later on Saturday mornings and don't always attend. Sometimes he says small things that don't sound like him. I don't ask him about them. We aren't to voice our doubts. If we did it would make room for Satan. It's strange sometimes to think what Marc and I would have if we didn't have God, Jehovah is the only thing we have in common. They tell you before you get married that that's enough, but sometimes it feels like weak glue.

Ash says something about cults, which she has been studying as part of her degree.

Oh, come on, I say as I laugh, it's not a cult. No one's controlling us. We're God's chosen people.

But then I remember the induction day at work, when they gave out a booklet full of company maxims and told all the new starters everything about the history of the organisation. When I took it home to show Marc, he said it looked really 'culty'. I laughed and told him it didn't, it just looked a bit like some of our literature. Now the idea begins to gnaw.

Ash goes quiet, and the next day she flies back to Edinburgh. A few weeks later she will disassociate herself, meaning she is no longer one of Jehovah's Witnesses. I'm not allowed to be friends with her anymore.

I can't think of life without Jehovah. Although the more I consider it, I realise that's not strictly true. When I do imagine it, I see a life without Marc in it because, without Jehovah, I'm not sure that we'd exist. Sometimes, when it's very late and Marc is sleeping, I sit up in bed and think about what the future would look like without him or Jehovah in it, but I can't quite make it come into focus.

One hot September evening, we go for dinner with Marc's bosses from the UK, who have come over to see him on his secondment. They're friendly and attentive and are also interested in the work I've been doing. I don't think there's anything wrong with talking to them about it over dinner. I notice Marc in the mirrors lining the wall, the cut-crystal chandeliers reflecting on into infinity. He is turning red. I don't meet his eye.

At the end of the meal they offer us a nightcap but Marc insists, No, it's late, we need to get home.

We're halfway across a bridge when he stops me, abruptly. Suddenly all the things he's wanted to say for years come out thick and fast and harsh. He tells me how unspiritual I am, how I'm leading him astray and have done for years, how I need to try harder to be a good wife.

I don't say anything. I just look at the water lapping at the canal's edge. I want what he's said to be ink so the rain when it comes can wash it from my skin. The worst thing is, I know he's right. He's only saying what the society says about women. I need to do better.

At home he lies down on the bed and takes his shoes off but not his clothes. He quickly falls asleep. I take my make-up off, avoiding looking at myself in the mirror. I can't sleep. I lie in the hot darkness imagining a long, narrow chest with enough drawers to keep everything he said inside it. I imagine slowly opening a drawer, putting his words inside, and closing it shut, so as to almost rewind and make it have not happened, so as to make living with him after this possible, or at least bearable. This is how I make myself safe.

Before we leave for home, I'm offered a permanent contract. I tell Marc, but he refuses to entertain the idea. This was the adventure, he says, we are going home now.

When we get home everything goes back to normal. We're back at the meetings all the time, back on the ministry, Marc is exactly how he was before, as if all his possible doubts have vanished. I don't need to think anymore of life without him or God in it. It stretches on, the same as it always has.

2. RUPTURE

'Is he willing to prevent evil, but not able?
then he is impotent. Is he able, but not willing?
then he is malevolent. Is he both able and willing?
whence then is evil?'

David Hume, *Dialogues
Concerning Natural Religion* (1779)

CHARCOAL, BONE AND ASH

2005

MY DAUGHTER LOOKS UP AT me with her round eyes. Her hands are beginning to unball themselves already, and sweat beads on her brow. In the seven weeks since she was born, she has taught me so much about herself. Things I know about her are that she has a deep, abiding fascination with her hands; she spends almost as much time looking at them as she does me. She gazes at her long fingers and so do I. She is calm and she is patient and she is beautiful. I've never seen anything like her.

On the television news, people pour from the tube, their faces glazed, cut and grey from ash and smoke, long hordes of them, just walking. In Tavistock Square a double-decker bus sits with its top blown off, the side of it hanging like the lid of a sardine can.

I don't want to keep watching, but I can't stop. I look down at Imogen as she feeds. She is so small and yet so wholly herself that I can't begin to think of the world outside. Its vastness. Its badness.

She wasn't supposed to happen. This wasn't part of the plan, Marc said when I discovered I was pregnant. Of course, we'd been going to have children, we'd chosen not to remain childless in the Lord, as some people did who preferred to have children after Armageddon. We just weren't going to have them yet. But children are a precious gift from Jehovah, and so she grew, and I grew, until my skin itched and I became lethargic and slow. I'm so surprised you're good at this, Marc said. It must be nice to have found your calling.

I didn't feel good at it. It didn't feel like a calling. I was sick with fear about having to give birth to the baby. For worldly people, birth seems straightforward enough, but for me, if I needed a blood transfusion I would have had to say no, and then I might die.

Once, at an assembly, a sister told the audience she'd been pregnant with a baby whose skull wasn't forming properly, and she refused to have a termination because that would go against Jehovah's loving commandments. The baby died at birth. As the audience applauded her loyalty, I tried to write the experience down in my notebook, as we were supposed to with important points in the programme, but I found I couldn't write the words.

It was strange being pregnant so soon after graduation from university. I had been thinking about what to do next. I'd never thought before about pregnancy and choice, pregnancy was just what happened when you got married, but sometimes I was so sinful that I thought I'd like to have a say in taking the pregnancy to term or not.

The elders helped prepare me for birth. They told me what to say to the doctors, how to refuse blood, how to remain steadfast under trial. Then there I was, one Saturday evening in May, leaning against the hospital wall, hardly able to stand and barely able to express the magnitude of the pain as Marc coached me to not get too carried away.

Try a bath, the midwife said, not too hot though. It might help take the edge off the pain.

The bathroom was grey – 'elephant's breath' or 'sea mist' is what they'd call it on the paint charts. I lay in the tepid water (Best for baby, the midwife said). I like my baths so warm I can't get into them easily. I feel like I'm submerged, as though I disappeared at the first antenatal appointment when they called me 'Mum'. I looked around, wondering if there was someone else in the room, then I realised the midwife meant me. I was Mum. I had been subsumed.

The shower curtain hung limply in the water, darkening at the end. 'Dead salmon' it would've been called if it was also a paint colour. I lowered myself into the bath, my taut skin reddening from poor circulation until it would be called something like 'circus candyfloss'. I felt the pain disappear, as if the baby was

251

holding its not-yet-taken breath. Marc pushed open the door and sat on the toilet lid.

I knew the possibility of my death was on his mind, because only a month ago a sister died in childbirth when she refused a blood transfusion. When it happened a brother in the Kingdom Hall said it would have been better if the baby had died too. I lay in the bath thinking about what he said and how right he was. It wouldn't be fair to expect a man to raise a baby on his own. That's what women are for. I wasn't sure my faith was strong enough to withstand pressure from the doctors if something did go wrong. I was scared, and Marc was too. I couldn't imagine how it must feel for a newly widowed father to have to raise his child alone.

Four hours later, I was pulled apart. You're not the same after that. They don't tell you that when you give birth it's not only a baby that's born in the room. She was born and I traded the girl I was for my daughter, held high and covered in blood; my tiny daughter, placed in my arms, making Grampa's shirt, which I wore as a silent prayer, red. She looked up at me, and although they told me babies can't see far I knew it was a lie. She widened her eyes when she first saw me and didn't take them off me until she found her hands; then she stared down at her fingers and unfurled each one slowly, deliberately, in turn.

I'd never let myself properly imagine this tiny golden promise. I was suddenly full of love, so pure and unasked for, as if I might burst, and this little creature, so small that surely they couldn't expect me to look after her. She was, is, so perfect. I whispered her name to her, and inhaled her strange interior smell, my blood matting itself on her hair, and in that moment, I broke the promise I'd made to Marc. He'd said, This baby changes nothing, and I'd nodded, but with her in my arms, I knew, this baby changed everything.

The reporter keeps talking on and on. Imogen mews at me, knowing instinctively how to get my attention. I look at her and she smiles, her whole face lighting up. I put her on my shoulder, pat tiny bubbles of air from her.

Things I didn't care about before feel like a big deal now Imogen is here. I sat and watched 9/11 unfold when we were on honeymoon, and said it was all part of Jehovah's plan; the same with the invasion of Iraq, when Marc had called protestors deluded for thinking they could change the world. Then, I didn't stop to think about what I thought. But now it's as though my skin has been peeled back: I'm raw and sensitive and utterly exposed. I don't know if I like it or not. It's like I'm turning into someone new. But I don't tell anyone about it. I don't want them to think there's something wrong with me.

The light's all wrong too. Sometimes my field of vision seems tinged with pink, like the corners of an old photo. Sometimes I see things moving at the periphery, almost-human shapes, unsettling disturbances. More things to not tell Marc.

The strangeness started in the days after Imogen

was born, when life became a circus of visitors bringing gifts. They brought tiny dresses bedecked with gold and ribbons, dresses I don't know how to contort her stiff, stubborn body into. I am suspicious of these overt gender significations. They brought boxes full of expensive scented oil to rub into her sparrow legs. On the fourth day, when I was full of hormones, leaking everywhere in stinking patches of milk and unbidden tears over everything, a sister handed me a rectangular box. She was all teeth and smiles as the paper crinkled under my hands. Inside was the familiar orange cover of *My Book of Bible Stories*. I thought it was the only book she really needs, the sister said. I smiled back. Yes, I said, it's so special, thank you.

Inside the book were the pictures I used to see in my nightmares. Noah's Flood, with animals being swept away and people clawing at floating tree stumps, their heads barely above the water; and wise King Solomon holding a baby by the feet, sword in hand, raised above the baby, its mother screaming, the imposter mother with her hands over her face. Towards the end of the book there are pictures of buildings falling, pavements cracking open, fire licking through the streets, and then, finally, the new system, people patting lions, everyone smiling, baskets of fruit everywhere. I put the book to the side. I bent and smelt the strange womb-fresh smell of Imogen's head and knew I could never read that book to her. I just couldn't.

And now, today's news. I can't settle. I am suddenly

bursting with thoughts. Things I want to talk about, but there is no one to talk to. I'm not allowed to talk about doubts; I can't ask why there are so many statements of condolence from other religious leaders and yet there are none from ours. I can't ask: if we're such a significant religion then why aren't we saying something, and if we're a charity, why aren't we helping? I wanted to ask the same things after the tsunami last year, but I was too scared. I worry I won't be able to keep all these questions inside for much longer.

I turn the TV off and put Imogen in her papoose on my chest so I can make dinner.

Marc's all excited when he comes home. Have you seen the news? he says. Awful.

I look up from setting the table. I know, I say, it's horrible.

Just, evil, he says. Imagine being cuckoo enough to believe what they do. He shakes his head. It's so obviously Satanic.

I take Imogen out of her papoose and settle her into her bouncy chair at the foot of the table.

I dish up Marc's dinner, giving myself exactly half of what I give him. This means I can't get fat. I don't feel like eating tonight, it's the meeting and I am always nervous before I get ready for it. Having to get dressed up on a Thursday evening exhausts me. But I can't say that.

Did you see the markets tumble though? he says. I shake my head; some things I don't pay much attention to.

It's chaos, totally wiped the value off everything.

He stops with his fork halfway to his mouth as though someone's pressed PAUSE. I sit wondering how long it's going to take him to move it again.

You don't think, he says with his eyes shining, that this might be the start of the end?

I hadn't thought. It didn't look like the end, it looked like a lot of terrified people. I shake my head.

I didn't think, I say.

Well, it all adds up, doesn't it. It'll make them turn on religion, and the markets are tumbling and, well, Bush and Blair. (He's really animated by now.) The G8 conference, they'll be talking about peace and security, I bet you. All the prophecies, they're all coming true. Just think, this could be our last summer before the new system.

I don't want to think. I just want him to stop talking.

It's not for us to speculate, I say. No one knows the day or the hour.

You're right, he says, I'm so lucky to have you. You're so much more spiritual than me.

I can't tell if he means it or not. I smile as I cut my food up into smaller and smaller pieces.

But did you hear what the group that did it said? he says. They said they did it in the name of God's peace. Poor Jehovah, having that attributed to Him. I bet He just can't wait to wipe them out.

I look at him. Does he not realise he wants the same thing to happen to the perpetrators as happened to the victims of the attacks? Does he not realise how like them he sounds?

Later, at the meeting, I feed Imogen in the back room of the Kingdom Hall, behind the screen the elders bought to protect my modesty. I'm the only new mum in the congregation who's breastfeeding. Some people are a bit strange about it.

Afterwards I take her over to the open sash and case window, where I can see people outside the gay bar opposite, the sound of their conversation and laughter making its way up to where I am. I watch them embrace each other in greeting, I watch their relaxed body language, their easy camaraderie, based on their differences not their similarities. I watch and watch, the same as I've watched at every meeting since Imogen was born. I like being in the back room; I like being away from the talks, and when I'm there I turn the volume down on the speaker so I don't need to listen to the life-giving instruction. I am being enticed and drawn out by my own desires, and I like it.

Sometimes I think I'd rather be out there with them than in here with Jehovah's people. I let my mind wander, wondering how it must feel to be them, before I go back into the stifling heat of the main hall, where everyone is sitting in long rows, the men with their identical haircuts and the women with their modest clothes, and for the first time, it looks deeply strange to me.

I sit, determined not to think about who's radicalised, or how all our beliefs are subject to change at the

Governing Body's say-so. I don't want to think about how this will act on Imogen, or to think about the things I've been told since childhood that I'm now expected to tell her. I wrap her shawl more tightly around her. Kiss the top of her head.

She looks up at me with so much faith in her eyes. Who will I ask her to place this faith in? In what ways will I destroy her innocence?

Something new stretches in me. It checks its limbs for strength, knowing one day, I will need it to help me run away.

After that, I begin to think new things. Sometimes I want to unthink them. I don't want to know my limitations, or how difficult it is to pretend that everything's fine when the whole life I've been living begins to look threadbare, a lie. I want to close my eyes to make it go away, but every morning when I wake, the feeling is still there, waiting. I wonder if I can live this life much longer.

I try to forget. I become a wind-up toy, going and going and going. Imogen doesn't yet know the way days and nights are arranged. I go for days on very little sleep. I don't feel tired, instead I feel invincible. I revolve the day around her feeds, I clean the house until it shines first thing every morning. When I take her out for a walk, I try to outrun the new parts of myself, pushing the pram faster and faster until my legs hurt. I take her home and feed her and lay her gently in her bouncy chair, and when her eyes shut tight I cook dinner so it's ready for later. In the long afternoons I put her on her play mat and clean the house, and afterwards I try to fill the dead hours before bath and bed with more walking. I take her to feed the ducks, but I'm scared by the swans and how powerful their necks suddenly look, how they could snatch a baby if they were in the mood to.

As summer intensifies the light becomes even stranger. It's too bright now, too clear, too white, becomes part of the strange disturbances at the edge of my vision, where it splinters itself into many parts, refracting into rainbows.

Everything is louder than it was before. The whole city hums when I'm out with the pram, static creeps under the old windows into the flat until it takes on a shape of its own and lurks behind me, biting at my heels.

So no one knows what's happening, I make sure Imogen looks good. She's always clean and always dressed in ribbons and pretty dresses, and I try to quiet the voice that wants her to be comfortable and look like a baby still, in sleepsuits all of the time. I smile at the meetings, and answer when I'm meant to, and I hand over magazines on the ministry. It's easy enough to let the emptiness swallow me. I've been emptying myself out for years and years and it's simpler this way, to keep pretending instead of turning to face the thing that's stretching, clawing, inside me.

HE WHO CAUSES TO BECOME

2007

IMOGEN GROWS. LIFE FEELS CERTAIN, settled. Sometimes I wake in the night, hyperventilating, as if from a bad dream, to realise I haven't been dreaming at all. This is the dream. I have everything I could want. A nice flat. A beautiful child. A husband with a good job. A degree, a research position. Enough money for holidays. What is wrong with me that it isn't enough? What is wrong with me that I don't want any of it.

I feel like I'm playing at being an adult. As if I'm trying on someone else's life and finding it doesn't fit. It doesn't matter what alterations I make; this life hangs loosely on me.

I am tired of polishing and baking and preaching and cooking and playing peekaboo and reading *The*

Gruffalo. I am sick of acceptable entertainment and modest clothes. I don't know if other people feel like this, because I can't ask anyone about it. We don't talk about our beliefs outside of the meetings. The elders say debating them is a bad thing, so we talk about mundane things: the weather, the latest magazines, other people in the congregation.

Imogen looks at me with her trusting eyes. She knows nothing yet of the circle she's been born into. She doesn't know that the life I have is the life she will have to have too, if we are to accept her forever. She blinks. I can't pass this on to her. I can't leave her. I play with her curls as she sits on my knee, resting her head against me for another nap. I will take her with me. She will come too.

I am scared. I am still scared of the dark, and the darkness inside my head that will not leave. I don't know how to build a bridge from one world to the next. How do I get there?

It is easier to not think about these things. It is easier to starve myself until my hipbones come back.

It is easier to polish the bathroom mirror every morning. It is easier to be a good Christian wife.

I slow my mind right down until I am a record played at the wrong speed, distorted and incomprehensible. But this is the life I've chosen. This is the best life ever. How can I not see it?

I do things I shouldn't. Ever since Amsterdam I've bought books I've either needed to keep hidden or I hope that no one else has read. Marc doesn't mind books on the bookshelves: Makes us look intellectual, he says, although he also says he couldn't bring himself to read fiction. Well-worn copies of *Young Adam*, *The Blind Assassin* and *Yellow Dog* are hidden in the bedroom. I visit Waterstones and am overwhelmed by the choices on the shelves. I'm too nervous to ask a bookseller for any help. Instead I stick to the books on special offer on the tables near the front of the shop. The best thing about breastfeeding is that it takes so long. I get through a lot of books.

Trying to believe in this life works until Imogen is nearly two.

My feelings are safely tucked away inside me when, one biting-cold spring day, there's someone new at the Kingdom Hall.

He stands at the front of the hall with his hair touching the top of the back of his cheap polyester suit. It's longer than it's allowed to be. He's tall. I like his profile when he turns to the side and then I remind myself I'm not to look at other men like that. Recently this is something that I have had to remind myself of often.

I'm talking to a sister when an elder comes over with him. This is Dieter, he says, he's here for the summer, from Germany. Maybe you and Marc could help settle him in.

Of course, I say. We start talking. He asks where I'm from and when I tell him he tells me I won't believe it but he knows someone from the congregation I grew up in. No way, small world, I say, the way

I often do when I meet a new Witness: we all seem to know someone who knows someone. The elders say this is what makes the worldwide brotherhood so special, that we are connected across continents by Christian love.

Before long we're swapping stories. When Marc comes over I say, This is my husband, and Dieter laughs then and asks if he has a name, and my husband grips his hand tightly and shakes it hard. This is so Dieter knows who's boss here. I'm Marc, he says, with a C.

After Marc walks away, I give Dieter my number. I'm around half the week, I say. If you want to do something, let me know.

June 2007

I do what I'm told and help Dieter to settle in. Perhaps I'm a bit too enthusiastic about my responsibilities, because one day Dieter and I sit at a pavement cafe in the same way we've sat in cafes, bars and pubs for weeks now. When I'm not working, I'm with him. Imogen isn't old enough to speak properly yet, so she keeps our secret safe. Or she would if there was a secret to keep. But I'm just being friendly. It doesn't matter that he makes me laugh, it doesn't matter if I admire his nose when his head's turned to the side, and it doesn't matter if I tell him things I've hardly ever told myself. None of it matters at all because I'm just showing him around the city and there's nothing else to it.

I order pizza, big enough for the two of us to share,

and a couple of beers. We talk about books. Later, when I come back from the toilet, he's writing in the leather notebook I've noticed him using a lot.

What are you writing? I ask.

Just things, he says.

He smiles, and looks at the polished tabletop, his reflection distorting back at him, the sun bouncing into his eyes. With his left hand he pushes his hair out of them.

He squints at me.

What about you? he says.

What do you mean?

Do you write? he asks.

I laugh. I don't write now, I say. I used to, when I was a kid. I won a stupid national short story competition when I was twelve. But I stopped when I met Marc.

Stupid? he asks.

Yeah, I say, just a silly competition for kids.

I stopped writing when I returned from Amsterdam. I knew it would only get me in trouble. Writing was the only time I could think clearly, and I didn't always like the thoughts that came out. Writing feels like a portal to a dangerous truth.

I think you could write, he says.

I laugh.

I couldn't write a book, I say.

You will, he says, you'll write something postmodern.

I don't know what postmodern means. Later, I'll

look it up in the dictionary and be even more confused, or more intrigued.

Come on, I say, let's go back to mine for a bit. There's a book I want to lend you.

See, he says, you're already behaving like a writer.

Imogen wakes and strains to sit up in her buggy, so I pick her up and lift her out onto my knee. Sleep-heavy she leans against my chest and stares at Dieter with her saucer-round eyes. Every time he talks to her she buries her face against my cotton T-shirt, but as soon as he stops talking, she turns towards him. She's torn between revulsion and fascination. Quickly this push-pull becomes a game of peekaboo until she's laughing so hard her whole tiny body is shaking.

She walks the short distance back to the flat, holding my hand, and Dieter tries to push the buggy, but every time he puts his hand on it, Imogen barks, You not touch my buggy! I hoist her up on one hip and push the buggy with my spare hand, and when I hit a bump in the pavement Dieter tries to stabilise the buggy but touches my hand instead. You not touch my mummy! Imogen shouts. We both laugh and are still laughing as I pull the buggy up the steps at the front of the flat and open the door.

Dieter comes into the cool, bright hallway and looks around, then walks into the sparse white sitting room, where books line the Edinburgh press to the right of the fireplace. He runs his hand over the two Habitat cubes I saved up for for months, before bending down to look at the books in them. I pull a book from the shelf.

This, I say, I want you to read this.

He turns it over to read the blurb on the back.

Brilliant name, he says, Safran Foer has a real ring to it, and what a great title. Maybe after this everything will be illuminated.

I wanted to call Imogen Safran if she'd been a boy, I say, but Marc said it was too effeminate. It's an amazing book. I didn't know books could be written like that. If you like it, I'll lend you his other one. It made me think differently.

In a good way?

That's up for debate, I say, as Imogen tugs at my hand. Me play garden, she says. I take her through to the kitchen and open the double doors so she can play in her sandpit. Dieter follows, taking in everything he sees.

It's a lot to lose, he says.

I don't know what he means. Or maybe I do. I don't ask him to elaborate.

I'm not sure how Christian our friendship is. It's not approved of for members of the opposite sex to be friends. I'm not sure if we are friends, exactly. I don't know what to call what we are.

We're together on another evening, having a drink at a bar. I've told Marc that other people are with us, but they're not. It's still light at closing time, and outside the bar Dieter decides he's hungry. I point him to the kebab shop down the road, where fat spits from rotating skewers. Dieter is suspicious. What is that? he asks. I tell him I think it's lamb. Looks a bit rank, I add.

Rank? Dieter asks. What's rank?

Like minging.

Minging?

Horrible, I say. You'd use 'minging' to describe something you think is pretty vile. 'Rank' is probably the same.

Ah, so it is another Scottish colloquialism.

Yes! I say, exactly.

We move forward in the queue.

Like this too, he says. Queuing is a very Scottish thing.

I guess, I say. Maybe we're just polite.

Or more easily rounded up?

He reaches into his trouser pocket; his hand comes out empty. My wallet, he says, it's gone.

We leave the kebab shop and run back to the pub, but by the time we get there it's locked up for the night.

It's OK, I say, I'll take you back in the morning.

But the next day it's not there. His ID card is gone, his money too. I take him to the police station where they take details from him, and then on to the German Embassy. Afterwards we drive around the city with the music turned up loud. Perhaps that's the moment when our relationship starts to look little less like Christian friendship and a little more like something else.

I am not sure how Christian it is to keep messaging him, or to hide my phone in a drawer so Marc doesn't see it, or to buy a notebook and to start to try to write things down again. I know it's not Christian to think of him all the time, to not be able to concentrate at work or to think of anything other than the next time I'll see him. It's especially not Christian to know I've crossed a line in my mind, and I never want to go back to the other side.

But I don't care.

I AM THAT I AM

July 2007

MARC SAYS I LOOK TIRED. You need a break, he says, I'll take Imogen to my parents' house for the weekend.

I'm surprised he wants to help, but I'm not going to complain. I'm not used to so much time to myself: two days feels like a lot to fill.

It's Friday evening and I call Dieter, who says he's going to the pub with Alex. You should come, he says. Alex used to go out with Ash, and he's been rootless ever since she left the Witnesses. I find it hard being without her too. I looked her up online a few weeks ago, even though I knew I shouldn't. She's still in Edinburgh. I really miss her. I really want to talk to her. It would be so easy to send her a message, even though I mustn't. People say Alex isn't a good association, mainly because he's at art school and it's supposed to be a hot-bed of sin, but I know better, having been to one myself. It's not really that exciting.

We sit drinking Jack and Coke until closing time when the lights flicker on and off to call last orders. Let's buy a bottle, I say, feeling extravagant, and we run across the road to the off-licence. Afterwards, we realise we have nowhere to go. We can't go to mine, because it would look bad to have two unmarried brothers up to the flat, and we can't go back to either of theirs because it would look bad for a married sister to be at a single brother's house. We decide to go to a friend's place. She has a crush on Alex, so she won't grass us up. Nevertheless, she's not amused when we turn up all whisky breath and giggles. We try to bribe her with a drink but she goes to bed annoyed. Don't make a mess, she warns us as she walks off, or do anything stupid.

Just before dawn, Alex falls asleep, his head resting on my shoulder. Dieter watches him. He doesn't say anything. He laughs when Alex sinks into a deeper sleep and his head begins to slip down my arm, before he startles, wakes a little, and lifts it back onto my shoulder. This happens again and again.

Sometimes I worry Dieter knows things I haven't dared to admit to myself. He watches me a lot. I think he knows I'm not happy. But I'm happy when I'm with him, it's just the rest of the time that's the prob-lem. I'm married to Marc though, and I can't not be married to him. I've made my choices in life, now I have to live with them.

Two weeks earlier, I was on holiday in Italy with Marc and Imogen and things were hard. Fourteen days felt like forever in the dust and the heat, which seemed to build every day, along with the air pressure. Every morning I tipped limoncello into my lemonade to help collapse the days into each other. On the worst afternoon, I lay in the hammock in the garden watching the black clouds roll over the horizon as they eddied themselves around the pool, the grass, the cotton, me.

That night, I went to bed in the near-pitch-dark bedroom, the shutters closed to the heat and the moon. I lay there. Eyes open, head blank. Marc came to bed later, full of wine and despair. He sat on the end of the bed and asked if I still loved him. I could see the outline of his back as his voice cracked. Do you? he asked. Just tell me if you don't, he said, I need to know. I said nothing. His shadow moved around the room. The door opened. Closed. Had I ever loved him? I wasn't sure. Had he ever loved me? I didn't want to think. Sometime in the early hours, the weather broke, and thunder cracked and lightning fought its way in through the slats of the shutters. The next morning it was as if none of it had happened.

Rain poured down the guttering, and never left for the rest of the holiday. We stayed in the house, playing old video tapes for Imogen, rewinding the same ones over and over. Life looped.

Now, in the room with Dieter, the Diet Coke runs out. We sit side by side and drink whisky neat, passing the bottle between us. As we talk, he stays facing forward. I like seeing him in profile like that. It makes it easier to talk, even if sometimes I don't remember what was said come morning.

He doesn't always answer immediately. He takes his time when he speaks and says things slowly and deliberately, like he really means them. I like not being rushed. I like having spaces to answer in. I like not having to fill the spaces with sound. I like sitting in his silences.

Outside, the blue lightens to morning. Alex stirs. Sits up. Rubs his eyes. Shit, he says, are we still here? We laugh. The whisky's finished. We need more. Leaving feels like an urgent thing to do.

We spill out into the morning. I shiver from dawn's left-over cold.

Where to? Dieter asks. Come on, I say, striding ahead, up the hill towards the New Town. I have no idea where we are going but it feels imperative that we walk quickly. I stride ahead of the boys. Slow down! they shout but I am nearly running by now. They catch up with me and put their arms around my shoulders, I put mine around their waists and we walk like this for a while up Dundas Street and onto Princes Street where we dart past night buses heading back to the depot.

I don't want them to know my legs are jelly by the time we get to the Mound. I don't slow down. I make it look like I know where I'm going. This side of town is a riddle. I like it. There are no people we know here. This morning, that's important. We need to stay unseen.

On the horizon the sea blinks brighter blue, not Edinburgh blue. I am in the blue of elsewhere. I am not here; I am not me. We walk on and up. I turn around, beckon, Come on, come on. I am still drunk; I am not drunk enough. I turn around: Pub, yeah? I ask. Not open yet, they shout back in unison. On and on. Up and up. My breath comes ragged. Past the Hume statue, the Elephant House. I stumble on glazed cobbles. You OK? Dieter asks as he bends down. I'm fine, I tell him. We reach the park, where mist hovers, grass gleams with dew. I bend down, it's too damp to sit; the haar begins to roll up the hill. I need a coffee, Alex says. Me too, we echo.

Coffee and food feel dangerous. They might bring me back to this city, into the limits of myself. I need something to take the edge off. I am edging off the edge, slowly, precipitously. I would like to stay like this. To be drunk, suspended in time.

Ahead of me now is Dieter, and I watch the back of his neck, caught by the sun. The length of his hair. Still too long. Sun-lightened. The length of his stride. His easy gait. His simple elegance. Something catches in my throat.

Dieter stops outside a cafe. I blink. He beckons me towards him. I am unwinding. His eyes are too blue. I am being wound in. I am. Have I thought this before? Not recently at least. I am. I am. What am I? Thirsty? Hungry? Wife? Mother? What else? What will I be next? Lustful? Sinful? Greedy?

I have been good for so long. And for what? Salve? Salvation? Deliverance? Deliverance from what? Deliver me into whose jaws? The foolish brag of my heart – insistent, pounding, too loud, too fast – it will be the ruin of me, as I always knew it would be.

Bite my tongue. Taste blood. Bitter. Sweet. Bitter. My blood. If it's my blood, can I do what I want with it?

I am a verb to conjugate. Past. Present. Future.

Are you coming? he asks.

He is magnetic north. I feel his pull.

At home, I stand in the shower and watch the water run down my chest, over my stomach and down to my feet. I feel it slip and drip from my sharp edges and I stand with the window thrown wide open to the garden, not caring that Marc says I'm not to do that because someone might see me. But he's not here; I can do just what I want.

Suddenly, I'm not afraid. I only want to feel like this, new and alive, forever.

I step out the shower, rub myself dry with a towel rough from the line. I lie back on the cool cotton covers and fall asleep with the windows wide and my hair still wet. I wake with my teeth chattering to a blinking phone screen. Dieter says he and Alex are going out again tonight and do I want to come. Sure, I text back.

I draw black lines carefully around each eye, deliberately smudging them, and then I find the shortest dress I own, one Marc says needs leggings underneath. I put it on, then pull on black tights and ankle boots. I smile when I realise how normal I look. I don't look like a Witness or a wife or a mother, I just look like anyone else. I don't know how I've pulled off this trick, but I like that I have.

It's midnight in the pub and they're ringing last orders. I don't want to go home. Where next? Dieter says. Alex smiles. Cab Vol, he says. I bite the side of my lip, smile at them.

We can't, I say, it's a club.

I don't get it, Dieter says. In Cologne we go clubbing all the time.

Alright then, I say. Tonight we are in Cologne.

Alex laughs. And what happens in Cologne stays in Cologne, right?

Outside, the fresh air hits me. Standing is difficult. Maybe I've drunk more than I thought.

Alex goes in first, bouncers parting like the Red Sea. Pharaoh in pursuit, they close in on me, and ask to check my bag. Inside are nappies, cartons of formula, a crumpled sleepsuit. Not what they're looking for. They wave me in. Stamp my hand.

Dance. Don't think of death. Bodies pressed. Moving. Holy communion. Don't think. There is just the bass in my chest. Just bodies. Just mouths on mouths. His wet mouth. My tongue. Symmetry. Look at the way we fit. Not here. Hands grab hands. Fingers lace. Back of the club. Booth. Fingers probe. Fabric. Zips. Stubborn buttons. Music moves through us. Kiss. Lick. Bite. We are emptied. I blink. SHIT. Wrong hands, fingers, mouth. Wrong boy.

Alex stands up. Grabs my hand. Says we need to find Dieter.

We find Dieter halfway down the Royal Mile. Alex says he's hungry. Outside the chip shop Dieter and I stand bathed in the glow from a neon leaping fish. I saw you, Dieter says. With Alex. What happened?

I try to think what happened and realise I can't remember the specifics of it. We were on the dance-floor and then we weren't, but what exactly we were doing or did I don't remember.

Will you leave Marc? he says.

I shake my head. Because you can now, Dieter says. Scripturally, I mean.

Something shifts, opens, a small crack of light seems to emerge. The only way I can escape my marriage to Marc, according to the rules of the elders, is to either die or to have sex with someone else.

We didn't, you know, I say.

I know, says Dieter, but you know touching also counts.

I didn't know. But still, standing there in the fresh Edinburgh night that even in July is cold, it seems that surely I can't leave, it would mean too much. Instead I need to keep this indiscretion quiet.

When I get home, I see bags in the hallway, light escaping from under the study door. I check my phone, and see six missed calls.

I tiptoe to the bathroom, scrub my teeth without looking in the mirror, scrub my hands, my face. After-wards I lean against the study door, trying to look sober. Hi, I say, you're home.

Marc does not look up from the computer screen.

I thought you weren't coming back until tomorrow.

It is tomorrow, he says.

You know what I mean, I say. Later.

I just thought you might like to see your little girl, he says.

He asks me where I was, and I tell him I was out.

I can see that, he says. Where?

I tell him where I was and hope that's enough.

You were clubbing?

We just wanted another drink.

Who's we?

Me, Dieter and Alex.

Just you?

Just us.

I see, he says.

I go to bed, but I can't sleep. Later, Marc creeps into the bedroom. I turn over, shut my eyes, tight.

The next morning, rain runs in long sheets down the windows. Imogen bangs her spoon on the table. Eggs boil and the kettle hisses. Marc says he needs to get some air, and takes out his bike, in spite of the weather.

I feel sick, but only because what happened didn't happen with Dieter. I feel like I've cheated on the wrong person. But was it a way to get to him? Was it a way of destroying everything so completely that Dieter became possible rather than impossible? What seemed so impulsive feels less so when I see it like this. What seems like a mistake starts to feel like it might, on some level, have been deliberate, even if I didn't really know it was. Am I more calculating than I think? I don't want to know. I say I want to be in the truth and call myself a servant of Jehovah, and yet everything I do seems to indicate otherwise. Not for the first time I remember how Mum always said actions speak louder than words. I'm just good at drowning out what it is my actions are telling me about myself.

I send a message to Alex: *I need to see you.* I leave Imogen with a friend, promising to be back soon, and we meet in a cafe, where we agree it was a mistake, that we'll never do that again.

Walking home, rain dripping down my neck, I think of the darkness Dieter says is in me. This might be it, leaching its way out until I am all black and black and black and I have stolen everyone else's colour and spun it into my own absence.

Something soon will break.

It's easy enough not to see Alex again. But everything intensifies with Dieter.

When I am not with him I need to be with him; when I am with him I can't think of not being with him. I don't sleep. My eyes become shadows. I don't care. My bones protrude. I don't care. I am lit up. We go for lunch and I pull long strings of melted cheese from between toasted bread, watch the fat drip from it and fold it into my mouth, chew and chew and chew, slurp juice from grilled tomatoes. Oil from olives lies thick and heavy and rich in my mouth. I am licking the salt taste of them from my lips as an elder and his wife walk into the cafe and they smile at us until they realise Marc isn't there. Then they stumble over their words, hurry to their table. Even then, we don't care. We are books and food and walking and drinking and we don't talk about what's happening between us because some things are best left unsaid, unnamed.

Without this maybe I could have gone back to being the dutiful wife; maybe I could have slowed my mind back down again and tried to unthink the things I'd begun to think about God and the religion, now my doubts are beginning to surface properly and become impossible to submerge. But Dieter wakes something in me that I'd tried to put to sleep so long ago by not eating, not wanting.

Now, I am made from hunger. I am raw and starving after years of denial. My appetite should scare me, but it doesn't. I've always known it would take me to dangerous places, I am ready to let it.

Early one Sunday morning, I sit in the bath with the windows open to the garden, the birds singing happily outside. What I'd give to be one of them out there in the fresh air. My head is heavy and dull.

Imogen sits between my legs, pouring bubbles from one cup to another. I play with her hair, stretching her damp curls all the way down her back. I didn't notice them get so long. She chatters away.

I am trying to piece last night together. Something went wrong, but I can't remember what.

When I woke earlier, I was still fully clothed, on top of the covers. The blind was open, and the sun was streaming in, but when I checked the time it wasn't yet seven. I rolled over to see if Marc was still sleeping, but he wasn't there.

Imogen wasn't making a sound. It was late for her to be still asleep. I lay trying to decide if I should check on her or not. If I checked on her, I ran the risk of waking her, but if I didn't check then she might be dead. Any time she slept in I had this same conundrum.

I padded down the hallway to the sitting room and pushed the door open. The blinds were shut. I could hear Marc snoring on the sofa, his breath rhythmic and deep. Certain things started to come back. I had been drinking, drinking too much, at a Witness barbecue. I began to remember a flowerbed and maybe even throwing up in it, the taste was lingering somewhere along the ridges of my molars. I remembered Marc finding me there and being bundled into a taxi. When we reached home, the taxi driver helped me from the car, asking if I was OK. I remembered the final click of the heavy front door and after that, nothing. Time stopped. It starts again with Marc lying on the sofa.

I didn't want to wake Marc. I ran a bath instead. I thought a drink might work. Hair of the dog. No one mentions my drinking. Not to me at least. Marc says people have spoken to him about it. About how sinful and wayward I'm becoming. No one asks why I do it. No one asks if I'm OK. All anyone's interested in is how bad someone else is being.

I wake Imogen, take her into the bath with me. As I balance my glass on the edge of the tub the ice clinks against the glass and the bubbles burst to the surface, the sun cutting through the crystal, projecting rainbows onto the far wall. Imogen says, Pretty noise, and I laugh, clinking them together again for her. We stay like that for a long time, until I hear the heavy sound of Marc moving around followed by the steady hum of him hoovering. Quickly, I'm out the bath. I rub myself dry, tip the rest of the gin down the sink and clean my teeth roughly. I lift Imogen out and wrap her up like a sausage roll, the top of her head peering up out the towel.

I carry her into the sitting room where the blinds are open, sunlight spilling into the room, picking out the shine on the wide floorboards. Marc is sitting on the sofa with a coffee in his hand. He smiles when we go in and says, I think I'll get a Sunday paper. He doesn't say anything about last night. He doesn't say anything about the meeting, it's just clear we aren't going to the Kingdom Hall today. He doesn't say anything about not sleeping in our bed.

I sit down, tucking my feet under me, and flick the TV on to find cartoons. Imogen settles herself on her little cane chair, dangerously close for her eyesight but I'm too busy trying to remember what happened last night to move her away.

I hear the front door close behind Marc and I settle back against the sofa. I try and try, but I can't remember a thing. Nothing is clear, just being sick and arriving home and that's it. Something must have happened to make Marc sleep on the sofa. The memory I'm missing holds the key to it, but I can't make it come back. There's only a blank that becomes static the more I try to see into it.

Did I tell him about Alex? Surely not. If I had, I'd know about it. Did I tell him about Dieter? Did I tell him about my doubts? Did I tell him how unhappy I've been for years? Did I tell him what a terrible wife I am, how the harder I try to be submissive the worse I am at it? What the hell happened? What the fuck did I do or not do? My head hurts. The pain creeps across the front of my forehead, and I rub my fingers over the frown lines there. I want to know and do not want to know and I also know there is no way really of knowing for sure. There is only sitting here, with the light burning the back of my hung-over eyes, and realising that I am quite, quite mad, as mad as everyone has always said I am.

Marc comes back, puts the paper on the coffee table and smiles at me. I know he won't fill in the blanks for me – why should he? It is my fault I can't remember. When he tells me I am not well, I know he's right. All these blanks, all this insanity, all of my own devising.

Two weeks later, on a Wednesday after Imogen's dance class, I do something I really shouldn't. The whole summer's been so full of things I shouldn't do that one extra thing doesn't seem like that much. I send

Ash a message asking how she is. She replies immediately. We arrange to meet in the back room of a vegan art cafe. I've been a few times, but when I took Marc he looked around at it and asked if I thought maybe there might ... you know ... be demons here? Then he refused to eat any of the 'weird' food. I like it. And it's safe. No one can see in. As Imogen sleeps Ash and I talk and talk and talk and it's as if she's never been away. I tell her everything. It just comes out, and afterwards, as we hug and promise to keep in touch and I walk home, I am lighter than I've felt in years.

At home, I pull the buggy up the shallow stone steps in front of the flat, and turning round as I put the key in the lock I realise that soon, all this will be gone. I just know. Soon Dieter will be back in Germany, his visit come to its end, and Marc will find out what's happened with Alex, he'll decide something's happened with Dieter too, I'll try to tell him nothing has, when really, what's worse? To cheat physically or emotionally? Marc decides we need to move, and finds us a new flat in Edinburgh's Southside. I'm trying not to think about. I just want it all to be over.

August 2007

The day it breaks is the same as all the days. You think it will come with drums and trumpets, that the skies will go dark. But it's not like that.

The city is bursting with tourists; it's the festival and they bring a new energy to the place. That combined with the heat makes me feel more alive, like I want to take risks. It's evening, we are at a party.

It is a stretch to call it a party. The flat is tiny, with the furniture against the walls, and people are dancing in the front room. The music is up loud, and everyone's keeping an eye on how many drinks everyone else is having.

It's a party for all the young ones in the congregation. I'm in the kitchen so I don't have to watch people dance, and so I can be close to the alcohol.

Earlier, in the sitting room people sat in stiff, hard-backed chairs lining the walls, swapping encouraging stories of people they'd met on the ministry and scriptures they'd found useful recently. Then the elders left and people began to dance awkwardly under the bright overhead light.

Alex and I are telling Dieter that whatever happened between the two of us was just a silly mistake, and he's listening intently, too intently to notice Marc, who coughs so we know he's there. The three of us look at him as he swings his body towards Alex, but Alex is small and quick and darts out the kitchen and down the spiral stone close and out into the twilight. Marc clatters after him. I look at Dieter and he folds his arms around me, telling the top of my head that it's OK, everything will be OK, and then, taking my hand, we follow Marc and Alex down the stairs.

What was I thinking that I started the conversation about what happened? How stupid am I? How desperate am I for Marc to find out, and set me free?

On the street, Marc has Alex's shirt collar in his hand. Dieter walks in the other direction, away into the night.

Startled by the commotion, other brothers and sisters arrive on the pavement, eager to know what's happening. At the sight of them, Marc lets go of Alex, tells me we're going home and takes my elbow. He steers me up the street. I don't want to go, but there is no alternative.

I know this is the end of the end.

I lie awake next to Marc as he snores. The laminate floor is cold under my feet as I make my way into the sitting room, my heart beating so fast I'm sure this time it will escape my chest. I sit, wrapped tightly in a blanket, and wait for the tears to come and the remorse to hit. But nothing happens. Eventually my heart slows. I feel calm. There is certainty now. There is a knowing for sure that soon all this will be gone. A lot to lose, Dieter said. But I didn't think of what I might gain.

I wait for morning. When it comes it fills the room slowly with its first soft light, the pink, red, orange flitting across the cold walls. I open the blinds to let it in.

I hear Marc's heavy feet, then splashes as he ablutes himself in the bathroom. Does he pray for absolution I wonder, or does he only say all his prayers aloud for everyone else to hear? Does he still carry his doubts around with him? Does he hope his outward shows of piety are redemption enough for him? I know how it goes, it's not like I've not been doing the same.

His wet feet flip-flop into the sitting room. I don't look up. He sits down, clears his throat. I keep looking forward.

We need to collect Imogen, he says.

I nod. I'll go, I say.

I hardly think my parents will want to see you, now they know what you've done to me.

He has called them, told them everything. He has told the elders too. He tells me he wants to get the ball rolling. We'll be seeing them soon.

I nod again. I'm not exactly sure what he means.

I don't want to go alone, he says, I'm not ready to start doing things alone. Get ready, we'll take the train. I'm still over the limit.

On the train he says how much he'd miss me; that he's thinking he might forgive me. I want to run away. I want to puke. I'm not really sure what to do about you, he says. Hopefully the elders will help me with my decision. After the stress of the move is over, they'll come to talk to us.

We arrive at the station. Imogen reaches her arms out to me, but Marc takes her. She screams and kicks. Mummy, Mummy, she wails, but he holds her tight. His father stays in the car. His mother hugs him, making a point of not looking at me. On the train Imogen wriggles free of his arms and crawls across the table to me. She sits on my knee, cuddling in tight as she eyes her daddy balefully across the table.

That week, I pack our life into boxes to move to the new flat across town. Better schools here, Marc said, and I nodded. I keep my books, my CDs, all my things, all separate from Marc's things, just in case. Then I tape them up with brown parcel tape that squeaks as I try to get it off the roll. It's cheap and doesn't keep the lids down. I hear it in the night, making a high-pitched squealing sound as the boxes come unstuck.

HERE I AM

LIGHT BECOMES TOO BRIGHT

THE SATURDAY BEFORE DIETER GOES back to Germany, Marc and I move to the new flat in the Southside. It's where the rich people live. It heaves with yummy mummies wearing skinny jeans, striped T-shirts and ballet pumps. I'm not sure I'll like it.

Dieter and I spend every moment we can together, knowing our time is running out. We're not in a relationship and we're not not. We just are. Neither of us have seen Alex since the night of the party. Sometimes Dieter makes jokes about what happened; my desperate escape bid, he calls it and I laugh, because it's both funny and not funny, like everything seems to be this summer.

We walk a lot. One evening as the sun sets softly in the west, bouncing off the Edinburgh sandstone, he tells me as he looks down at the pavement, his sunglasses obscuring his eyes, that his mother has never told him she loves him. Not even once? I say. He shakes his head. Never. Is that why he's such a puzzle to me? Something I'm trying to work out.

I think about when Mum visited recently to help me pack up the old flat. She sat back on her heels, surrounded by bubble wrap, and asked me if I loved Dieter. He'd been there when she'd arrived and she'd sensed something, like mums do. I'd nodded and she'd smiled and some sort of understanding seemed to pass between us then. It felt like a strange time for acceptance. I want to tell Dieter how I feel, but I don't know how to say it. I don't want to sound like an idiot so I just nod when he tells me about his mum and don't offer anything in return.

I know there's a difference between telling someone you love them and showing them. Mum told me she loved me all the time, but it feels like a precarious love, hinging on me also expressing love for Jehovah. How messed up it all is, none of us really understand what it means to love or to be loved.

Dieter leaves on a Friday. I drive him to the airport. Marc took the car keys to work, by mistake he said, and I had to traipse across town to get them from his office. He had forgotten, he said. He had also forgotten to tell me the elders are coming over tonight . I try not to think about this as I set out for the airport.

We drive at speed, with the music loud and the windows rolled down. The words of the Walkmen's 'The Rat' blare through the speakers: 'When I used to go out I would know everyone that I saw. Now I go out alone if I go out at all.' Dieter turns it up. That'll be you soon, he says. No shit, I say. We both laugh. It helps to try to see the funny side, though it's not really funny.

At the terminal, he writes his German phone number for me on a napkin, with his name at the top. In case you forget it's mine, he says with a grin, as if I could. And then he slings his backpack over his shoulders and walks towards the departures gate and I bite the soft flesh on the inside of my bottom lip. Imogen waves at him, as he turns around and raises his hand in one final salute, and is gone.

A SHREWD PERSON ACCEPTS CORRECTION

As I wait for the elders to arrive, I swing my legs back and forward and work my shoe on and off. I can't stay still. I walk round the sitting room, running my finger over the top of the furniture to check everything shines and sparkles for them. There's no dust to be seen, each wooden cube either side of the fireplace is neat and clean, all the books carefully arranged by subject and height. I've made sure none of them are books the elders could disapprove of, the others are hidden under my bed. From over the mantelpiece Marc's favourite red painting leers. I hope they forget to come. I feel so sick. I just want it over with. Naturally, they haven't told me what to expect.

I prayed earlier. Part of me thinks it's a useless endeavour. The other part of me is too scared to risk it. If He's real and I don't pray to Him, then I'm screwed. If He's real and I pray to Him, then I'm hedging my bets. If He's not real, then praying is at least a sort of a way of working something out. It's beginning to feel as if serving Jehovah isn't really the choice I thought it was. I don't have anything outside of the religion. And the religion feels like an uncertain thing: my membership of it is now provisional, and about to be decided by three men who I don't properly know. There isn't a choice in that either.

After I dropped Imogen off with friends earlier, I washed and put on a clean skirt. I'm sure it sits lower on my hips than it did the last time I wore it. I like the coolness of the silk against my skin, although Marc says it's immodest because the light shines through it.

I go for a walk around the block, my lungs struggling for air when I think about what's going to happen next; I tell Jehovah I'm sorry for everything I've done. I hope he's listening but not too hard. From an open window, I hear the sound of a piano; whoever's playing falters and starts the piece from the beginning, only to stumble again in the same spot. I lean against the stone wall opposite the window, hoping the overhanging bushes, their leaves turning to russet already and pockmarked with berries, will hide me a little. The piano player repeats the section, but still makes the same mistake, over and over. There's something soothing about these repetitions. I would stay if I could, but I can't. Instead I go back to the flat, where Marc brushes the stone's chalky dust from the back of my blouse. You're a mess, he says.

They knock on the door and I jump, even though

I know they're coming. I open it and smile at the three elders on the doorstep, welcoming them.

Brother Ardman comes in first; as he passes me, he stretches his damp hand to take mine. He grips it limply as he shakes it up and down; it seems like forever until he lets my hand slip from his. As he bends to take off his shoes, I wipe the sweat from his hand onto my skirt.

Brother Gillespie and Brother Heikkinen decide to leave their shoes on. I gesture them to go into the sitting room and in they go. They are sitting on dining-room chairs, laid out in a row to face the sofa, with their suits and ties on when Marc comes into the room. He is wearing a clean shirt I starched for him earlier, his thinning hair plastered to the side of his head and his cheeks pink from his second shower of the day. He shakes each of their hands in turn. I notice that Brother Gillespie has brought some mud in with him. It's a tiny patch, which has settled just in front of his feet, but as I look at it, it seems to grow and grow. I want to hoover it up immediately. To stop myself thinking about the mud, I look at my hands crossed in my lap. I sit like that, hoping I look repentant; I know they are looking at me, I can feel their eyes on my skin. I don't want to look up, but when I do, I see Brother Heikkinen with one eye squinting in the opposite direction, so I'm not sure if he is looking wholly at me or maybe is interested in the people walking past the window. He takes a folded handkerchief from his lapel pocket and dabs at his watery eye before folding it and putting it back, limply, where it was.

The three of them remind me of the foxes I saw early this morning. I went for a run to try to shake off all the adrenaline. I was running along a wide tree-lined street, filled with detached houses full of sleeping bankers and lawyers, when suddenly shadows began to move, coalescing first into the body of a young fox then separating into two others. As the three of them stood staring at me, spanning the road, I worried they wanted to eat me or perhaps ask me to join them. I turned and ran back to the flat with the rumble of a rubbish truck coming from the main road, and further away the sound of sirens. I love being outside as the city wakes.

Brother Ardman clears his throat. I decide that someone needs to say something, and no one is saying anything, so in a voice too bright and too shrill I ask if anyone would like some cake.

No, thank you. We are not here for cake, Brother Ardman says, making it clear that he'll be the one to do the speaking for them, in the same way he speaks on behalf of the whole congregation. Would you like to tell me why we're here, he says.

I swallow. I can't tell them I'm not exactly sure why they *are* here. Marc said it would be a good idea to ask them up – a clean slate, he'd called it, to tell them about what happened before we were married. It has been on his mind, he explains. It would be good for both of us, he said. I don't know if he's told them about Alex and Dieter. I don't know what they will ask me. Now here I am, being asked to tell them why they're there. It feels like a game I don't know the rules to. I look out the window until Brother Ardman clears his throat again. Let us pray for Jehovah's guidance, he says.

We all bow our heads in prayer. How strange we must look to everyone walking by, how odd they must think we are with our bowed heads and our folded hands, and them, sitting in a row, facing me.

Dear Jehovah, Brother Ardman says, we pray that you can give us your guidance and blessing as we are gathered here together. We pray that you can listen to our dear sister and that you can discern her heart condition. We pray that you can soothe her husband and give him the comfort he so sorely needs. We pray that you can extend your love to all those in your care who err and sin. We bear in mind we are only men sent to do your will, and we pray that we do your will this evening. In Jesus's name, amen.

Listening to this, my head feels full of static. Knowing that the supreme being in the universe is being asked to be present here in this room is too much. I can't comprehend it.

The sound of our amens echoes around the room.

Now, please tell us why we're here, Brother Ardman says again, leaning forward and resting his elbow on his knee. It would be good if you could make it clear to all of us what you would like to talk about.

Brother Heikkinen uncrosses his legs before crossing them back the opposite way. He's never liked me much.

I'm not too sure how to begin, I say, and turn to Marc. Would you like to go first?

Brother Ardman frowns. This is clearly not what he was hoping for. No, he says, we need you to go first. Thank you.

Outside the sun begins to set. I wish I was out there with the people on the pavement and the birds singing dusk. Marc shifts around at the far end of the sofa, but he doesn't say anything. He coughs gently but stays quiet.

Silence becomes the sixth person in the room.

We did some things before we were married, I say at last, some things we shouldn't have.

Heavy petting, Marc says. I'd call it heavy petting. I wanted to confess, he continues, it's been such a heavy burden to live with. I can't keep it to myself any longer.

He looks over to me, and I think I can see the triumph in his eyes.

I felt terrible, I hear him say, but then his voice seems to drift further away. I tell myself not to think of Dieter, I can't let myself wonder what he'll be doing or who he'll be doing it with or how it'll be too late with the time difference to text him after this is over.

I watch as Brother Ardman hands my husband a tissue. I know it's hard, he says softly, and we really admire you for telling us this. Your bravery is to be commended. Is there anything else you'd like to say?

Well, Marc says, on a roll now, there was this time once in Spain before I was married. He laughs, high-pitched. Lads' holiday, he adds.

I sit forward and look at him. I didn't know about this.

I'd had too much to drink, but I was young, he says. Only twenty or twenty-one, and she was local and drunk. She seduced me. I know there are no excuses.

I remember the way he quizzed me before we got married. I never let slip about any of the other boys.

That's fine, Brother Gillespie says. It was a long time ago and you were young.

I think about Simon and the boys from school and wonder if their reaction would be the same if I told the elders about them. I wonder what they'd say if I confessed about them.

How about you? Brother Ardman says, turning to me. How did you feel during the things you did?

I'm not sure I understand, I say.

What I mean is how did you feel physically during the things you did? he says. Did you enjoy it? Did you get pleasure from it?

I don't want to answer. I suppose so, I say, it was OK.

Right, thank you, he says, and then, detective-like, he begins to take notes in his notebook, even though he didn't write anything down the whole time Marc was talking. I notice he was never asked about his 'pleasure'.

Just when I think they might be finished, Brother Heikkinen frowns and takes up the baton. Where were his hands, he asks?

I swallow. They were . . . they were . . . I lick my lips and worry my voice will crack. They were in my pants, I say.

Pants, Brother Heikkinen says. And by pants do you mean trousers or underwear?

Underwear, I say quickly.

And your hands, he says, where were they?

They were in his underwear, I say.

What were they doing there? Brother Heikkinen asks.

I was touching his penis, I say.

Now it's Brother Heikkinen's turn to take notes, and he sits nodding as he does so, as if he's suddenly pieced something together. I'm not sure if I've given the right response; I'm pretty sure right now there are no right answers.

My chest feels heavy. I already felt like a weight was on it, but it's getting heavier, crushing me now. Dark creeps into the sharp edges of the room. I ask if they would like a lamp on. Just put on the overhead light, please, says Brother Ardman. I get up and have to walk past Marc to get to the switch. His face is so red. He doesn't look back at me, instead he just sits staring straight ahead at the fireplace, as if the painted Delft tiles hold his interest more than the conversation does.

Brother Gillespie, do you have anything to add? asks Brother Heikkinen.

Yes, there are a few gaps I'd like you to fill in for me.

I nod. OK, I say.

I'd like to know how pleasurable you found it, on a scale of one to five, he says.

I don't know what to say. Too much pleasure and they'll hang me for it, too little and Marc will hang me for it. I go for the middle, knowing I can't win.

Three, I say, let's call it a three.

Right, Brother Gillespie says. Good, thank you.

He looks less comfortable than the other two do, when he talks to me, he looks at his knees, not my eyes.

How much did you try to persuade him to do it again, he asks.

I think how it wasn't me who did the persuading. Not that they will believe me.

I don't know, I say, maybe once or twice.

And did he give in to you? Brother Gillespie says.

Oh, no, I say, no, he stood quite firm in his resolve.

Well, thank you, says Brother Gillespie. He doesn't take any notes but the other two are still writing it all down.

Brother Ardman looks up. How did the guilt affect you? he asks.

It made me lose a lot of weight, I say quickly. I think it was that that made my anorexia come back. I think the guilt was eating away at me.

I am learning to play the game.

Of course, Brother Ardman says, yes.

It doesn't occur to me that this is an imposition, or that I don't need to answer their questions; to me this is part of a God-ordained process and Jehovah is peering into me as I answer, searching my heart.

I hope God doesn't see what I thought earlier, when I drove to Mum's house after dropping Dieter at the airport. I wanted to see her one last time in case the elders decided to disfellowship me tonight, in case I can never see her again, whether I want to or not. Traffic was down to one lane on the bridge, the smell of bitumen coming in the open window as Imogen slept in the back. I turned the music up to drown out her snores and inched the car forward, hoping it wouldn't overheat. Through the sides of the bridge, I could see the Firth of Forth far below. As I watched the grey water, I thought how comforting it would be if there was no God, no devil, no grand plan, no eternity of Witnesses and Marc's round face. For as long as it took to cross the bridge, I let myself wonder how it would feel to book tickets to Cologne and to tell Dieter how much I need him and his ideas and the books he reads. I let myself think how it could be if we both left and made a new life for ourselves. And then I put the thought away. I can't leave.

At Mum's, her husband took Imogen upstairs to his studio to paint as I told her what I'd done. I was terrified about all the things she might say, but she didn't say any of them, she just told me I'd not been myself for years, and this summer she'd seen glimpses of me coming back. She didn't say that what I'd done was acceptable, but she didn't say it was wrong either. I was relieved after I told her. I didn't tell her about the elders' imminent visit. I was too embarrassed to tell her they were having a judicial committee for me. That was too humiliating, and perhaps it would be a step too far for her.

I sit in front of them and tell myself I must try harder to be pure. I must try harder to push these thoughts away. I must accept this loving discipline.

Well, thank you for this, says Brother Ardman. I think we've covered everything about you and your husband. Let's move on, he says, to the next part. I know you have more you need to tell us. Your husband has already spoken to me, but I need to hear it from you.

I don't know what Marc has told them.

I kissed another brother, I say. We didn't mean to, but we did.

I look at my husband at the end of the sofa, his red face glowing.

Would it be possible for him to leave the room? I say. It's not really fair for him to have to listen.

Brother Ardman shakes his head. He's your husband, he says, and as the head of the family he needs to be here. It's his right to listen; please continue.

My lips begin to tingle, and I worry I'm suffocating. Through the open window I can hear people laughing.

It's like I said, I say, we were in a club, we were on the dancefloor and then, well. I shrug, hoping that will say enough.

Ah, says Brother Heikkinen, suddenly alert, a club. And did you pay to get in?

I nod. Yes, we paid, I say. I know this will get me in more trouble.

He makes more notes, his hand passing over the page faster and faster, as if possessed.

Let's get back to the matter in hand, Brother Ardman says. We need the mechanics of what happened. So, you kissed another brother. Can you tell us who it was, please?

It was Alex, I say. It was only once.

We aren't really concerned with how many times, Brother Ardman says. We need to know what happened and how much you enjoyed it.

I think I'm going to fall over, even though I'm sitting down. The hairs on the backs of my arms begin to rise, and I rub them as the elders run through all the questions from before, but it is worse this time. They ask where his hands were and for how long, and I try to say I'm not exactly sure of the specifics of what happened, but it's clear that Marc's spoken to them already and that they have an idea they're attached to. There is no way I can explain that it's hazy and difficult to remember without sounding like I'm trying to get off the hook. There isn't anything I can do to absolve myself. This is the only way out of my marriage, to confess to something I'm not sure about. I can't tell them how unhappy I've been for years, they wouldn't see that as reason enough to leave, and so this all has to be my fault and mine only.

As they're asking questions, I can see Marc out of the corner of my eye. It's impossible not to be worried about what might happen after they leave. I thought confession was supposed to make you feel better. Lighter. Absolved. All I feel is incriminated. Judged. Degraded. I know this is all I deserve to feel. This is divine justice. I'm meant to swallow their judgement whole.

I keep my eyes fixed on the elders. I try to forget Marc's there, but his presence is too large, his anger is too big.

And have you and your husband had sex since you told him? Brother Ardman asks.

No, I say, no, we haven't.

My husband clenches his fists. I sit back. I hope they're finished.

We also need to talk about Dieter, Brother Ardman says. What happened with him?

We were just friends, I say. My voice catches and turns ragged at the back of my throat.

How am I am supposed to reduce any of the complexity of the summer into simple answers for these prying men, desperate for titbits they can recycle later when their wives are sleeping and they're so deeply ashamed to be grunting into toilet paper.

I hardly even know what happened between us, but if I tried to tell them they might think it was a worse betrayal of vows. They don't know how easy it is to fuck someone, how much harder it is not to. They don't know how Dieter made me write after years of blank pages. I will not tell them how he's made me wake up and how hungry he's made me for a different life. I will not tell them how, now he's gone, I don't want the life I had before him. I will not tell them I can't go back; I will never be who I was before. That life is over. None of their questions are designed to help me explain this. They aren't really here to listen, only to judge. They have reduced me to physical sensations only.

We were just friends, I repeat. They look confused. Disappointed, almost.

Are you sure? Brother Gillespie asks. I saw you together often.

Marc sits forward. I know he thinks there has to be more.

Yes, I'm sure, I say.

You don't have to protect him, Brother Gillespie says.

I'm not, I say, there's nothing to tell.

Let's get this clear, Brother Ardman says, if more evidence comes to light regarding you and him, then we will have to come back and go through the same process again. It would be far better for you if you told us everything now.

I have, I say, I've told you, he's my friend. There's nothing more to it.

If you're sure, says Brother Ardman, sighing, then we will just have to take your word for it. Please remember Jehovah is watching.

I know, I say.

If you could leave the room now, Brother Ardman says, we need to talk to your husband.

In the kitchen the strip light above me vibrates, emitting a tiny, low hum. A fly hovers around the light's plastic casing before finding a way in. Once inside, it beats its wings faster and faster, until I can hear them above the sound of the light. The noise becomes frantic, rising to a higher and higher pitch until suddenly its wings stop beating.

I get up and turn the light off.

Finally, Marc comes in, flicking the light back on as he does. I see the dead fly inside. I ask him what's been said, but he won't tell me. They're still debating me. We sit at the table until Brother Ardman comes and says my husband can go back into the sitting room. It's after 10pm.

My eyes are heavy, and the black-and-white Habitat clock behind me loudly ticks each minute away. I'll be sure to give that to Marc when he leaves. It's a wedding present I never liked. Design classic he called it; tacky, I wanted to say. I rest my forehead on the white Formica table, hoping the cold of it will keep me awake. Just after 11pm, my husband comes back in. Come on, he says, they need you now. They've made their minds up about you.

His face is blank, I can't tell which way things have gone.

The elders watch me as I come into the room and they watch even more closely as I sit down.

Let us pray again, Brother Ardman says.

We bow our heads, all of us lit up for the neighbours in the house opposite to see. I wish I had drawn the curtains.

Dear Jehovah, Brother Ardman begins, we pray now for your divine guidance and blessing to determine our sister's guilt and repentance from her sins. We pray that you guide us to arrive at the right decision and we pray that our sister will accept your loving discipline and that she can see it as the blessing it is. In Jesus's name, amen.

I look up.

Have you repented of your sins? Brother Gillespie asks.

Yes, I say, yes, I'm very sorry.

I sound like I'm seven and have been caught stealing sweets from the newsagent.

Brother Heikkinen wipes his eye again and, tired of folding his handkerchief, stuffs it into his pocket. One of his eyes looks at me, the other at Brother Ardman. What exactly are you repenting of? he says.

I know this is a trick question, just as I know everything hinges on my answer. I'm sorry I hurt my husband, I say, but I'm sorrier that I brought reproach on Jehovah's name.

I hope I've remembered it correctly: God above everyone else.

And what works do you plan to do to show your repentance? Brother Ardman asks.

I'll listen to Jehovah's instruction. I'll study more, I

say in a rush, trying to remember what else I should do. I'll focus on re-establishing my relationship with Jehovah. And of course, I'll listen to your instruction too, I add.

Brother Ardman's face remains impassive, then he frowns as he tells me dryly that it hurts Jehovah's heart to see a marriage fail. He catches me unawares when he asks if I'm prepared to make mine work.

I didn't expect this. I feel as if their hands are round my neck. I feel as if I'm submerged and am drowning. I feel as if the water is not water, but steel, and not steel but concrete blocks in my lungs, pulling and keeping me under. How can I tell them how scared I am of my unhappiness and what it might make me do to myself? How can I tell them how for years and years I've been made to feel smaller and smaller and less and less significant, until this summer, when I met Dieter? And that he was willing to see me, and not some manufactured, desirable version of a woman? I can't say any of that because that's not what they're here for – there's no way to escape from any of this other than to do what I might or might not have done with Alex, and if I don't get out of this, I don't know who I'll become. I know I can't live with Marc anymore. I know I can't keep raising Imogen in this damaging religion. And yet. I don't know how to escape from either without losing everything. I am trapped. I want to be sick.

Now Dieter is gone, all my life will be ministry, meetings, prayer, endless rounds of Christian association. I don't want it but I don't know what I'm supposed to do without all of it. How am I supposed to think about building anything new when leaving would mean losing everything? How does anyone begin a life all over again, from nothing?

I say, Yes, I'll try to make my marriage work.

Actually, Brother Ardman says, after a protracted pause, it's up to your husband to decide what happens next. It's not your decision to make.

I feel like I've been tricked. I'm too tired to work out how, I'm too scared to think they might be playing games, I'm too blind to see that, power-drunk, they might even be enjoying themselves.

We've reached a decision, Brother Heikkinen says. I'm sure you'd like to hear it.

I swallow. I nod.

It's not been an easy evening, Brother Ardman says. It's been hard for us to listen to all the details of your transgressions. We're still not sure we've got to the bottom of what happened between you and Dieter, but we'll have to leave that for another time. We've decided you're allowed to remain as one of Jehovah's Witnesses, although it was a close call. I think it's important for you to know it wasn't a unanimous decision.

I keep my eyes fixed on the floor. It hardly feels like Jehovah's judgment if it's not unanimous. Surely someone's channel was blocked, or one of them interpreted something wrongly?

There are caveats, he continues. You can't answer at meetings, and we think it's best if you sit at the back of the Kingdom Hall to limit your association with everyone else. The outcome would have been different, I'm sure, if it weren't for your husband here explaining about your fragile state of mind.

It begins to rain outside. I can hear it hitting the pavement with such a ferocity that it bounces back up. It has that baked summer smell to it. Some pressure begins to lift.

I nod and agree to everything as they pack their notebooks into their briefcases and stretch out their legs, stiff from the hours of sitting. I realise how close to the edge I was and how lucky I am to have been pulled back. In this moment, I truly believe, whatever I have thought before. It doesn't feel like the most loving organisation on earth, but it's all I've got. I need to make myself turn away from the cracks that are beginning to show, I need to make my faith stronger, I need to try harder to sustain this belief. I need to do this so I don't lose everything.

They shake Marc's hand and tell him they are so, so sorry. In the hall Brother Ardman kneels to tie his shoelaces and looks up at me as he does so. He doesn't smile, he doesn't frown. He just stares and I look at him, thinking of all the things he now knows about me.

Finally, they're gone. I'm going to stay with a friend, Marc says, barely looking at me. He leaves quickly. I shut the door, and then I sit on the floor until I'm cold from the hard hallway tiles. I'd rather be here than in the sitting room, with the three chairs still all laid out in a row.

3. DELIVERANCE
AND EXILE

'An alien resident I have come to be in a foreign land.'

Exodus 2 v 22

THE RED SEA

2008

Time has lost its meaning now it's only me and Imogen and our own way of doing things. The days take on strange new shapes. As the months passed we found our own rhythm. I still push her buggy across town to the Kingdom Hall when I have to – just often enough that they don't ask why I'm not there – but I don't like to.

As winter falls, we play in the park until it gets dark and the big lamp in the middle of the park comes on, lighting us up as we seesaw up and down. Her laugh cuts through the sound of cars and buses on the road next to us, and when she shouts she's going to the moon, we both throw our heads back and laugh. We sing our 'going to the moon' song and suddenly, it's everything I imagined it could be. I've done it, even if

I'm not sure exactly what I've done or what comes next or how the hell I get us there, but fuck it, we're going to the moon. I feel the hot prick of tears at the back of my eyes as she sings her song over and over and complete unfettered joy spills from her, her tiny curls bounce golden in the sodium-lit park. I am alive and whatever comes and whatever I've been through, she is here with me. Somehow, I'll keep her safe from everything else.

I try not to think about the things that led to us being here. They are still too much. The Sunday after the elders left, Marc phoned to tell me I needed to come to the meeting. When I arrived he smiled at me. Extra-special talk today, he said. I sat there, in the sweating, stifling heat of the Kingdom Hall, as Brother Ardman stood on the platform and warned the whole congregation about me in a public talk. He didn't name me, but he made it pretty clear what had happened and who'd done what to who. He told the congregation – my friends and some strangers – that they could decide if they wanted to associate with this errant sister or not. Afterwards, everyone lined up and shook Marc's hand, gave him hugs. No one said anything to me. Then, outside the butcher's shop with the line snaking itself around the corner of the block, Marc told me he was done with me.

He took my phone and used it to call Dieter, telling him he'd tell his elders about what happened. I knew he had every right to do that according to our religion's rules; I was still his wife, the house was still his, my phone still something he was allowed to look through. When he threatened to take Imogen I knew I had no right to expect to have the majority of access to her. I believed everything I thought I owned was really his, my freedom just a worldly idea I was too attached to.

After six months, Dieter emailed me to say he was afraid of Marc and that what had happened between us was wrong. Even though he had a point, it hurt. Still hurts.

Our afternoons in the park are hard-won. It makes me like them even more.

Let's get chips as a special treat, I say. In the glass-fronted chip shop with the blue illuminated fish stranded in the window, I lift her up and let her feel the warm steel countertop. She keeps her hands there to heat them up, watching as the woman behind it heaps sizzling, fat-laden potatoes into the paper container. Ketchup? the woman asks, and Imogen lisps back, Yeth, pleath. She clutches her chip poke as she sits in the buggy on the way home, amazed by her tiny wooden fork. I wish things could stay like this.

But in these long days, the tiredness that's always lurked around my ragged edges gets bigger, more awful and powerful than I knew tiredness could be. Some mornings I'm too tired to take Imogen to nursery; instead we spend the day watching Disney films. I can't concentrate. I try to focus on underlining the right paragraphs in the publications for when Brother Gillespie's wife comes to study with me.

Trying to save me, I suppose. I try to behave when I'm on nights out with the few sisters who still talk to me, but I want to escape. I want to be like the other people, the ones on the outside.

I email Ash about it all. I wake up to messages from her most days, as she's in Australia now, so she sends them overnight. We are trying to figure out our new lives through each other somehow.

Mum's been so good too since it all happened, and our relationship, so difficult when Marc was around, now seems fresher. I don't want to lose her again. It's as though when I was with Marc she went away for a while, and now she's back. Marc phoned her to tell her I was always getting drunk and flirting with every man I saw. She thought it was funny, especially the part when he said I was rolling around in the gutter. Straight out of Oscar Wilde, she said, very desperate. She told him she already knew, but he told her my version of events wasn't exactly the truth, before he elaborated further, telling her I tried to sleep with anyone who'd have me. Still, there are limits. She remains devoted to her faith. I know I'll lose her if I leave. So I must stay too: I can't doubt the organisation and keep her.

I often think about God. I think about how we are told that the organisation is evidence of His love. But it doesn't feel loving to me. It feels harsh and cold, domineering. I try not to think this, just like I try not to think of the sign I saw on the back of a public toilet door once that said DOMESTIC ABUSE: THERE'S NO EXCUSE, and then went on to list a lot of things that felt familiar. Things the elders had told me were meant to happen in a relationship. Everything I've been taught about love my whole life has been warped and twisted.

This is why I like the days in the park. They are easier than thinking these things. It's easier to play with Imogen and to pretend the rest of the world doesn't exist.

One day, there is a crash on the doormat. A brochure full of evening classes. We were always warned that our spare time was to be devoted to Jehovah, and evening classes were an unnecessary distraction. Although, now I think of it, they didn't mind us going to the gym. Maybe it was thinking there was a problem with. Creative writing is one of the classes on offer. I've been writing constantly ever since Dieter. To begin with I wrote emails to him, and then after Marc voiced his objections, I wrote in a notebook every time I missed him. I filled up those notebooks pretty quickly. And I write weird stories about people trapped in towers, stories about crumbling walls. I still write to Dieter in it. I still want to figure out things through him, even if it's a strange way of going about it.

The creative writing class sounds interesting. I have no idea if I'm good at writing or not, it is more like an instinct; I don't know if what I'm doing is creative. I tell Mum about it, and she encourages me. You have to do it, she says. Having a little something just for you would be good. I can look after Imogen.

The first night, I'm really scared to go. I don't know what the course will be like. I don't know if I feel safe, walking in the dark alone. But outside the cold air is refreshing as it hits my face, making me remember how it felt to have somewhere to go.

The campus is a rabbit warren. Each building is identified by its own number; the only problem is I can't find the number I need. I don't want to look lost out on the dimly lit side street. Glancing around, I take the campus map out my bag, and try to line its schematics up with where I am. A voice behind me makes me jump, Are you looking for the creative writing class? Yes, I say, I am. Come on, he says, this way.

Inside the room four desks have been pushed into a hasty horseshoe. When the course facilitator comes in, she's dressed in long linen clothes. I'm not sure if she's wearing a dress or a skirt or even trousers, the fabric just flows around her. Her wooden beads click together as she speaks. She talks a lot about writing and self-expression and its healing powers and I listen impatiently; really, I only want to know how to write a book. The last thing I'm after is self-expression. She sets us a task, and we all bend our heads to the desk and begin to write and write and write, the sound of our pens on paper in harmony with the noise of the wind rattling the loose windows. She bends her head too. Every time I look up at her, she's pushing her glasses back up her nose. Later, she asks us to read our work to her. I hadn't expected this. She starts at the other end of the table, and everyone reads their hastily assembled paragraphs, to which she offers feedback about arc, metaphor, powerfully emotive sentences. I'm lost. I don't have a clue what she's talking about.

Too quickly it's my turn. I didn't know what to write, so I wrote about last week. About how long it took to get ready in the morning, about losing Imogen's hat and taking forever to find it and then fixing it to her head and finding it didn't fit anymore. I had to pull it hard over the top of her ears to make it stay in place, and then I'd gone into the bathroom to clean my teeth and Marc's stupid toothbrush was still there, frayed and used at the edges, standing in its glass.

I feel like I'm going to throw up the whole time I'm reading it to the class. Like my insides might escape onto the desk, or worse, like they already have.

She goes silent, brings her brows into a frown. It's good, she says, I like the analogy. Maybe lose the toothbrush though, laying it on a bit thick. I really don't know what she's on about. His toothbrush was there, that's why I included it.

It's the first time since I was young that I've trusted anyone with anything I've made. And it feels good. She doesn't laugh or point or say how stupid I am. No one tries to make me feel small to make themself bigger. My feet feel light as I walk home.

As I stand at the crossing waiting for the lights to change I see something sparkle in the window of the antique shop to my right. Peering in I see an old pharmacy chest with rows and rows of tiny drawers, each inset with a round crystal handle. It's beautiful. It's also eerily familiar, exactly like the one I imagined when I was in Amsterdam.

Those traffic lights were the scene of another revelation. A few weeks earlier I was standing, waiting for them to change, when I realised my life had no specific purpose at all. All my life I'd been told my life had a purpose, which was to be a Jehovah's Witness. But I realised, as the lights flashed green, that that alone wasn't a purpose; it did nothing to explain who I was, or what it was I was supposed to fill the years with. I don't want to think like this. But I can't stop.

I tiptoe into the house, taking care not to wake Imogen. It's OK, Mum says, she was fine. I curl up next to her and tell her about the old chest I saw. I say nothing, have said nothing, about my doubts.

How much is it? she says.

I don't know, right now anything's too much, I say. She laughs.

I remember how that felt, she says. Just after I left home when Zoe was little, Grampa bought me really good knives and pans. It made me feel special every time I used them.

We both go quiet. I'm thinking about Grampa. I don't know what she's thinking about, until she says, I still have that knife. It's a great wee knife, handy for all sorts of things.

She leaves. Two days later she sends me a blank cheque with a note attached, it says: 'For the chest, don't worry about how much it is.'

I stand with the cheque in my hand and look at it. I want the chest so badly. But Mum doesn't know who she's buying it for, not really. She doesn't know about last Christmas and how I bought gifts for Imogen, wrapped them carefully and left them in a stack in front of the fire. I couldn't say they were from Santa, I couldn't run the risk of her telling Marc, or of this betrayal of our beliefs getting back to Mum somehow, but when she woke in the morning she clapped her small hands together. Oh, Mummy, she said, Santa is real! He's real Mummy, when Daddy said he wasn't.

I can't tell Mum who I am, just as I can't tell Imogen Santa isn't real.

The next day, I buy the chest.

Winter begins to crack. The days are grey and blustery, the watery sun barely able to make its way through. It snows on my 28th birthday. I feel really lonely that day. I decide to go for a walk to see if it helps ease the feeling. I tuck the analogue camera, another gift Mum gave me earlier in the year, under my arm. I walk and walk and walk. I get a takeaway coffee and let its hot bitterness burn my mouth. I find an art gallery I've not dared to go in before and browse its walls. Hanging just near the back is a print, with blue letters constructed from hundreds of tiny other shapes against a white background. The letters say: EVERYTHING IS MADE FROM SMALL THINGS. I peer more closely at it; in the bottom right-hand corner is a tiny 28/50. I take this as a sign. I've been looking for signs all winter. I need things that point me in the right direction and cheer me on. I also need new signs, not just war and earthquakes and famine heralding the Four Horsemen of the Apocalypse. I want the universe to tell me I'm going in the right direction. I talk to Ash about this a lot. We talk about tarot and mysticism and magic. I need to make sense of things. All these new ways of looking help more than God ever did.

It begins to snow as I walk. I take a photo with my camera even though I don't really know what all the buttons do. Everything feels still, paused. I realise there's a space in me. The religion filled me up. They always say people who leave are left with a God-shaped hole, but it's God who makes the hole. My whole life I've only known who I am in relation to who I am not, but that isn't an answer, it just creates more negative space. Maybe everything that's gone wrong in the past was because of this space I didn't know how to fill, and God couldn't either. I need to find something to fill it with. I don't want to be empty anymore.

Every time I do go to the meetings, I feel displaced. I try to keep doing works that befit repentance but they feel like meaningless repetitions. God's love feels cold when I see sisters grouped in a huddle at the back of the Kingdom Hall with their backs to me.

They like to look at me as they talk to each other in hushed voices, before laughing loudly. They never talk to me, but they like to stare me straight in the eyes when they walk past. I always look away first. Brother Ardman's wife is the worst; she loves being an elder's wife, she loves the certainty of a life lived properly. At one meeting she comes up to me, and I think she might be about to offer me a lift home, so I don't have to walk home in the dark, but instead she looks at me with her top lip turned up into a sneer and says, I really want to help you: just to let you know, I've been thinking about how Imogen won't ever really be well adjusted as an adult, passed between both parents as she is, like some sort of unfortunate parcel. Then she smiles at me. Just so you know, she says again as she walks away. As if I've never entertained the idea of Imogen's wellbeing in any way before. This kind of Christian love feels a lot like contempt.

On the way home I stop at the red light, glancing to my side I see the illuminated sign outside the synagogue, it says: IF NOT NOW, THEN WHEN?

Later that night, I can't stop thinking about this phrase, because really, if I don't do something now, then when will I?

The year blurs.

It's summer again. I still miss Dieter.

I hide at the back of the same cafe every day and sit with my hood up; that way I think I'm invisible. I write and write and write. Everything makes sense on the page. Nothing makes sense outside of it.

I wear warm socks and lots of layers as a buffer between myself and the outside.

I don't feel strong enough to stop going to the meetings. But brothers and sisters have begun to give up on me; they back away from me as if I'm infectious and they might catch my worldliness from me. Brother Gillespie's wife phones with an excuse not to come for my Bible study most Fridays now. Maybe my flat's a contamination zone. Brave ones poke me on Facebook. Brave or nosy. Depends which way I look at it. I'm tired of being chewed up and spat out, a piece of gossip regurgitated later.

Marc tells me the circuit overseer's visit is coming up, and because he's so important and gives such encouraging talks, I need to make sure I'm there. It's his weekend with Imogen. I can't wait for the divorce to come through. I look strange dressed for the meeting now.

The circuit overseer is a big deal. He's in charge of all the congregations in the South of Scotland. When he visits every Witness makes sure to go to the meetings and fawn over him. He looks at everyone's report cards so he knows exactly how long we've all spent on the ministry and how many magazines we've placed, and from our records he can see if we've been reproved or have had to attend a judicial committee. There are so many written records of my life I never said they could take. This means he knows everything about everybody, and all the brothers and sisters want to have him to their house for lunch. It's a bit like having Jesus come to visit.

I walk across the city trying to stop myself feeling sick.

When I stop for a takeaway coffee I realise I'm shaking, my teeth chattering hard by the time I get to the Kingdom Hall. Even the stairs look daunting but I swallow, will my feet to walk up them. I go into the toilet where the speaker is turned up, and through it I can hear the circuit overseer speaking. I try to breathe normally. The meeting's already in full spate when I go in. People turn to look at me. None of them smile. I find a seat at the end of the back row and sit down.

From the platform the overseer watches as I sit down, as though he's expecting me. He keeps his eyes fixed on me as he carries on with his talk. He asks everyone to turn to their Bibles to hear Jehovah's views on divorce. He reads a scripture and somehow makes it sound like divorced people will never gain Jehovah's favour. Never. As simple as that, I realise there's nothing I can do to get back into God's love. Why didn't they tell me that a year ago? Why have I wasted my time?

I want to get up and leave right now, but I don't. I won't give them the satisfaction of being able to say later that I stormed out. I won't let them think I'm angry. I sit still until they all stand to sing the middle song. I lean forward and carefully put my Bible and my song book back inside my bag, I stand up, and I walk out the main hall into the foyer where I find my coat and an umbrella I left there months ago, and I leave. I know I'll never set foot inside a Kingdom Hall again. There is no love there. There is no God there either.

I get home, and pace around. I need to do something to mark this as an ending.

I get a black bin liner and put all my Witness publications in it. I don't put my Bible in, no one ever throws Bibles away. I worry that if I do somehow God will come and get me. I hedge my bets, and instead push it to the back of the shelf.

I put all my modest clothes, my high-necked tops, my too-long skirts, my not-too-high heels, in the bag too. My sensible ministry bag and coat also go in. Then I tie the sack up, drag it out onto the street and heave my whole life into the communal rubbish bin.

Back in the flat I'm exhausted. I go into my bedroom, find my way under the heavy duvet, and sleep.

2009

All winter, things feel heavy and impossible. When Mum comes to visit, I try to hide from her the fact that I'm not going to the meetings anymore. I tell her I'm going to a new Kingdom Hall, to stay away from Marc. She says, That's a good idea, and I hope she doesn't see through me. I think she doesn't ask questions because she doesn't want to know the answers.

Now I'm on my own, the outside gets scarier. I know it's somewhere I need to learn to live but I'm not the same as the people in the world. I'm scared of them all. I've been told they're sinful for so long that I find the thought of being friends with them impossible. Not because I don't want to be, but because I don't know how.

I talk to other adults so seldomly now that my voice sounds strange when I speak. This loneliness begins to feel like a comfort and trap.

I'm so used to books telling me how to live that it feels really strange to have no crutch to depend on. I have no rules and no guidebooks. Sometimes it feels like floating. Other times, closer to falling.

I'm still not sure if the world is going to end. I see it in my dreams and I wake screaming, my heart pounding. Some days I have a heavy sense of impending doom that grows and grows over days. I can't shake it. I try to convince myself that if the Witnesses are wrong about being God's people then they might be wrong about everything else too. I know there are websites bursting with apostates who could help me, but I know they won't be objective. I know they've been led astray by Satan, and I don't want to be one of them, because if I am, then Mum won't talk to me anymore.

Meanwhile, the newspapers are full of Obama's campaign trail. I've never been allowed to be interested in politics, nor to vote. But now I read the news all the time. I find I have opinions, even though I keep them to myself. I realise now it's pointless to say you're neutral, because everything's politics. I love Obama's message of change, even though it feels like a wildly optimistic thing for me to achieve.

In January, the month of two faces, one turned to the past, one to the future, I watch as he fumbles his inaugural oath. It makes him more human somehow.

Imogen dances around the room, singing, Obama is king. When's he getting his crown, Mummy, she asks. I sit transfixed as he says, All are equal, all are free, and all deserve a chance to pursue their full measure of happiness.

What would life look like if I dared to pursue my freedom? What it would cost?

LAND OF MILK AND HONEY

OLD HABITS

WITH MY LEGS WRAPPED AROUND his I feel his taut calves with the soles of my feet. I am sweat-soaked like I always was with him. He is too. Some things never change.

Afterwards, Simon lies at my side, his head on the new pillows of my new bed, the room bathed in the light coming through the cracks in the shutters. He smiles at me, and I smile back at him as we both float into sleep.

It was always going to happen, that he'd be back in my bed. They warned us about the dangers of social media and casual hook-ups. The elders made it sound so easy, it was inevitable that I'd look up Simon just to see what he was up to. And I saw that he was in Edinburgh and so of course I sent him a message and of course we spent the afternoon in the

THE LAST DAYS

pub and then another afternoon and another and then he was back at mine and we were reminiscing about old times.

He sat on the grey wool sofa Marc was still paying for and looked around the room. You need something to make it feel more like home, he said. I looked and saw the room through his eyes: tightly controlled and perfect, but like a stage set – not like somewhere you'd want to spend too much time.

Trouble is, I said, I don't know what my taste is.

You could try some giant parasols, he said, like my mum used to have hanging up.

I've spent so long being told what's right and what's wrong, and how it's wrong to be individualistic and materialistic, that I don't have a clue what I like. And last year, once everything happened, I really didn't have a clue about anything at all. Time was an awful thing, stretching on and on, especially the weekends when Imogen was away. To try to fill time I'd come up with things I could do: Sunday mornings I'd write and read and often do it over brunch in a cafe, drawing out my coffee for as long as I could; and Sunday afternoons I'd walk to the cinema to watch old black-and-white films. It's so odd, Marc would say, when he dropped Imogen off, to see you playing at being something you're not. But it seemed like he had it the wrong way round. Maybe Marc's the one who's playing, him and everyone else. That year was like watching my own death or rebirth. Difficult at times to work out which.

Before he goes to sleep Simon moves across the bed to me, folds me into his arms; in them I feel small and almost safe. So strange that this has been forbidden, that my whole life sex came with rules attached to it, with shame and caveats, that I was to surrender my body to my husband with no questions asked until it wasn't mine but his. Sex was a transaction, a weapon wielded against me, and here I am now, trying to reclaim that – not just trying but finally seeing that sex is the closest thing to God we have. It's the best way of leaving your body for a while, of breaking the bounds of your own form and becoming something else, and this is why they warned us about it; not because it's dirty or dangerous or sinful, but because it's a way of communicating without language, of making us wholly human, only flesh; we don't need spirit to transform us. Sex is the opposite of death, it's a way of forgetting it and cheating it, if only for a while, and that is why they didn't ever let me, us, all the women, enjoy it, because what a knowledge to have, what power to wield, that sex is pure and raw and nothing to be ashamed of. If they were wrong about this, what else were they wrong about?

These realisations are easy in the dark; these are equations I can make balance. But morning brings old thoughts and bad habits, and when the following week Mum comes to stay and Simon sends a message asking if he can come over, I send one back saying I'm sorry for what I've done, I can't keep seeing him.

All these sins of the flesh, these barbed crowns, so difficult to take off.

UNDER TRIAL

I LIE ON THE BED, WATCHING feet moving below the curtains around the cubicle.

The woman next to me has been pacing for the last hour, up and down and up and down. At least she's quiet. The woman on the other side keeps letting out howls, terrible long sounds, as if she is being torn up.

It's getting sore now, like the nurse warned it would earlier, when she asked me to lie back on the bed. Flop your legs to the side, she said; it'll be just like a smear test. But it wasn't. Her fingers were cold as she pressed the pills in place inside me. All done, she said with a smile, it'll start to work soon. Might be a wee bitty sore, but nothing you can't handle.

I've brought my book. I made sure it was a difficult one; reading something difficult makes it easier to disconnect from what's happening. Which is what I need to do. I can feel a tightening in my stomach. A pulling up my legs. It feels too familiar.

A few weeks ago in May I thought I was brave when I took the train over to Glasgow on my own, going to a gig and knowing no one, but not caring. The guy next to me looked like he was there on his own but it turned out he wasn't. He was mates with the band. He was in a band too. He bought me a drink. I bought the next one. And so it went until after the show we sat on the low wall in the lane at the back of the venue as the band loaded their gear back into their van. Above us gulls mewed and swooped like paper cut-outs against the cobalt sky. We passed a bottle of whisky between us. I was already drunk enough for the first heat of the alcohol to feel like nothing at all. I shrugged when I realised I'd missed the last train. We hailed a taxi back to his and it was the feel of skin on skin, limbs stretching and us burrowing into each other, wanting and being wanted, my lines blurring into his to make new shapes.

The tightening gets worse. I ball myself up. I will not cry.

I didn't see him again. I didn't need to. I just needed to know I could do it, that I could look the same as other people. I was getting good at that too; I had skinny jeans and a leather jacket and I dyed my hair and had a fringe cut in and I looked convincing. Then the line turned blue on the test, and shit. I had to think then. Actually think. Dieter told me once that my thinking apparatus had fallen asleep. He wasn't wrong. I'd sleepwalked through so much of life. I've only been thinking for about a year, and bang, now there's something big to think through.

What I thought was, I don't have enough love in me for two children. I'm not very good with Imogen: I love her so much, but I have many flaws. Marc says she's got no hope, that she'll end up mad like me. A second child would drive her mad. And she'd be the lucky one, she'd be the one who got to go to her daddy's house and get presents and treats and fancy dresses; the other kid wouldn't know their dad and how would that make them feel? It often felt like Mum couldn't stretch to loving two at a time. She would let me sit on her knee until Zoe came home and then she would tell me to get off; the love would go to Zoe, and I'd be left alone. I can't repeat that. If I had a baby, I'd have to creep back to the Kingdom Hall because I wouldn't have anyone to help me. I'd have to sit at the back and be judged by everyone for eternity. I can't do that. Mum would find out what I'd done and she'd be so disappointed, and she'd try to give me advice and read the right scriptures to me. There isn't mother enough in me to let this happen, or maybe there is too much.

I phoned the clinic. I dropped Imogen at nursery in her new coat and patent shoes, kissed her on the forehead. I got the bus to the other side of town. I pulled my hoodie up, knowing Witnesses lived there, and looked around me as I went inside. The nurse was friendly; she didn't say anything judgemental to me. I expected questions and recriminations, forgetting she was not an elder. After I told her everything, she made an appointment at the hospital for the next day.

Now it hurts. I pull my knees up to my chest. It hurts really badly. The nurse said it would feel like a period. But she's wrong. It feels like giving birth. They should have warned us. I feel blood coming out me, and rush to the toilet. I put the metal bedpan they've given me over the lid. Afterwards I gaze into the mess of it, hoping to see something discernible. There's nothing there but lumps and clots mixed with the stench of my own insides.

The nurse puts her head round the curtain. Everything OK? she asks. I shake my head. She leaves and comes back with two painkillers in a plastic beaker. She sits on the edge of the bed as I take them. If it's bad you can stay, she says. It's OK if it's sorer than you expected. I can't tell her I'm not crying because of the pain or for the not-baby. I'm crying because of the line I'm crossing and can't go back over. I'm crying for the way I'm here alone and have no one to call when I leave. I'm crying because the next time I phone Mum I will have to add this to the list of things I need to keep from her. I'm crying because what sort of woman, what sort of mother, what sort of animal sits expelling a part of her, a thing she helped make, and cries only for herself? I'm crying for all the years I thought the rules in the Bible were enough to save me from the complexities of life.

The pain rips and splits. I welcome the way it

inflicts punishment on me as if maybe the baby has lived, grown, come to term and to terms with the raw deal it's been dealt, with its inheritance of a mother.

You can go home to finish it off, if you need to, the nurse says. I nod thanks.

There's someone to take you, isn't there? she says. I nod again. Yes, my mum's in the cafe. Next time I talk to Mum all I'll be able to tell her are lies. I am not a proper daughter. And I know if I keep behaving like this, soon enough she won't be my mum either.

At home that afternoon, Imogen sits with her tiny legs under her watching her favourite fairy film, her eyes barely moving from the screen when I tell her I need the toilet. Her not-sibling slips out of me more easily than I thought it would. There is no mistaking what it is, or was, or might have been. I cover it in toilet paper, the red blotting through before I flush it away. I go back into the sitting room and cuddle Imogen tight. She snuggles in under my arm, as if she thinks I can keep her safe.

There needs to be a pay-off for what I've just done. I need to make it mean something. I need it to be worth something.

What needs to happen next is all of life, all the time. No more stagnating.

October and its damp has worked its way up into the old town. It hangs around the streetlamps in wisps as we run down closes through the night. My feet slip on the wet cobbles. We need to get to the venue before the last song.

After everything earlier in the year, I got a new job. I'm not sure how I did it, but I'm working in events. I've organised a music festival using all the smaller venues in town and I'm running the lead singer in one band to one of them, so he can sing the last song with his friend in another venue. We get there and it's packed; we elbow through the crowds of his fans in the bar, some of them stopping to ask if he's who they really think he is. But it's too busy in the gig. He doesn't want to push his way through.

When I told Mum about the new job, she was not happy. Bad associations spoil useful habits, she said. But she's wrong. The organisation is wrong. All the worldly people I was warned about aren't terrible. In the last few months I've met some of the best people I've known. I've had some of the best conversations I've ever had. No one waiting to trip me up. No one trying to catch me out.

I leave the singer in the bar and tell him I'm going in anyway, and I'll see him at the afterparty later. I make my way through the crowd to the front where my friend – a new one who has helped me organise this – is standing. She smiles at me and we watch the final song together. Then the crowd disperses as the lights flick on, the beer-soaked floor sticking to our shoes. We've done it. We've fucking pulled this mad thing off. I've done something for me. I am on the other side and it's better than I ever thought it would be.

Christmas comes and this year I do it properly. I'm still too scared to buy a tree. I'm still scared about Mum finding out about this. Instead, I arrange fir boughs along the fireplace, interspersing them with fairy lights that glitter all the long evenings. Imogen begins to get excited about Santa coming again, and when she says her dad says he's not real, I tell her, You'll just need to wait and see: some big people have forgotten how to believe in magic.

The night before Christmas Eve I go to a party; I am filthy hung-over the next day as I elbow my way through shoppers to get the last doll's house in John Lewis. On Princes Street the sky behind the castle is snow-fat. I stop to stand still and watch as white, thick flakes of it fall. I could cry for the beauty of it all. Later, I wrap Imogen's presents with the curtains open and tealights dotted along the sill to light the winter dark. It looks right. The following morning, Imogen squeals as she rips the paper from her gifts. We spend the day building her new doll's house, taking great care to arrange the furniture exactly how its tiny inhabitants demand. I roast a chicken, the smell of it fills the kitchen. Solemnly we set the table, putting green and red candles in the middle just like Granny would. When we sit down to eat it feels strange to be pulling crackers just the two of us, knowing families are all gathered together elsewhere, but it's also slightly magnificent to think that I've made this for Imogen. I look at her flushed cheeks, see the excitement dance in her eyes, all the loss is worth it for this, more gain than I could have dared hoped for.

The last night of the old decade comes. I put on a tiny silver dress, stuff my heels into my bag and put rings on every finger. I shiver my way over to new friends. Their house is full by eight, bodies making condensation on the windows, people packed and pressing against each other everywhere, the music loud. I mix gin with champagne and take over the music at the mixing desk. Just before the year ends, we tumble out onto the street and someone wraps a coat around my shoulders. We climb the hill to the duck pond, slipping, sliding, trying to find our drunken feet. I clutch my second bottle of champagne of the night for comfort. Premature fireworks whizz damply into the deep blue night sky. The pond is frozen, and pissed-off swans wander around people's legs; some of them look like they might bite. Imagine owning all the swans, my friend says, and I laugh at him. I'd put them in a pie if I was the Queen, I say, and we're giggling when the fireworks start, great bursts of them shooting and firing into the sky. Just gunpowder, I say, but something has happened: I've outlived my own ending.

The bells ring in the new decade, the cheer of the crowd carrying on the winter air. I am alive. I am I am I am, as Dieter said to me in his second-to-last email. Deep breaths, the old brag of my heart again. I am here. I am not scared to live.

THE BLESSING AND THE MALEDICTION

2014

Y EARS PASS. LIFE FILLS UP. I see the joy in it. I fall
in love. I meet someone else, and we have a baby,
Alexander. He is the most beautiful thing I've ever
seen, just like his sister before him, and his younger
brother and sister will be too. They are all fiercely
beautiful.

Two years ago, I did a master's degree, and all the
reading and writing freed me. Now I know why Witnesses are told to stay away from philosophy and
critical thinking. On the course, I was too ashamed to
say I had been a Jehovah's Witness. I kept my former
life a secret, but the remnants remain. My tongue is
tied for as long as I can't face the past. I am scared of
what Mum thinks of me now.

I hardly see her. She disapproves of my new life,

though she still appears occasionally. I am scared to lose her entirely. I don't know exactly why, given our lives are so different now. Maybe it's the finality I'm afraid of. Maybe she's my only thread back into the past, now the rest are severed. I am sure that, now I have left the religion physically, it is enough. I don't realise that their teachings are still in my heart. Or maybe I just love her.

I see her at Granny's funeral. Zoe sits in the pew in front of me, doesn't sing along with the hymns. I see her looking at me, but she doesn't speak to me. She's not spoken to me since two years after I broke up with Marc. The first inkling I had that anything was more distant than it usually was between us was when Facebook suggested we become friends with each other. I never knew we weren't friends. She didn't send me a message, didn't say a thing. She just wasn't there anymore.

Mum is distant when she talks to me now. It feels like dancing around an elephant when I try to tell her about my life. I can't tell her who I am or what I'm doing. I begin to try to reconcile myself to the idea that one day I'll lose her to her religion, but I push that thought away. That can't happen.

FOUR WINDS

2014

IN THE SPRING OF 2014, Avery is born, blue and spluttering. He is something else, is one never to be beaten, is craning his head to sit only days after birth. Days feel ephemeral, time becomes translucent, I'm too tired to hang on to things. I want all of this to last as much as I want it to be done; the paradox engulfs me.

Summer turns long and lazy, I feel invincible. That I can have three children and know what to do seems almost incomprehensible. Life begins to feel perfect.

Too perfect.

In the middle of July, I meet up with friends. I take Avery, who sleeps curled in his car seat. I'm bursting with the future; life has that strange hue it tends to have when suddenly things I never could have imagined before are happening.

On the way home, I tuck him into the back seat, clipping his car seat in place. I kiss his tiny face and head south into the sun. I'm waiting for the lights to change, drumming my fingers on the steering wheel, when over the radio comes news that a plane has been shot down over Ukraine. I'm going to be sick. I will throw up. I don't know how I know but I know this is the beginning of the Great Tribulation. This is the start of the times of distress the Bible warned me about. The city will be cut off and walled up and there will be no meat other than the fat little thighs of my children, just as happened in Biblical times. Mobs will ravage. People will pillage and rape and plunder just like Mum said they would. The Witnesses are right. I know this. It is too late.

A car honks from behind but I can't get the right gear. I miss the lights. My legs twitch. I want to run. My vision blurs. A mist descends. I manage to get us home and up the stairs and into the flat, though I can hardly carry the car seat since I'm suddenly weak. I need to throw up. Are you OK? my partner asks as I drop the car seat at his feet, and run into the bathroom, lock the door, throw up right there and then right to the bottom of my guts and

we
will
all
die.

★

All the people I've let myself love and want and need will be dead. It'll all end because that's what God does, He takes everything away whenever he wants to. My whole new life will all be swept away, just as it was in the time of Noah. When I come out of the bathroom my partner asks if I'm OK again, but I can't tell him. How can I, how can I say what's in my head and what's to come? All I can do is hope it's quick.

Days and days and weeks and weeks, I watch the news, scroll through it on my phone, listen to it on the radio, I can't tear myself away. Avery doesn't know how to sleep yet. He becomes increasingly fretful, sore and full of colic. Every feed makes him sick; I suddenly become convinced he doesn't love me, and how can he after I've brought him into a world only for him to die a few months later? I am shortsighted, selfish, imprudent, stupid: all the things I've always known about myself are true.

Weeks pass. I can hardly eat. People talk about World War Three. I don't know if they're joking or not. I become scared to go outside. It's easy to spend time inside when you have children, easy to make excuses of their health or a bad night and not go to baby groups or story time or any of the places I'm meant to be. Everyone will turn on everyone else soon enough, I know that's what's foretold to happen at the end. At least I know what to expect. My partner thinks I'm tired from the children. How can I tell him the truth without sounding mad?

October: I'm still waiting for the end to come. I sit

on the edge of the bed trying to get Avery back to sleep as dawn nears. I've been up with him all night, but he wants to stay wide-eyed and alert. In the soft gloaming his pupils widen as he looks at me. He smiles his first real smile, right into my eyes. It feels as if I'm seeing him for the first time. I've been so scared. I've been so far away. His button nose, his almond-shaped head, his wide-set sea-blue eyes just the same as Grampa's, his white-blond fuzzy hair; my son; my baby. I smile back at him. I hold him close. I know what I have to do next, even though it's something I've stopped myself from doing for years.

I carry him into the sitting room, my heart thudding hard.

I tuck my legs up underneath me and put a cushion on my knee, cradle him in my arm; soon his eyes become heavy, his long lashes resting on his cheek. I flip open my laptop, its blue screen glaring at me, already admonishing me for what I'm about to do. I search for the apostate websites I was always warned not to read. I've been told they're full of lies about Jehovah and his organisation. I have to do it. I can't stay like this forever, with all the fragments of everything I was told just waiting to collide whenever anything bad happens.

I read and read and read. I read for weeks, I discover things I never could have imagined to be true. I read about child sexual abuse scandals and cover-ups. I read about money trails and various legal entities created by the organisation to provide indemnity in the face of lawsuits. There's so much that I can't take it in at first. It will take me a long time to unpick everything. By turns I'm breathless, angry, doubtful, I'm all the stages of denial and grief in the short space of a few weeks. I realise that it was all a trick, that the religion is nothing more than a business entity masquerading as a religion. I've been duped for so long. I want to reveal this world to Mum, but I know I can't. I know she'd say that apostates are mentally diseased, just like they say from the platform. I know she'd say they've been led astray by Satan. I know she'd say this is part of the persecution; and worse, I know she'd say she could never see me again. When we do talk, I skirt around the details of my life as much as I can. There is so much I have to keep from her already, and now I have to keep quiet about this too.

I walk around knowing these things about my old religion. It feels wrong to know them and not speak. I want to write about it, but I can't. I don't want to be called an angry apostate. The problem is that when I do try to write, I find I'm always writing around it, as if it's a subject I can't quite get to. Mum asks me questions, and I evade them; in theory I could go on like this forever, always keeping this part of myself hidden from her. But then something happens.

In the summer of 2015, as the city fills up for the festivals, our friend Chris comes to visit. We met him a few years ago through mutual friends, and Chris and I bonded when we both realised we were ex-Witnesses.

It felt a bit like coming home, to finally find someone who understood. All the previous times I saw him, we'd sat up late talking about the process of breaking free and the absurdities of growing up in such a strange, closed world. But this time, Chris is changed. He's quiet, withdrawn and angry. He speaks of getting revenge on his parents who've shunned him. He makes me feel uncomfortable. Nothing I say to him seems to make him feel better about the situation he's in. It's as if the grief he's experienced has done something to him, and he isn't the person I remember him being.

In the late winter of 2016 the news of Chris's death reaches us. He's died by suicide. I feel ripped apart by this waste of life. He needed his family and they shunned him. The severance of leaving everything behind leaves you feeling disjointed and out of place. Chris couldn't find his new place. He was so concerned with looking at what had been, he couldn't see what could be. I am so angry. I look at my sons and can't begin to understand how his mother could do that to him. I can almost understand why, but not the mechanics of it.

There are so many things I know about the organisation and how shunning kills people, how messed up it all is and I've never wanted to write about it. How can I when it's the last thing I can ever talk about? And yet I can't watch anymore, I can't read things online and stay quiet. I'm done with biting my tongue and being good and complying with their rules. All I can do is write.

I start a tiny blog and tiptoe around talking about the religion. It's safe enough. It's not like anyone's going to read it anyway.

DISTANT HAMMERS

I WANT TO STAY LOYAL TO JEHOVAH

THE ANTICIPATION FOR THE CONVENTION would've been building for months. Mum would be so excited about all the congregations across Scotland joining together in the one place for three days. All the special talks and meetings, the instructions about how she was to conduct herself at the convention, the clothes she should wear, the places she should avoid, the safety briefings, the volunteer sessions would all be over. The main event would be about to begin.

The Witnesses would have given out invitations on the streets. So many unfaithful people would hurry past the cart, unwilling to take one, too hard of heart to accept Jehovah's ways. Every once in a while someone would stop and take one only for them to discard it on the pavement later.

They'd all be saying it would be the best convention ever, the same as they said every year. In anticipation, Mum would have made her clothes weeks ago. She'd have sat in the summer evenings sewing the buttons onto new dresses. She did the same thing, year after year, all these little repetitions to mark the seasons; this, the biggest event of the year, demanded a new outfit for each of the three days it lasted.

Everything has to sparkle and shine for Jehovah the holy God.

She would be apprehensive, thinking of the sisters who would shake her hand with their sad eyes, never asking about her youngest daughter. She'd scan the audience hoping to see her ex-son-in-law, and run up to him at lunchtime, asking how her granddaughter was, if he was still teaching her Jehovah's life-giving ways. She would try to keep the tears in, but they'd fall easily when she thought if only her daughter could have been faithful, if only she'd realised how protected she was by Jehovah's loving organisation.

She would settle in her seat a good 15 minutes before the programme started, the way they would have been encouraged to in the meetings in the lead-up to the assembly, when the elders ran through how they were to behave and all the essential points to keep in mind during the convention. They'd have been told they had to wear their name badges at all times. To behave in an orderly manner. To witness to the people they met in town when out for meals in

the evenings. To remain seated for the whole programme. To take notes. To applaud the speaker. To
follow all the directions given to them.

Looking at the programme she collected on the
way in, she would write FRIDAY at the top of the first
page in her new notebook, keen to note down all the
instructions. On the front of the programme she'd see
the theme of the convention was CHERISH LOYALTY;
she would copy that down in her notebook. Her
husband would be doing the same, leaning over and
telling her how Jehovah's chariot was moving at such
a pace; she would nod as she read the headings for
each symposium of talks, remaining loyal in thought,
in word, in action, remaining loyal even to death.
She would nod again, because she knew her loyalty
to Jehovah was so firm it couldn't be called into
question.

The music video signalling the start of the session
would begin and the younger ones, still talking, would
scurry to their seats. A hush would fall over the arena
as nearly 10,000 brothers and sisters would all rise at
once and in unison all sing the opening song:

> 'Rather than condemn the weak,
> We should bear in mind
> How much we can strengthen them
> By our being kind.'

Maybe someone would cough, maybe a child
would laugh or a baby cry and be carried out by its

mother. Then the song would finish and they would all bow their heads in prayer to Jehovah, the sovereign God of the universe. The elder would pray into the microphone, his eyes tight shut and his voice powerful, asking God to bless their gathering together and to help the dear brothers and sisters to open their hearts to listen to the life-giving instructions that would be administered over the next three days, and a resounding, AMEN, would ripple around the crowd. The prayer would end in Jesus's name and dresses would rustle as everyone sat, and then the chairman would take to the stage to admonish the crowd that Jehovah deserved undivided loyalty.

Mum would be taking notes, the same way she always had, with her head bent low in attention. She would not notice the teenagers slipping off to volunteer to clean the toilets, the concourse, anywhere where they could scout out the talent, where the young sisters would eye up the brothers and the brothers would parade peacock-like in their new suits with their freshly cut hair. She would not see this or hear the laughter backstage, or see the backslaps and the handshakes; instead she would listen and write and would be attention personified. She would learn all the ways to build her loyalty and to maintain it, then she would sing in her flat voice how she must live up to her name as a Jehovah's Witness by doing all that Jehovah and his spirit-directed slave directed her to do, and then she would sit for the closing session.

And then they would play the film they'd all been waiting for on the giant screen behind the platform. On-screen parents telling their teenage daughter she couldn't live with them anymore after she'd started to pursue a sinful course. Quite right, she'd whisper to her husband, and he would nod.

Does she think about going to the toilet? Does she think about blowing her nose? Does she want this bit to be over? Or does she just take notes and nod in agreement? Does she join in the applause at the end of the film?

What does she do during the next talk when they describe disfellowshipping and shunning as an expression of true love? Does she write this bit down?

Does she think how Jehovah will reward her strength and loyalty with eternal life? Does this feel like enough of a trade-off? Does it sound like compensation enough for what she now knows she will lose? When does she decide what she's going to do next? Is it then, or is it days later, when her eldest daughter sends an email telling her that she doesn't really want to be the one to do this, but has she seen what Ali is doing now? Does she know immediately what she has to do when she follows the link and sees her younger daughter's written that disfellowshipping isn't love? How dare she contradict the organisation. How dare she question the values she was raised with. How dare she question everything she was taught to hold dear.

What's certain is that she'll pray about what she

does next, because she doesn't do anything without her Father's direction and blessing. She'll pray and she'll sleep on it until she feels Jehovah's answer deep within her, and then she'll know what she's doing has His divine blessing.

As soon as she knows she has His answer, she'll act.

She wants to show Jehovah the extent of her loyalty and that nothing is too much to expect her to do. She will do whatever it takes to get into the new system, even if that means sitting down at her laptop just after lunch, typing her daughter's email address into the addressee line and writing the easiest or the hardest email she's ever had to write. She will sit down and write:

I have heard that you have been writing derogatory comments about Jehovah and His way of dealing with people who, after saying that they are going to serve Him, leave His ways. If this is still how you feel about Jehovah, then I do not want to keep in contact with you until you realise that Jehovah's ways are a protection and a blessing. I want to stay loyal to Jehovah even when it is at such a great sacrifice to myself. Mum

Just like that, with only 83 words, you end my world.

BOOK THREE:
REVELATIONS

1. IN SEARCH OF

'Let me rise up, please, and go round about in the city,
in the streets and public squares, let me seek
the one whom my soul has loved.'

Song of Solomon 3 v 2

THIS IS HOW MY MOTHER *goes missing. I think that's what it's called. She's not dead. She's not lost, I didn't leave her somewhere. She just isn't here.*

I don't know what to do after I read her email.

I go into the kitchen. It's cooler there than the sitting room. I pull my cuffs over my hands and stand in the middle of the room, watching dust float. There's something I should be doing, but I don't know what.

I'd give it all for one afternoon with your sewing machine hitting pins, the Shipping Forecast, Jane in the red room, Peggotty's buttons. Listening to your heart; waiting for it to stop.

I pace a bit. I think I might be sick. I can feel it sitting there in my stomach.

I will make lunch, so it's ready for the boys when they wake up from their nap. I pull the long stringy pieces from sticks of celery, peel carrots, wash cherry tomatoes. It is suddenly important that I have food ready for them. It's difficult to cut things, my hands won't stay still. My stupid fingers are shaking. I put the knife down.

I'd trade it all for that. My birthright for a bowl of stew. See? The Bible never leaves. You taught me well.

I will burst if I don't do something. But what can I do? My mum is gone. She's gone and there's nothing to do. There's no funeral to arrange, there's no death notice to post, there's no one to call to tell, she's only gone from me.

This doesn't make sense. It's just another summer's day outside. The boys were pelting each other with water balloons yesterday, all their brightly coloured remnants littering the path. The paddling pool's still out, they'll want to go in it when they wake up and I'll have to put their swim nappies on and rub sun-cream into their arms and dab it onto their noses. Their granny, who was never quite there, is now finally gone, and how do I ever begin to explain it to them?

I creep into the sitting room. Avery is sprawled on his back, his mouth a perfect O. Alexander's hair is soaked with sweat. Their soft other-worldly breathing is sending their chests up and down. I love them best like this, abandoned to the world. I sneak out again with my laptop under my arm.

There is only one way I know to bury her. There is only one way I know how to make her listen.

In the kitchen my hands shake as I type a blog

post. I've never felt so hot, a burning comet ripping through my chest. I write it all out, and I press POST. Maybe she'll see this and more likely she won't, but it's out of me and on the page and that's where I'm learning to put everything, so that's where I put her. I have been silenced for so long.

You kept my baby teeth, my sun-blonde hair, what changeling will you make with them? What age will you bring me back at? Before you taught me to read, I'm guessing. Before I could hold a pen?

You drew smiley faces on my plasters. You wiped my tears. All of it, only ever conditional. How could you be both mother and executioner?

You can keep your afternoon. You can keep all your yawning afternoons. You can keep your hands running the fabric through the sewing machine.

You can keep your hands. Do not touch me again.

It doesn't make it better. It doesn't even help. I put my hand to my face and find it is wet; when Alexander wakes he asks why I'm crying. How do you explain to your own child that your mother doesn't want to see you again?

ALI MILLAR

Something loosens around my edges. I don't feel quite right. When I'm out, I start seeing her places I know she can't be. I see her walking towards me on the bridge as I push the children in the buggy; I see her coat open to the wind on a blustery morning; I run out the newsagent after her. But it is never her.

I think she must be hiding. It's a game. It's hide and seek. I need to look for her. We are still together, she's just pretending we're not.

*T*HE FIRST PLACE SHE'LL BE *is home. Our home, the one I grew up in. I need to go back. That makes sense. She'll be back at the house. How stupid I've been to not think of that. Of course.*

I pack the car, telling the children and myself we are going for a picnic at the river. I use what's left of my rational mind to convince myself I am simply taking the children for a picnic. The other part is so excited to be going home, to be in search of Mum.

I cut cucumbers into long strips, put them and carrot sticks and celery into glass jars, screw the lids on. Baguette for the children to share. Juice, apples, ham. It looks enough like a picnic to call it one. Blanket, straw bag, towels, change of clothes.

We drive east with the sun in my eyes. My heart thuds for the entire journey. I might be crying behind my sunglasses but it's hard to notice now I do it all the time. I turn the music up loud, so the children sing instead of arguing. Slowly the boys' voices slur and stop. I see them in the rear-view mirror, their heads lolling and rolling against their little chests, rising and falling in sleep rhythm. I turn to Imogen and say, Just us then. Let's go somewhere else, and I drive to where I was always going to go.

I go back to the village I lived in, along the narrow street rising up the hill, past cars parked outside houses blocking my right of way, past the shuttered shops and the bakery, also shut, past kids at the bus stop leaning smoking against the graffitied wall. It may as well still be 1996, it's just the same as it was the last time I was here. I turn right to go down the hill, past Mrs Lyon's house, a pharmacy now, and then another right past Mrs Cow's house and notice the doctor's surgery is gone, a wide gaping space where it once was. I turn left and I am on the same street I used to run down in the dark with the sound of my feet filling my ears. My street. The houses are smaller and shabbier and the gardens messier than I remember them being. As I round the final corner, my tongue is stuck to the roof of my mouth. I see the house that is also not the house, and there is Grampa, running along the street chasing his hat as the wind lifts it. Aunty Liz in her pale pink wedding dress, and I am bending down to buckle my shoe. My cat is even on the road. But I see the cat is not my cat when it stands and stretches and the tip of its tail is white in ways it never was, and the house is not the house either. The pond is filled in and the plum tree gone, and the white harling faded to dirty cream after so many years, and there are no curtains at the window and only a FOR SALE sign propped up outside. I am too late. Mum is not here.

I park the car and Imogen looks at me. Where are we? she asks. I can't say it. I can't tell her who we've come for or how late we are or any of the things that happened here. Instead I say, Just somewhere I used to know.

THE NEXT PLACE IT MAKES *sense to look is the town where we used to preach. That's where she was when she wasn't at home.*

I suggest we go to the beach, thinking the boys can run around in the fresh air. I try not to think that after we can go into town, and I can look for Mum. It sounds too mad to think, never mind to say. We bundle the children into the car. I don't bother with a picnic this time.

By the time we get there the tide is all the way in. The wind is ferocious, the waves high white horses pounding themselves against the cliffs. I think about going down, trying to walk into them, but that would be silly. Silly.

Let's go into town instead, I say. There's a chance, I think – a slim one, but still a chance – that she might be here. She might have taken it into her head that this was as good a day as any to go back, to take her husband for a walk along the walls or to go for coffee and a scone. It is a long way for her to come, but maybe she's here for the weekend. How funny, I'll say when we bang into her, to meet you here, and we'll laugh and the past will be forgotten, or, even better, will never have happened.

We drive up the hill away from the beach and down the long stretch into town. It takes me a moment to get my bearings. There's a Mountain Warehouse where a petrol station once was, the leisure centre extended with flumes and slides protruding out its side only to disappear, ouroboros-like, back inside. A retail park with more units empty than filled, an optimistic Marks & Spencer, a more realistic Poundland, an abandoned Argos.

We drive across the bridge, widened now, with gilt faux-Victorian streetlamps that weren't there 20 years ago. The town's seen better days but I'm unsure exactly when these were. Maybe the fact of my being there constantly meant I couldn't see it properly. It used to seem so big and now it's tiny, a collection of a few streets, boarded-up shopfronts and too many chip shops. Was it big because it was the centre of my world? Would it still seem big if I hadn't left, if I hadn't learnt the scale of other cities, if I didn't have something to compare it to? Does it seem big to the people who stayed? Will it seem big to Mum when she comes back?

I read once that limpets return to the same spot on

a rock until the rock erodes the limpet's shell, so it fits exactly to its one spot; but in turn, over time, the limpet erodes the surface, leaving its own mark. This mark is called a home scar. I can't help but think of it now, the ways home mars us, marks itself into us, how it erodes us, shapes us painfully into new forms. My mother, my first home.

We park the car. Should we stay? my partner asks, eyeing groups of skinheads who appear to have arrived for some kind of nationalist rally, endgame England on perfect display. We can't leave, this is the right weekend, she'll be here for sure. Let's stay, I say, we'll be fine.

He gets the buggy out the boot, and I carefully pick up Avery, who's now sleeping with his head slumped down on his chest the same as his brother. I barely worry now about them sleeping that way, whereas when they were little I used to turn around in the car and fix their heads all the time, worried they'd crush their windpipes. All the tiny baby things passing unnoticed.

The wind lifts Avery's hood as I strap him into the buggy. He stirs and, opening his eyes, strains to sit up. He looks around wide-eyed at this place he's never seen before, and I tell him this is where Mummy used to ... and then I don't know what to say. I didn't live here, but I was always here; Sundays, Thursdays, Saturdays. This is a town I used to go to, I tell him, and still full of sleep he lies back against his blanket as Alexander screams at being woken, shouts he's hungry. It's

OK, we'll get something to eat, I say, and point them towards the high street. It still smells the same, chips, fags, the encroaching seaweed-damp stench of the sea.

Time melts. I could be 36 or I could be six, and either decades could have passed since I was last here or it could still be the 1980s, it could be Christmas or it could be early spring. I could be pushing the buggy down the street in search of snacks or I could be clutching my mummy's hand walking past the town hall, ribbons of light stretched between buildings and me unable to see higher than the waists of passers-by, while from the shops comes the chant of 'Jingle Bells' and 'Do They Know it's Christmas'. In my head I will sing all the words and hope Mummy doesn't know what I'm thinking as she pulls my arm so we can get back to the Kingdom Hall, where it is safe and where Brother Llewellyn is waiting to give us a lift home after we have done our shopping. I remember once that the lady behind the counter said, Merry Christmas, in a sing-song voice. Actually, Mummy said, as loud as she could, we don't celebrate Christmas. The lady gave Mummy her change back very quickly, saying, What about the child? and Mummy said, I think that's none of your business. The lights and the songs made me feel sick and sad and far away for the want of them to be good things, not pagan things, not things that would take me away from Jehovah, not things that made me a bad little girl—

Where do you want to go? my partner cuts in.

I breathe. I am back. For now.

The skinheads have grouped themselves around the town hall, waving cardboard signs with GO HOME painted in large letters, some with flags facing away from me that I'm pleased I can't see. Police vans arrive.

They jostle each other, as dogs bark at ankles, their anger won't get them anywhere other than a night in the cell, but they have to put it somewhere. Over to the right is a Witness cart with two sisters I knew years ago looking the same but greyer. Maybe they've seen her, maybe I could ask them. Maybe they wouldn't answer me.

There is a little boy among the crowd, his hair buzzcut close to his skull and his eyes a fierce blue. He stops in front of Alexander and, staring at his hair down to his shoulders, shouts, Fucking faggot! Mummy, what's a hucking haggot, Alexander asks as I pull him away from the crowd. My fingers are freezing, my lips feel tight, my tongue fat. This child, these people, all indoctrinated with so much hatred. That was me. I am pulling my child away from a homophobic little boy who has no idea what he's just said, he just wants to be like his daddy. I just wanted to be like my mummy. All I ever wanted was to make her happy.

Of course I know where she'll be.

Let's go over the bridge, I say, there's an art gallery in the old Kingdom Hall.

We tuck ourselves in on the narrow bridge, made for horses not pedestrians with too many children. Cars pass close to us, eager to escape the crush of the town. Once over the bridge Avery clamours to be out of the buggy, and as the children run on ahead, I tell them to be careful of the swans, a great group of them up ahead, murky white. The swollen river widens and hurries to the sea and the swans, finding it more appealing than the empty-handed boys, are drawn to it. The old auction house beside the river has lost its windows and is boarded up now, the scrapyard is locked with a dozen padlocks. Our feet hurry past it all.

We go around the same corner the car rounded every meeting night, and there is the Kingdom Hall. It looks the same, the garden slightly more overgrown perhaps, no longer shaped and manicured into submission every weekend but instead left to grow as well as it can with the salt and the rolling mist. We walk towards it.

The boys push the gate open and of course it squeaks. We follow them in, and they point and laugh at the statue of a young boy pissing in the garden. I laugh too, thinking how mortified the elders would be to know the garden they used to make sure we carefully tended had been defiled by a statue like this. Next to the front door is a sign telling us to press the buzzer. I think of my old tricks; maybe I don't need to press it, maybe I could turn and run away, maybe I should have stayed in the city, maybe I should never have thought I was strong enough to do any of this, but I need to press the buzzer. I know Mum's here.

An older woman opens the door, her grey bobbed hair obscuring her face. I knew it, I knew she'd be here. Then she looks up and she might be my mother if I squinted hard enough but she's too thin and she smiles too readily. She holds her hands out and says, Come in, come in, welcome.

The foyer has the same foam ceiling tiles, the same concealed strip lighting, the same layout, but now the walls are white. There are no imaginings of the new system on the wall, there is no terrible grey carpet. But it's not different enough for me to feel safe; I think I'll throw up. I need the bathroom, I say and run into the toilets that are in exactly the same place they were, leaving the woman who opened the door staring after me.

In there, it's easier to breathe. The room isn't what it used to be. The tiles are gone, the blush-pink washbasins, gone, the speaker so we don't miss any of the meeting, also gone. I check, but Mum isn't in any of the cubicles.

When I finally leave, the woman is waiting for me. She smiles. You've been here before, she says, her voice both a statement and a question. I have, yes, I say, and then it tumbles out: I used to come here when I was little, I was a Jehovah's Witness. This is the first time I've said it to someone other than my partner or to close friends. I tell her what I was and I expect something from her, some condemnation perhaps; I don't expect the hand she places at the base of my spine and her warm eyes smiling at me. Ah, she says, I see. Come on, I'll show you the main hall.

I show her where the literature desk used to be, explain how the chairs were laid out. The platform is still there, but now it's for performances. There are windows now with light streaming in, spoiling the art. There's nowhere for Mum to hide, there's nowhere for her to be.

As we leave she tells us we must come back and I tell her I will, but of course I won't. I've looked for Mum and she is not there. I am running out of places she could be.

*T*HERE IS ONLY ONE PLACE *left to look. She'll have gone to see her mum and dad and her sister; she'll be in the kirkyard.*

It doesn't matter that it's been raining. It doesn't matter that the road's flooded. I buy flowers and tell my partner I'm going to visit their graves. I keep Mum out of the equation because I don't want to sound unhinged.

I swerve great wide puddles, take corners as carefully as I can. I see the chimneys of the old schoolhouse Granny and Grampa lived in before I was born. I drive up the short main street past the pub and the village green, past the community centre where Grampa used to judge vegetable-growing competitions, past the old church with yews with low entwined branches at the entrance. I park opposite the kirkyard.

Now I've arrived, I don't think she's here; surely not. But I need to make sure; I need to just check.

I walk along rows of gravestones, some small and black, some tall and slanting, the grass perfectly manicured, past fresh mounds of earth covered by wilting flowers and messages of love, and I stop to read every stone, every date, every hard-carved inscription. I delay finding her. I'm suddenly so nervous. What will I say when I see her? Will she run at me with her arms stretched out, like in the illustrations of the dead coming back to life after Armageddon?

I can't remember where their graves are. I weave quickly between stones, and the rain comes back, spits itself against my face as I try to find Mum or Granny or Aunty Liz or Grampa. I can't find the right row. I get to the brow of the hill and see the planters in front of Aunty Liz's grave. I run towards the grey matte stone, kneel to trace the words, getting harder and harder to read. Grampa's is thick with moss. Soon people won't know who lies there. I start to panic. What if she *is* dead? What if she's dead and no one has told me, what if one of the graves is hers. I read the rest of the gravestones, carefully and methodically again. She is not here. She is nowhere to be found. My mother has hidden herself completely.

2. NEW DAWN FADES

'I am with you always, even until the end of the world.'

Matthew 28 v 20

*I*T WAS THERE AMONG THE *truly dead that I realised you were gone. There is now no way back to where we were. I have by turns been sad, angry, driven mad by your absence and the lack of name and ritual for it. Grief and love, the two are inseparable. You exist as a noun only now all the action of a verb has been lost.*

I wanted ritual. I wanted to build a funeral pyre for you. I wanted sackcloth and ashes. I wanted to sit shiva on the floor, but if I had, I wouldn't have been able to get up. This book became my ritual, this is where I put my grief for you.

This summer, I read a line that made everything easier. It said: 'But it is for us to distinguish, to see the difference between wrong done to us and equal wrong done by us.' It felt important to think about this in relation to you. I realise now the extent of the harm done to you by the religion you believe to be God's. You've been manipulated, lied to, robbed of money, time and love. The harm you did to me pales in comparison to this. I can't be said exactly to forgive you, but I understand you now. And I can extend this to Zoe and to Marc and to everyone else held captive by a corrupt organisation. You've all been and all continue to be exploited.

I've delayed writing this ending. I don't want to stop being here with you. I've written many different ones. I wrote them as the heat outside intensified, I wrote them all the long nights I couldn't sleep, I made notes on my phone as I walked. I have constantly been preoccupied with how to finish and also not finish. I know, when I end this, I will leave you behind, again. It's raining today. The parched earth smells relieved. I sit at the window as I write, looking out over the garden at plants you'd know how to name – see, you are always absent – and I will make bread using your recipe – see, you are always present – and I will have finished writing this because it is exactly here that it ends with nothing fixed, each of us in our own hinterland, where we will stay, always, even until the end of the world.

Author's Note

ALTHOUGH THIS BOOK IS MY story, while writing it I was acutely aware that my experiences echo those of countless numbers of people around the world who grew up as one of Jehovah's Witnesses. They also reflect the experiences of people who are still in the organisation, many of whom are devout, many who have doubts or who have long ceased to believe, but who can't easily leave without losing family, friends and livelihoods. It takes a certain amount of guts, time, stamina and selfishness to fully leave – I know. In many ways the story is not only mine, but one readers will find themselves in.

This was not an easy book to write. For two years I felt as if I'd crossed the Styx and was communing with the underworld of memory and of loss. It was not the best place to be. At the outset, before I knew what I was letting myself in for, I was motivated to write this book because I didn't feel that any of my experiences were represented anywhere. Leaving puts you at a certain cultural disadvantage, where you're not part of the world you knew, but you're also not fully a citizen of the world you're trying to join for a long time. Any time I'd seen Jehovah's Witnesses portrayed I felt like it wasn't done properly, until I read Grace McCleen's *The Land of Decoration* about an unnamed sect that bears a startling resemblance to Jehovah's Witnesses. It was this book combined with the failings of others that made me think I could write my own story, and in turn, write a story to represent and communicate the lived experience of millions of members. I know I won't have got it right either, but I hope I've come close. At times it feels strange that only a few years ago I couldn't tell anyone I'd been a Jehovah's Witness without feeling uncomfortable, and now I've written this. In many ways this is an act of reclamation.

This is a work of memoir. Which is to say that memory itself is fallible, eroded by time and trauma, but it is written in the best faith. I know too that my narrative lens is limited: I couldn't tell everything from everyone's perspective. I have tried to be even-handed and fair and have done my best to conceal the identities of the people in the book. All names have been changed; no descriptors have been used. This book is in no way an attempt to exact revenge on any individuals or of criticising members, it is instead a way of illuminating the cult tactics they are subjected to, as well as dramatising the difficulty of leaving.

As the book became progressively more difficult to

write, I was, ironically, motivated to continue by a Bible verse that had been drummed into me since childhood. In James 4:17 it says, 'if anyone, then, knows the good they ought to do and does not do it, it is a sin for them'. I knew the good I had to do; I knew the carefully crafted public face of the organisation to be a deception designed to conceal the realities of life inside the religion. I knew the moral imperative was that I speak out, regardless of the damage inflicted on myself. I know leaders of the organisation have over time used the excuse of religion to raise vast sums of money that currently sit carefully invested in off-shore tax havens; I know they have consistently exploited people's capacity and need for belief to secure their income sources; I know they manipulate the truth and erase uncomfortable parts of their history; I know members are repeatedly subjected to coercive control; I know no concern is shown for vulnerable members of the organisation, any apparent concern is only expressed to protect their charitable status; I know the motivations of leaders revolve around money and only that, with express disclaimers buried deep in their website designed to legally get them off the hook should members refuse blood transfusions or follow advice and end up seriously injured, critically ill or dead, it's all designed to create indemnity; I know they have repeatedly and consistently refused to comply with requests from inquiries and court cases to provide information; I know they violate the second part of Article 9 of the Human

Rights Act while using the first part to protect their preaching work.

I know this is a corrupt and immoral organisation. I couldn't keep this knowledge to myself. In the end writing this wasn't a choice, but a necessity.

Acknowledgements

Invaluable to the existence of this book, in this form, are the following:

Matthew Marland, at RCW, who took a chance on a very different manuscript. Robyn Drury, my editor and co-conspirator at Ebury, whose insight, patience and tenacity made this book something more than I ever thought possible. Laura Nicol, for her enthusiasm, insight and tireless championing - thank you. Diana Riley, for her extensive marketing expertise and many brilliant ideas. Sarah Whittaker, whose visual interpretation of the book created the perfect cover. To the legal team at PRH, for their guidance and knowledge. Alice Brett for copyedits and Jacqui Lewis for proofreading. And Stuart Kelly, for believing long before I did.

Debts of gratitude also go to Gavin Ritchie, Catherine Simpson, Ever Dundas, Lee Brackstone, David Keenan and the rest of the Monument Maker reading group whose company lessened the difficultly of arduous edits. And S.H, whose kindness worked as a sort of transportation from one world to the next.

Works whose influence were key during both the gestation and the writing of the book include Maggie Nelson's *Bluets*, Michel Faber's *The Book of Strange New Things*, Joan Didion's *Blue Nights*, Seamus Deane's *Reading in the Dark*, Sylvia Plath's *The Bell Jar* and Stuart Kelly's *The Minister and the Murderer*.

I couldn't have written this without music ferrying me between the past and delivering me safely back in the present. Largest thanks and heaviest rotation goes to Cassadaga by Bright Eyes. Dan Willson who unwittingly delivered the title in his song, Providence, at a gig in Edinburgh's Portrait Gallery.

And finally, to Euan, for lending me his stubbornness all the times I needed it most.